Sunset
Mexico
TRAVEL GUIDE

*Snorkelers on Cozumel Island slip into the clear waters of the
Caribbean, home to the world's second largest coral reef.*

By the Editors of Sunset Books
and Sunset Magazine

Lane Publishing Co. • Menlo Park, California

Research & Text
Barbara J. Braasch

Coordinating Editor
Suzanne Normand Mathison

Design
Viki Marugg
Lea Damiano Phelps

Maps
Roberta Edwards
John Parsons, Eureka Cartography

Our thanks...

to the people and organizations that assisted in the preparation of this travel guide. Special appreciation goes to Gabriel Huerta and other members of the Mexican Government Tourism Office and to Exploration Cruise Lines for their valuable assistance.

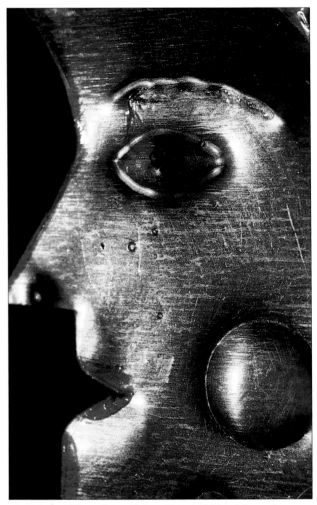

Painted replica of pre-Columbian gold burial mask is a fine example of Mexico's handicrafts.

Cover: With a swirl of her skirt, Mexican dancer captivates the eye. Lively music and dancing delight visitors, as do other expressions of Mexico's colorful culture. Photography by Cliff Hollenbeck.

Photographers

Morton Beebe: 49, 74 top. **Barbara J. Braasch:** 138. **Jon Brenneis:** 143 bottom. **J.Y. Bryan:** 25. **Dick Bushnell:** 113, 131. **Glenn M. Christiansen:** 10, 15 top, 18, 34 top, 39, 142. **Betty Crowell:** 40 top, 74 bottom, 81. **Lee Foster:** 15 bottom, 17 right, 90 top. **Gerald L. French:** 58 bottom. **James Griffin:** 24, 104 left, 120, 127 top. **Enrique Hambleton:** 8 bottom, 16, 17 left, 65 bottom. **David Hartley:** 127 bottom. **Cliff Hollenbeck:** 8 center, 42 top, 47, 57 right. **Dave Houser:** 1. **Ellen Kadelburg:** 82, 98, 103, 122 top. **Martin Litton:** 33 top. **Jack McDowell:** 7 left, 9 top left, 31 top, 55 top, 73, 79, 87, 88, 89, 95, 97, 121, 135. **Peter Menzek:** 71. **Mexico Ministry of Tourism:** 80. **Jurgis Motiekaitis:** 26. **Don Normark:** 9 right, 42 bottom, 64, 66, 104 right, 105, 143 top. **Norman A. Plate:** 8 top, 9 bottom left, 41, 55 bottom, 58 top, 63, 134, 139. **Norman Prince:** 32, 130. **Gil Pruitt:** 90 bottom, 111. **Bill Ross:** 7 top right, 72, 114, 122 bottom, 128. **Dick Rowan:** 40 bottom, 57 left, 112 top. **David Ryan:** 2, 7 bottom right, 34 bottom, 48, 50, 56, 65 top, 96, 119. **Carol Simowitz:** 23, 31 bottom. **Tim Thompson:** 106, 112 bottom. **Ken Whitmore:** 33 bottom.

Editor, Sunset Books: Elizabeth L. Hogan

First printing October 1988

Contents

Special Features

¡Bienvenidos!
A Warm Mexican Welcome

You'll feel at home in Mexico from your first *bienvenidos* ("welcome") to your last *hasta luego* ("until next time"). And there will be a next time for travelers who fall under the spell of this colorful country. Mexico can be whatever you want it to be. It's a diverse country that offers just about every vacation ambience. Add to this its proximity, accessibility, and low prices, and you have a travel destination that's hard to surpass.

Fun in the sun? Mexico offers countless resorts along its 6,000 miles of coastline. Peek into the past? View ancient ruins hacked free from the clinging jungle. Nose for nostalgia? Revel in cities impressed with a Spanish stamp and follow the route of this country's struggle for independence. Enjoy shopping? This is a land of handicrafts; schedule stops at village markets for browsing and buying.

From spectacular game fishing and skin diving to boating on high plateau lakes and playing a round of golf on almost-deserted courses—the range of activities is unlimited.

And you won't have to travel far to find the contrasts of this land. In short treks from Mexico City, the country's cosmopolitan capital, you can visit tranquil mountain spas, sparkling seacoast resorts, quaint Indian villages, picturesque artists' colonies, historical haciendas, and awe-inspiring archeological wonders.

Meet the people

Fairly early in your visit, you'll realize that Mexico's people are one of its greatest attractions. To understand the country, you'll need to know something about its inhabitants. Historically speaking, they are a new race, with roots dating back thousands of years to the Aztecs, Mayas, and other Indians who originally inhabited this area, to the Spanish who conquered the land if not the people, and to the French who ruled it briefly.

Mexicans are expressive and exuberant in music, architecture, crafts, and other types of art. Bold colors and powerful forms are characteristic of both ancient and modern artists.

Your introduction to Mexico

Mexico appeals to almost everyone. We hope this book will lead you to happy discoveries in this land of variety. Consider it an introduction to the country, its people, its customs, and its atmosphere.

The "Essentials" section in the back of the book reviews accommodations, transportation around the area, tours, and entertainment for each of Mexico's seven regions (see pages 149–158). Maps in each chapter are accompanied by "Details at a Glance" features offering general facts on getting to the region, its climate, and appropriate attire.

The last chapter in the book discusses tourist cards, custom regulations, money, language, and health considerations. But your best bet before setting out on any trip to Mexico is to check with a travel agent for the most current information.

Totonac Indian musician

Massed Mexican flags

Patio fountain at the National Museum of Anthropology in Mexico City

Acapulco's native dancers

*Colorful
carved fish*

8

*Classic encounter
in the bullring*

Vibrant bougainvillea

Chapultepec Park balloon vendor

Brightly painted pottery

Massive rocks frame sandy stretch of beach at Baja's tip.

Baja California

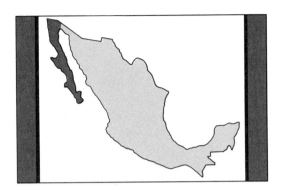

Baja presents two faces to the visitor: One is of a rugged outback of rocky arroyos and steep-walled barrancas, thorny cactus forests, and towering peaks mantled in pines. The other is of an inviting winter playground, with pristine beaches, fish-rich seas, and palm-shaded resorts.

Not many years ago, most of Baja was the preserve of venturesome pilots and drivers of all-terrain vehicles. But since the completion of the 1,127-mile Transpeninsular Highway (Mexico 1) in 1973, Baja has become a magnet for large numbers of visitors. Today, the modern two-lane roadway, stretching from the U.S. border to Cabo San Lucas at Baja's southern tip, has made the whole peninsula a motor route.

The Baja experience

Beyond the hubbub of its border cities, Tijuana and Mexicali, Baja offers no elaborate cathedrals, large marketplaces, or brassy night life. Only Ensenada and La Paz qualify as real towns; other spots are little more than villages. But everywhere between lies an unforgettable landscape—of pastel deserts and startling green oases, of deep blue waters and crashing surf, and of supreme peace and quiet.

Attracted by some 850 species of fish, anglers flock to the 800-mile-long peninsula. Campers pitch tents and park rigs along its lovely beaches and, in winter, whale-watchers congregate around Scammon's Lagoon, breeding ground for gray whales.

Conquerors, colonizers, and developers have found Baja California's rugged terrain inhospitable in the extreme. Even today, a good portion of the peninsula remains uncultivated, unmined, and virtually uninhabited.

A peek into the past

Since the days of its discovery by the Spanish, Baja has changed little. Whereas the rest of Mexico was rapidly explored, mapped, and subjugated by the Spaniards, the peninsula continued to be an enigma until the end of the 17th century. For many years it was thought to be an island.

Hernan Cortes sent the first exploratory mission into Baja in 1532, and traveled there himself in 1535 after hearing of fabled pearl beds. Though no permanent settlement resulted, his last envoy, Captain Francisco de Ulloa, explored it thoroughly by sea. In 1697 a Jesuit missionary, Padre Juan Maria Salvatierra, landed on Baja's eastern shore to establish a chain of missions.

After more than 400 years of exploration and settlement, these fortresslike edifices are among the few permanent artifacts of civilization.

Though Baja today is an exciting destination, it was long shunned by tourists. Its Indians were among the poorest and most despised, and its deserts the harshest and most feared in all of Mexico. In fact, had Baja been less trackless and forbidding, it might not belong to Mexico at all. In 1847, the United States forces that conquered Alta (Upper) California had an equally secure grip on Baja California. But they let it go: Nobody considered Baja worth keeping.

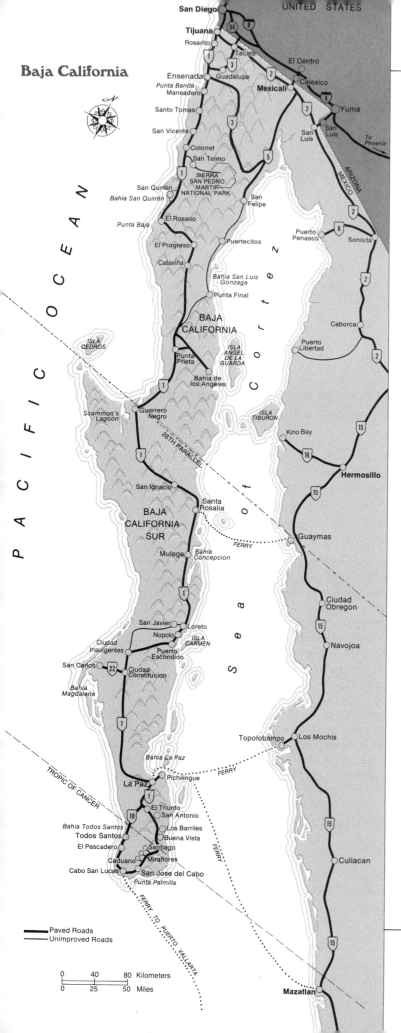

Baja California

DETAILS AT A GLANCE

Baja California

How to get there

Millions of people cross the border into Baja for a day or so of shopping or sports; some drive down the peninsula to fishing resorts along the Sea of Cortez. The drive is easy with a little planning (see page 17).

By air. Scheduled airlines serve Tijuana and major Gulf Coast settlements (Loreto, La Paz, and Los Cabos); commuter lines cover resorts from La Paz to Los Cabos. Almost every resort has a landing strip for private planes. A comprehensive travel service provides Baja pilots with air charts and resort reservations. For information on out-of-the-way resorts, write to Patti Senterfitt, Baja Reservation Service, 1575 Guy Street, San Diego, CA 92138, or call (619) 291-3491.

By bus. A popular trolley connects San Diego and Tijuana, and Greyhound and Mexicoach provide service between Los Angeles or San Diego and Tijuana. Autotransportes de Baja California links Mexicali with San Felipe, Ensenada, and Tijuana, while Tres Estrellas de Oro serves towns along Highway 1.

By boat. Private boats will find good harbors. Car ferries crisscross the Sea of Cortez between Santa Rosalia and Guaymas, between La Paz and the mainland ports of Topolobampo and Mazatlan, and between Cabo San Lucas and Puerto Vallarta.

Tours

A growing number of outfitters and organizations lead nature expeditions to Baja—through the high desert, along the Pacific shore, on the Sea of Cortez, and among wild islands of both coasts. Gray Line Tours offers trips from Los Angeles and San Diego. Exploration Cruise Lines offers 8-day sailings from autumn to late spring between La Paz and Acapulco and January to March whale-watching cruises from La Paz to Scammon's Lagoon.

Accommodations

Modest hotels, scattered trailer parks, and campgrounds stretch up and down Highway 1. Larger cities, resorts, and guest ranches offer additional choices (see page 149).

Climate & clothes

It's best to visit Baja's high northern mountains in late spring, summer, and early autumn. From La Paz to the peninsula's tip, it's very hot in summer. Sport clothes are all you'll need.

La Frontera

For many residents of the southwestern United States, Baja California is just a few hours or, at most, a day's journey away. It is not unusual, say, for a San Diego family to drive down to Baja for a spur-of-the-moment shopping spree.

La Frontera (Mexico's border) is the first and often only impression many *norteamericanos* have of Mexico. Because of the concentration of visitors along the border, towns there are an often strange composite of U.S. and Mexican elements. Atypical of the rest of the country, they provide an easy stepping stone to the real Mexico beyond.

Travelers should have no problems with language or currency. English is understood almost everywhere, and dollars are welcomed.

Tijuana

Every year, visitors from the north make millions of crossings over the Tijuana River into the tourist haven billed as "The Most Visited City in the World." From here they can catch planes and buses to points all over Mexico, or join expeditions into the Baja interior. But most visitors simply come to shop and play.

With a population of over 1 million, Mexico's fourth-largest city is growing in new directions. Shops, restaurants, promenades, and a hotel are located at or near Plaza Rio Tijuana, an area once characterized by tumbledown shacks that were periodically washed away by the now-channeled river. Paseo de los Heroes—built to rival Mexico City's Paseo de la Reforma—boasts landscaping, *glorietas* (traffic circles), and statues of Mexican heroes as well as one of Abraham Lincoln.

Crown jewel of the new zone is the $35 million Tijuana Cultural Center. In addition to a fine museum and a variety of shops displaying handcrafted goods, the modern complex contains a spherical Omnitheater, where a film on Mexican culture, history, and tourist attractions is shown several times daily. The center is open daily from 11 A.M. to 8 P.M. For information, call (706) 684-1111.

Avenida Revolucion, the traditional shopping street downtown, had a face-lift recently: it was remodeled with underground wiring, off-street parking, trees, and benches for people-watching. Colorful street vendors, narrow old *paseos* and arcades bulging with all manner of Mexican-made goods and duty-free imports, and good restaurants add to the area's appeal.

Shopping here can be fun and truly rewarding if you know what to look for. Finds range from the best in folk art at two government-sponsored stores on Revolucion

(Fonart and one with goods from the state of Puebla) to the gaudiest of tourist horrors. Because Tijuana enjoys free-port status, some of the best buys are imports—cosmetics, perfumes, jewelry, and fabrics. The shop at Calle 4, Sara, has long been noted for imports such as crystal, porcelain, and clothing.

Plaza Rio Tijuana has three major department stores and a number of specialty shops. Follow Agua Caliente Boulevard southeast of town toward the race track to reach another modern shopping mall.

Sporting events draw sizeable crowds. Attractions include year-round horse racing and greyhound racing at Agua Caliente Racetrack; Sunday-afternoon bullfights from May through September at El Toreo (Agua Caliente, 2 miles east of downtown) or the bullring-by-the-sea, Plaza Monumental (6 miles west); jai alai at the spruced-up Fronton Palacio, Friday through Wednesday evenings; and *charreadas* (Mexican-style rodeos) almost every Sunday afternoon from May through September at any of four *charro* rings. Check the tourist information center at the border for current schedules of all sporting events.

You can also play tennis and 18-hole golf at Tijuana Country Club, off Agua Caliente east of downtown.

Other attractions in Tijuana include a verdant city park that few north-of-the-border people visit; in summer, band concerts take place in its tall central pavilion, donated by Tijuana's sizeable Chinese colony. One of Baja's largest cathedrals, Nuestra Señora de Guadalupe, stands at Calle 2 and Niños Heroes, on Sunday mornings the city's busiest intersection. Open stalls are heaped with colorful produce at Mercado Miguel Hidalgo (Calle 6 and Negrete); popular market buys include vanilla, cinnamon-laced chocolate bars, braziers made from license plates, and piñatas.

Ensenada

From Tijuana, the 66-mile drive to Ensenada takes you along a scenic coast reminiscent of California's cliffside stretch near Big Sur, though much more developed. From Tijuana, follow the signs for Ensenada Cuota (1-D), a well-maintained toll highway. In addition to housing developments, sights along the way include the resort village of Rosarito Beach, once the site of a famous gambling casino; Puerto Nuevo, where virtually every house is a lobster restaurant; and Cantamar, where Southern California's hang gliders gather on cliffs and beetle-brow the beaches.

If instead you follow Ensenada Libre, the old road from Tijuana, you pass farms and dairies in the La Joya valley before reaching the coast north of Rosarito Beach. The road is slow, narrow, and curving; most motorists prefer the expressway.

... La Frontera

Casual Ensenada differs widely from bustling Tijuana. With its scenic setting on Bahia de Todos Santos, it is both a busy seaport and commercial hub as well as a top tourist resort in northern Baja. Cool ocean breezes keep the climate temperate year-round. Visitors can find a wide choice of charming small hotels, at rates much lower than on the U.S. side of the border. Fresh seafood is always a fine choice in the handful of good restaurants.

Getting around town is easy. Shops, hotels, restaurants, and sport-fishing boat rental offices line the main street, Lopez Mateos. You can follow this thoroughfare south to the airport, to Estero Beach (resort and shops, 6 miles from Ensenada), and to La Bufadora, the famed blowhole on the coast at Punta Banda (20 miles south of Ensenada).

Lazaro Cardenas, a waterfront esplanade to the west of Lopez Mateos, leads to a civic plaza lined with 12-foot-high busts of Mexican heroes. It also provides access to the pier, fish markets, and marina.

Shopping can be rewarding in Ensenada since it, like Tijuana, is a free port. Both imports and Mexican goods can be a bargain. To get an idea of typical pricing for Mexican handicrafts, stop first at the government-owned Centro Artesanal de Ensenada on Lopez Mateos, adjacent to the tourism office.

Lopez Mateos and the streets crossing it are the main shopping areas. Stores contain everything from wrought-iron furniture and papier-mâché to pure junk.

Fishing is the area's star activity, especially from April to November. Catches include yellowtail, barracuda, albacore, white sea bass, bonito, and halibut. Bring your own boat, rent one of the many available, or join a fishing party. Check established catch limits, closed seasons, and license requirements. You'll find places to have your fish cleaned, iced, packed, or smoked.

Other attractions include visits to Bodegas de Santo Tomas winery (daily tours at 11 A.M., 1 P.M., and 3 P.M.), Hussong's Cantina (a turn-of-the-century watering hole), and any of the hot springs in the mountains behind town. Isla Todos Santos, just opposite the shores of Ensenada, is open to adventurous visitors for hiking, fishing, and swimming. Winter surfing at Estero Beach ranges from good to excellent. At kilometer 39 off Highway 1, a 4- to 12-foot surf breaks half a mile out.

Ensenada annually celebrates Mardi Gras (the 4 days preceding Ash Wednesday) and Cinco de Mayo, a holiday commemorating Mexico's defeat of the French in the Battle of Puebla on May 5, 1863. Hundreds of yachts sail into the harbor on May 5 (the day on which the annual Newport–Ensenada International Yacht Race is completed.)

An upper Baja loop

The paved road (Highway 3) between Ensenada and San Felipe gives motorists an opportunity to cover a wide area of Baja Norte—an area including its three largest cities. The drive offers many scenic surprises.

San Felipe, on the east coast of Baja, nestles between the Sea of Cortez and the foothills of the Sierra San Pedro Martir. It's a quiet, relatively unheralded haven for sport fishers and RV campers seeking a bare-bones beach resort for a warm-weather winter getaway. Tourists have a choice of several moderately priced beach hotels and campgrounds, a few restaurants, and some shops.

Winter days are consistently in the 80s and 90s; nights dip only to 60°. It does get windy during the day, but the welcome breezes take the edge off the arid desert heat (most years, the area gets less than 2 inches of rain).

There's good fishing all year for bottom dwellers such as sea trout, corbina, and baya grouper. Punta San Felipe (north of town) is a fine spot to try your luck ashore, or you can rent a boat and equipment at your hotel or at the north end of the beach promenade. Large boats take passengers for a day of fishing around Gonzaga Island (18 miles out), as well as to Punta Estrella or Punta Ensenada Blanca. Fishing boats can be chartered for trips to Bahia de los Angeles to the south.

Mexicali, 125 miles north of San Felipe on paved Highway 5, is Baja California's state capital—but little known, as border towns go. Though it once had a reputation for vice, dating back to U.S. Prohibition days, Mexicali's bawdy past is hardly evident today.

Bullfights are held twice a month, from October through May. Colorful weekly charreadas take place on winter weekends at one of two charro grounds. Visitors usually come down for a day to wander among the shops and try one of the city's many Chinese restaurants, or stay overnight (several good hotels) to attend a bullfight or play a round of golf at the country club south of town.

Tecate is small, simple, and clean. Located at the junction of Highways 2 and 3, it's a pleasant place to stop. Pick up a map and visitor's guide at the tourist office on the south side of the plaza on Callejon Libertad. Highlights include the bakery, candy store, tile shop, and Centro Artesanal de Tecate (on Highway 3 about 1 mile south of Highway 2), which sells handcrafted items. Tours of the Tecate Brewery's imposing structure are offered the first three Saturday mornings of the month.

A short paved road connects Tecate with California State Highway 94 across the border. South of Tecate, Highway 3 heads up and over the mountains, joining Highway 1 about 6 miles north of Ensenada. Though members of a Russian religious sect settled the village of Guadalupe along the way, little remains of their heritage.

Downtown Tijuana's handsome Fronton Palacio is the evening setting for fast-moving jai alai games.

Flopping fish fill a net at San Felipe. From shore or boat, fishing is good here year-round.

Northern Baja highlights

From Ensenada it's 375 miles to Guerrero Negro at the boundary of the states of Baja California and Baja California Sur—an easy 2-day (or grueling 1-day) drive. You'll probably be tempted by several attractive detours along the way. A few miles below Ensenada is the checkpoint of Maneadero for validating tourist cards—the first place you'll need them in northern Baja.

Scenery along this stretch of Baja varies widely, from Pacific coastal views to green farming valleys and towering peaks. The high desert is alive with tall, tapering *cirio* (boojum) trees, grooved *cardon*, graceful *ocotillo*, and tortured elephant trees.

Sierra San Pedro Martir

Among Baja's surprises are its high mountain ranges. It's only a few hours' drive from the border to virtually un-

explored vacation retreats in the Sierra San Pedro Martir, site of Baja's first national park. The easiest way to reach these mountains is to turn off Highway 1 at the signed road to San Telmo (8 miles south of Colonet). From here a graded road—passable by standard cars in good weather—heads into the foothills to two ranches offering guest facilities. (Both have airstrips for fly-in guests.)

The road ends at an astronomical observatory (not open to the public) high in the mountains. From this spot you are rewarded with spectacular views of the Pacific Ocean to the west and the Sea of Cortez to the east. Directly below lie the barren plains of the San Felipe Desert; looking southeast, you'll see the precipitous, double-peaked Picacho del Diablo (10,126 feet)—the highest point in Baja.

The national park's piñon and ponderosa country is ideal for hiking, camping, fishing, and backpacking (entrance fee for overnight stays). Because the park has no developed facilities, you may prefer to make one of the foothill ranches your home base for exploration.

Meling Ranch, one of Baja's pioneer cattle ranches, looks much as it might have at the turn of the century—with the exception of modern guest accommodations that include a family-style dining room and stream-fed swimming pool. Horses and guides are available for pack trips.

Mike's Sky Rancho (also accessible from the road between Ensenada and San Felipe) is a more modern resort with motel-type accommodations and family-style meals. Campers will find developed sites along the San Rafael River below the ranch.

San Quintin

One historical account credits the explorer Cabrillo with naming the region in 1542. Because of a sheltered bay nearby, San Quintin attracts visitors who come to fish (especially for surf perch), dig for clams, hunt for black brant, or enjoy the wide sweep of sandy beaches. Bird watchers stop here because the marshes are a major resting area along the Pacific Flyway. Near El Molino Viejo (an old mill) and in the weathered cemetery, you'll see reminders of an English attempt at colonization in the late 1800s.

The high desert

Before Highway 1 was built, El Rosario (south of San Quintin) was the jumping-off spot to the rugged heart of Baja. Now the paved road cuts sharply east and up on the edge of Baja's high central desert where you'll catch your first glimpse of cirio and cardon.

A palm-studded oasis, San Ignacio breaks up the harsh Central Baja desert landscape.

How's the highway? That's one of the first questions asked of motorists who have just returned from a trip down the Baja peninsula on Highway 1 from the U.S. border. The usual answer: pretty good.

Sea of Cortez prize

It can be an enjoyable experience these days to drive the 1,127-mile length of the peninsula. What was formerly accomplished only by jeep or pickup is now easily managed by an ordinary passenger car.

■ Arm yourself with a good road map and a mile-by-mile guidebook. *The Baja Book III* by Tom Miller and Carol Hoffman (Baja Trail Publications, Huntington Beach, CA) offers maps keyed to road logs, and descriptions of major towns and beachcombing and fishing opportunities. Other sources include *The Baja Adventure Book* by Walt Peterson (Wilderness Press, Berkeley, CA), the AAA and Automobile Club of Southern California publications on Baja, and Dan Sanborn's *Mexico Travelog* (available from Sanborn insurance offices).

■ The Transpeninsular Highway is slightly narrow, there are no shoulders, curves may be poorly banked, and *vados* (creek beds that cross the road) may hide not only water but cattle. The moral of the story: Don't drive at night!

■ Fill up with gasoline wherever you find it—the next service station may be "just out." It's still difficult to find unleaded gas outside the border cities. Carry Mexican pesos or small U.S. bills.

■ Carry a complete set of tools and such replacement parts as a fan belt, spark plugs, points, condenser, and extra motor oil and radiator coolant.

■ Travelers should always bring extra food and at least a gallon of water per person.

■ If you plan to travel anywhere off the main highways, you'll be on gravel or dirt roads. It's a good idea to carry a shovel and tire chains, and to put inner tubes in your tires—cactus spines can puncture a steel-belted radial tire.

■ Keep a lookout for green utility trucks with emergency lights on the top and repair kits in the back. These are the "Green Angels"— the traveler's friend. A fleet of these trucks is supposed to cruise all sections of the highway at least twice a day to help motorists. Service is free; you pay for parts or gas. In a true emergency, they will relay messages by radio to your family at home.

To get service, pull off the highway and raise your car hood.

Secluded Bahia Concepcion camping site

Pool terrace of Hotel Hacienda overlooks the rocky coastline at the mouth of Cabo San Lucas harbor.

Dining is delightful on the flower-filled patio of Los Arcos hotel in La Paz.

... Northern Baja

Turn off at El Progreso to view the ruins of Mission San Fernando, the only Baja mission founded by Father Junipero Serra. (Get a four-wheel-drive in wet weather.)

For desert lovers, the following 104 miles can be the most fascinating part of the trip. The high desert is best glimpsed after winter rains, when the desolate land blooms with kaleidoscopic color. Cataviña is right in the midst of the most spectacular part of the boulder-strewn desert. Nearby lies rustic Rancho Santa Ines.

Bahia de los Angeles

South of Cataviña 65 miles, a paved road leads across the narrowest part of the peninsula to Bahia de los Angeles on the Sea of Cortez. This incredibly beautiful bay is usually the first goal of people who pilot their own boats and aircraft down the gulf side of the peninsula.

The mountainous length of Isla Angel de la Guarda rises only a quarter of the way across the bay, forming and protecting a coastal channel filled with fish. There are yellowtail, cabrilla, and grouper all year, with dorado as well during the summer and early fall. Large schools of porpoises and whales move through the channel.

Campers have a wide choice of sites north and south of the village at the bay; there are only two motels and trailer parks at present.

Guerrero Negro

On the 28th Parallel (dividing the state of Baja California from the state of Baja California Sur) sits Guerrero Negro.

From November through February, hundreds of California gray whales head for Scammon's Lagoon to breed and nurse their young. To reach the lagoon, follow the road marked Parque Natural de Ballena Gris about 5½ miles south of town.

Central Baja highlights

Loreto and Mulege (*moo-lay-HAY*), this region's largest villages, attract sports-minded vacationers lured south by good weather, water, scenery, and comparatively low-priced resorts. The Sea of Cortez has some of the world's best fishing—marlin, sailfish, roosterfish, grouper, and others.

San Ignacio—a desert oasis

Date palms introduced by Jesuit colonists spread a shadowy green roof up and down a valley, a signal to southbound drivers weary of desert driving that they have reached the attractive town of San Ignacio. On its charming plaza lie a well-stocked store and a massive stone church built by the Dominicans in 1786 and still in use. In autumn, racks of drying dates line narrow streets behind the plaza. Mule trips take passengers to mysterious cave paintings in the nearby mountains.

Santa Rosalia—a ferry terminus

Once a French-owned copper-mining town, Santa Rosalia still retains some of its French names and customs. The prefabricated metal church designed by Alexandre Gustave Eiffel (of tower fame) for a Paris exposition, ended up here around the turn of the century. A ferry operates three times weekly between Santa Rosalia and Guaymas on the mainland. An airstrip lies just south of town.

Mulege—gateway to Bahia Concepcion

As far inland as you can see, the valley of the Santa Rosalia River is a forest of majestic palms where you can hear the rustling of breeze-stirred fronds, the trickling of water, and the calls of tropical birds. Just upstream from the sheltered village, the river is dammed and partly diverted to irrigate citrus, mangoes, papayas, bananas, and date palms. Downstream it's a brackish tidal estuary where big snook lurk—try for them if you can resist the lure of the Sea of Cortez beyond.

Mulege is so small that, even at a stroller's pace, you can visit all the shops and displays in a few hours. Highlights include the restored mission, built in 1766 on a high point upstream from the rest of town, and the imposing state prison (often unoccupied), on a hillside north of the plaza.

Everyone who visits Mulege should spend at least a day on an excursion (preferably by water, though you can get there by road) to Bahia Concepcion, deservedly famous for its fine white beaches, sheltered, warm water, and good fishing. This is the place for the getaway-from-it-all beachcomber.

Detours from the main road lead to several trailer parks and a choice of overnight accommodations (including a fly-in resort) at public and private beaches.

Loreto—Baja's first city

Leaving Bahia Concepcion, the highway snakes up into spectacularly rugged mountains before dropping down to photogenic Loreto on the gulf. Loreto (founded by Jesuit priest Juan Maria Salvatierra in 1697) was Baja's first city and its capital for 132 years. It still enjoys its one-time prominence and is rapidly gaining a new reputation as a favorite haunt for fishing enthusiasts. Located here is Nuestra Señora de Loreto—Baja's first mission—rebuilt again and again, and most recently restored in 1941. It was from Loreto that Father Junipero Serra began his northward march in 1769.

Fishing is great. In proportions that vary with the seasons, all of the valiant game species are ready to do battle—yellowtail, marlin, sailfish, roosterfish, tuna, bass, sierra mackerel, bonito, cabrilla, pompano, and others. For shellfishing and shore casting, head south of town a few miles to where the hills come right down to the water, forming headlands and sheltered coves.

You don't like to fish? Visit the mission museum (closed Sunday and Monday) to see the artifacts collected from all over Baja; stroll the side streets to discover the mud-and-brick oven of Loreto's original bakery; visit the few shops for souvenirs; sit in the plaza and people-watch; or lie in a hammock and look out to sea.

A visit to San Javier, a little community hidden back in a spiny mountain gorge, takes almost all day, although a new road (completed in 1982) replaces the original track. Ask your hotel to pack a lunch; then hire a truck or four-wheel-drive vehicle and driver and allow 2 hours each way for the 23-mile trip. The goal of this rough but beautiful trip is to see the finest example of mission architecture in Baja—the only original mission church remaining intact. It was finished in 1758, has never been restored, and still serves the ranchers and townspeople.

South of Loreto at Nopolo Bay, an ambitious new resort development similar to Cancun and Ixtapa is under way. Now on hand are a beachfront El Presidente Hotel, lighted tennis courts, and the first nine holes of an 18-hole golf course. Several other hotels await completion.

Farther south along the 223-mile drive between Loreto and La Paz is Puerto Escondido, a natural harbor where you can rent a boat at the marina or fish off the dock. Beyond Puerto Escondido the road swings inland; Ciudad Insurgentes and Ciudad Constitucion are the two principal inland towns.

To Los Cabos

From La Paz to the tip of Baja you're in resort land. Unlike the rest of Baja, which is camper country, this area receives most of its visitors by air or by water, exactly as if it were an island—about 100 miles long and 50 miles wide, with sea and land mixed in most agreeable proportions. It is a desert island, though, and that is one of its special qualities. Cactus comes right down to the shore, even at the tip of the peninsula (which extends into tropical latitudes). Many of the beaches are as deserted as Robinson Crusoe's. Going inland usually means going up a little (peaks are over 6,000 feet), so you're always looking out to sea.

Private pilots make Baja's tip a favorite target. Surprisingly luxurious resorts south of La Paz have their own strips—also used by the air taxi service from La Paz. This city is also the home port for Exploration Cruise Line's *North Star*. The ship makes regular 1-week voyages between here and Acapulco with stops at Cabo San Lucas and several mainland ports (see page 39).

You can make a loop trip from La Paz (rental cars available) down the gulf side of the peninsula to Cabo San Lucas, and then up the Pacific side by way of Todos Santos. The entire loop is paved. Along the route are campgrounds and hotels; this is a major area of Baja's new development.

Friendly La Paz

La Paz, colonial capital of Baja California Sur, lost part of its drowsy charm when it geared up for tourists who arrive by ferry from Mexico's west coast resort cities and by jet from the U.S. No longer a backwater town, La Paz is an intriguing city of over 100,000 that most visitors remember fondly. The city's major attractions are within 2 or 3 blocks of the coconut palm–lined waterfront drive—a circumstance encouraging strolling, even though cabs hover about.

The life of the city centers around the water. Even the bandstand—traditional center of the Mexican town plaza—adjoins the malecon (Paseo Alvaro Obregon) in La Paz. Two piers serve sportfishing and commercial boats; the state tourist office is located at the sportfishing wharf. Ten miles to the northeast is Pichilingue, terminal for the Mazatlan and Topolobampo ferries.

Around town. More than a few of the city's buildings are quaint and almost Victorian in appearance. On the south side of Plaza Constitucion stands the original mission, a large rose-pink church. Bilingual plaques describe the history of the church and the city's early settlement. The Museo Antropologico (corner of Ignacio Altamirano and 5 de Mayo) contains interesting exhibits on the area's history, geology, anthropology, and folk art.

Shopping. La Paz is a free port, so you'll find good buys on both imported goods and Mexican handicrafts. Most stores are along Paseo Alvaro Obregon, also the locale for Seri Indians to display their fine wood carvings. In Casa de las Artesanias you'll find many locally-produced items, including leather goods, black coral jewelry, and objects fashioned from seashells. La Perla and Dorian's stores have the largest stock of goods. Visit The Weaver (Fortunato Silva) on Highway 1 for cotton and woolen items and the pottery workshop on Chiapas at Calle Encinas.

Water sports. Superb angling is what brings most people to La Paz. You can rent fishing equipment, boats, and guides from the sportfishing pier near the center of town; reservations are advised from April through June.

Snorkelers and scuba divers will enjoy waters that are warm, wonderfully clear, and teeming with brilliantly colored fish not at all frightened by human presence. Around the rocks near the beaches, you'll find legions of hermit crabs or enormous chitons, and starfish with 20 or more feathery rays.

A pleasure boat offers all-day excursions to the sandy beaches of Espiritu Santo Island; check with the tourist office for details.

Accommodations and dining. Several hotels face the malecon; others are located in the northwest corner of town. Fishing resorts and RV facilities are also found to the south of town (see page 149). Major hotel dining rooms and a few other restaurants sprinkled around town provide good seafood.

Countryside villages

From La Paz, the highway through El Triunfo and San Antonio—towns that whisper of a mining past—climbs gradually into foothills pocked with prospector's holes and draped with yellow-flowering *palo de arco* shrubs. A tall smokestack, landmark of El Triunfo, towers black against the distant sky. Two yellow church towers rise between the smokestack and mine buildings on the hill where once $50,000 worth of gold and silver was produced monthly. San Antonio, now a cattle ranching center, possesses a church of rare simplicity—one of the most handsome in the region. From San Antonio come the baskets, hats, and ornaments sold in the shops of La Paz.

A turnoff 65 miles south of La Paz takes you to the small town of Los Barriles and the Sea of Cortez. Here several fishing resorts (see page 149) provide comfortable accommodations for anglers, many of whom arrive by private plane. (Taxi service and rental cars are also available from La Paz.)

Inland, past the high peaks of the cape region's jagged blue ranges, you'll come to Miraflores, well known for its fruits, cheeses, and leatherwork. Craftsmen here make fine saddles, belts, shoes, and holsters; practically all the *cueras* (leather gun belts worn by cowboys throughout Baja) are made in Miraflores. Nearby Caduano also turns out leatherwork. Goods bought in these two towns cost slightly less than they do in La Paz. Whether or not you're shopping, take time to stop and watch the artisans.

Los Cabos

The end of the great Baja peninsula comes into sight at last. Gradually the desert shore curves westward toward the green splash of San Jose del Cabo, then on and on to the final tall rocks that stand apart and unapproachable—The Friars.

Here Baja California reaches a climax of sorts, not only in geography but also in the beguiling settings, extravagant spaciousness, and elaborate embellishments of its resorts. Prices don't really soar until you get past San Jose del Cabo, a neat, sunny little town that invites exploring.

Between San Jose del Cabo and the end of the cape you'll pass many protected coves with small white beaches that, unfortunately, are often fenced off and inaccessible to the visitor. In bygone years, pirates lay in wait, planning to loot the richly laden Manila galleons, trading ships on annual voyages to Acapulco with stores of Oriental finery and sometimes a fortune in gold. After the long voyage of 6 months or more, ships headed for the mainland put in at San Jose del Cabo for fresh water and supplies. Frequently, bold sea dogs—Thomas Cavendish among them—made off with the rich booty. (A wreck on the beach just east of the cape is the Japanese longliner *Inari Maru No. 10*, lured aground in 1966 by local fishermen using a radio transmitter onshore. Old traditions die hard.)

San Jose del Cabo, a pleasant little town with an attractive church and parklike plaza, has a number of small shops and restaurants. Along the beaches just south of the village is a new resort development, currently boasting 4 hotels, a golf course (9 holes open at present), tennis courts, and the cape's jetport. Bird watchers will enjoy the freshwater estuary adjacent to El Presidente Hotel.

Turnoffs along the 23-mile stretch of beaches between San Jose del Cabo and Cabo San Lucas lead to a line of deluxe accommodations (see page 149). The resorts (several with private airstrips) start with a Moorish mirage at Punta Palmilla, followed by other deluxe establishments around Chileño Bay—spreading grandly and improbably on a desert shore where a few years ago only an obscure ranch stood.

Cabo San Lucas, at the very tip of the peninsula, at first glance still resembles the small cannery village it was before word of its fame as a fishing destination got out. The older section of the town lies inland from the bay formed in the shelter of Baja's southernmost headland. A handful of luxury establishments, several more modest hotels, a trailer park, and a couple of good restaurants are located near the new marina. Cabo San Lucas is the terminal point for the Puerto Vallarta ferry and a shore port for ships cruising along the Mexican coast.

Avid deep-sea anglers put Cabo San Lucas on the map, and they return year after year to pit their skills against the big ones that managed to escape the last time. Families come along, trying out the latest in swimwear around improbably shaped pools, most of them complete with swim-up bars and underwater stools.

Though fishing is the name of the game, you'll find tennis courts and shopping arcades. At the marina, an open-air market has good buys in silver, ironwood, and rare black coral. Small boats, called *pangas*, ferry passengers out to El Arco, a natural arch in the sea where the Sea of Cortez and the Pacific Ocean meet. A multitude of beaches and clear waters nearby provide endless scope for snorkelers.

A loop through Todos Santos

From Cabo San Lucas, Highway 19 heads north along the Pacific side of the peninsula before turning inland to connect with Highway 1 at a point 19 miles south of La Paz. Now that the 87-mile road has been paved, it's usually the preferred route between the cape and La Paz (about 1½ hours less driving time). Several small villages lie along the way.

For the first 50 miles the road parallels the Pacific, sometimes within view of the water, sometimes inland. Several dirt roads branch off to beautifully unpopulated beaches. At Playa Los Cerritos, 44 miles north of the cape, camping is permitted; Playa Punta Lobos, farther north, is a popular place to stop for lunch.

After you reach the farming community of El Pescadero, it's about 7 miles to Todos Santos, a village surrounded by a verdant valley. Tall mango trees, light green and shiny-leafed, line the roadway. Sugar-cane fields and towering palm trees mark fertile lands.

The mission (founded in 1732, rebuilt in 1840, and remodeled in 1941) retains evidence of age in its hand-carved doors and handhewn benches; a bell-ringing rope hangs down from the high tower within hand's reach.

Todos Santos is about 50 miles from La Paz. In spring and after the summer rains the desert glows with yellow clouds of *palo verde* flowers, pink blossoms come out on the *cholla*, and the wands of the *palo adan* (relative of the ocotillo) are tipped with red flowers.

A few miles from Todos Santos on the Pacific side is San Pedrito, a languorous beach with dangerous waves—swim here with caution.

The West Coast

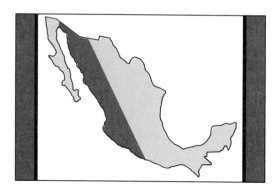

The Golden Coast and Mexico's Riviera—these are two of the names bestowed on the western side of the Mexican mainland. Mexico's west coast offers the nearest tropical destination for motorists from the western United States. It is also the closest by sea, and is regularly visited by cruise ships from San Diego, Los Angeles, San Francisco, and the East Coast. The cost of air travel from the western U.S. to Mexico's west coast is comparable to (or even slightly less than) airfare to the next-nearest tropical destination—Hawaii. Ferry service to and from Baja makes it an increasingly popular leg on a triangle trip from California or Arizona.

Attractions

Great mountain ranges, grand canyons, lush jungles, and sparse deserts—they're all found along the west coast. Its bay-notched coasts are edged with superb swimming beaches, and its many rocky points lure anglers. Mixed emotions greeted the building of Highways 15 and 200, which made these formerly remote spots easily accessible. This "sunshine route" continues all the way down the coast to the Guatemala border.

In many parts of western Mexico the bare feet on once-secret ribbons of sand belong not to native fishermen but to tourists. Luxurious hotels cover spaces where fishing huts once stood. Here you'll find swimming pools, restaurants, and a wide range of activities to fill all your waking moments.

If you're an adventurous traveler ready for a change from the commercialism of Mazatlan, Puerto Vallarta, Manzanillo, Ixtapa, and Acapulco, you can find unspoiled locations where rural Mexico is right at your elbow. A number of smaller and less expensive resorts dot the Pacific coast's southernmost 1,000 miles. Here, gourmet restaurants are scarce, shopping is limited, and you'll need to dust off your Spanish. South of Acapulco, less-developed beaches invite intrepid, self-contained campers.

A sunny land

With some of the most dependable sunshine in North America, Mexico's Pacific coast is at its best from November through April, with congenial waters, balmy nights, and days so sunny that the midday sand sizzles.

Weather is best during winter and early spring; the "in" season is from November to May. Hotel prices drop sharply during the rest of the year and many a canny traveler braves the warmer temperatures and intermittent rains to sun at half the price. One exception is Guaymas: You pay more in the summer for rooms there because of the added cost of air conditioning.

Waves scallop the sandy arc of Zihuatanejo Bay.

The Northwest Coast

One of the most accessible portions of Mexico is the northwest corner of the state of Sonora, which includes the 253-mile stretch of Highway 15 from Nogales to Guaymas.

The desert in this area is spacious and almost unscarred. Flying over the desert or driving through it, you'll see how light civilization's touch has been—out toward the coast, vast areas have never been inhabited; in many regions, European culture and industry gained footholds three centuries or so ago, but the only traces of them now are ruins.

The people who still live in the desert have attempted to transform their environment, though they and their goats and cattle are scattered too thinly to change the look of the land much. The brown adobe houses, barns, and corral walls blend easily into the desert setting.

Nogales

Nogales, Arizona, and its Mexican counterpart, Nogales, Sonora, are primary entry gateways for Mexico's west coast beaches. The customs offices at the border are open 24 hours a day; here you can acquire tourist permits, if you haven't already (they're not necessary if you're visiting only this city). The Southwest's fifth-largest border crossing, Nogales, Sonora, has dozens of American-owned factories producing everything from sunglasses and luggage to computer parts and underwear. It's also the biggest crossing for Mexican fruits and vegetables bound for U.S. tables.

But it's the sheer joy of shopping that brings most visitors to Nogales. Along the 6 blocks nearest the border, small shops jammed floor to ceiling spill out onto the sidewalks with ironwood animal carvings, gaily colored serapes, handloomed wool blankets, leather goods, papier-mâché parrots, onyx chess sets, piñatas, and embroidered dresses and shirts. Among the newest malls are El Cid and Plaza San Miguel.

The U.S. side of the border offers a better selection of trailer facilities, motels, and hotels.

El Gran Desierto

Mexico's Highway 2 follows the border on the Mexican side from Tijuana through Mexicali and San Luis to Sonoita, and then turns southeast to meet Highway 15, the route to Hermosillo.

Colonial ruins can be explored on day trips from the colonial town of Alamos.

Crumbling remains of original Kino mission at Cocospera

Over 300 years ago an Italian Jesuit priest, the incredibly tough and daring Father Eusebio Kino, settled in the vast Sonoran Desert and endured thirst, hunger, and hostile Indians while exploring (often alone) great stretches of northwestern Mexico and what are now Arizona and California. By the time he died in 1711, he had founded 22 missions.

In addition, Father Kino converted seven Indian tribes to Christianity and taught them how to farm, survived a bloody uprising, wrote two books, and built an ark in Caborca with the idea of sailing to Baja. He discovered the Gila River and was the first to chart the surrounding countryside. He was also the first to prove that neighboring Baja was a peninsula—not an island.

In fact, no single person has had more influence on this area.

Cocospera. The only traces of the original mission structures are the crumbling, weathered adobe walls of the Cocospera mission, on Highway 2 (follow signs to Cananea), 24 miles northeast of Highway 15. It was one of the three missions Kino himself tended, visiting once a week by horseback.

Most of the rest of the existing missions were rebuilt nearly a century after Kino, under Franciscan direction during the same era as California's missions, 1780 to 1820.

Magdalena. In 1966, Father Kino's remains were discovered at Magdalena de Kino (6 miles south of the town of Magdalena and about 1 mile west of Highway 15). Around fiesta time, from late September through October 4, the route from Nogales to Magdalena is congested with foot travelers on pilgrimage to recharge their spiritual batteries.

Magdalena offers very little in the way of sightseeing except for the attractive plaza surrounded by arched, missionlike buildings housing restaurants and shops.

The other mission locations are Imuris, San Ignacio, Oquitoa, Atil, Tubutama, Pitiquito, and Caborca. Best accommodations are at Magdalena and Caborca.

. . . the Northwest Coast

The thin track of Camino del Diablo (now Highway 2) once wandered uncertainly for some 126 miles along the Arizona–Sonora line, among the rocks, cactus, and soft sand between San Luis and Sonoita; it was no place for the casual traveler. Today there's still a long gap between gas stations, but the smooth pavement of Highway 2 invites—and gets—high speeds.

From San Luis, Highway 2 heads east into the flat, silty desert. The road reaches out for the nearly featureless horizon ahead; on your left you can see the Gila Mountains of Arizona, and far off to the right, the faint blue line of Baja California's 10,000-foot-high backbone.

It's wise to take certain precautions when driving long distances on barren roads: never drive at night, don't sleep in your car, and don't pick up hitchhikers. Take along plenty of water and extra gas. For a less hazardous and tedious trip, drive to Baja California and take a ferry across the Sea of Cortez.

El Golfo de Santa Clara, a hamlet 70 miles south of San Luis on a paved road, sounds more impressive than it is—a remote fishing village in an unspoiled, natural setting on the Sea of Cortez. Wide white beaches with soft, clean, inviting sands stretch for some 56 miles. Tides are among the world's highest, rising as much as 25 feet. Fishing is the prime attraction, but you can also explore the beaches in a dune buggy, or swim and sun. Facilities include a gas station, drugstore, grocery store, restaurants, and trailer parks (no hookups).

En route to Sonoita, the highway forsakes its straight-arrow course out of San Luis to wind easily among some of the cinder cones and basalt mesas of Cerro Piñacate. It's hard to find a more massive volcano than this anywhere in the world. The volcano's broad, symmetrical, black lava mass, studded with hundreds of cinder cones and pocked with explosion pits and calderas, lies south of the highway, which cuts across some of the lava flows. U.S. astronauts practiced here before their first moon mission.

A corking good fishing port, Guaymas stretches along a deep bay.

The paved road to Puerto Penasco (also called Rocky Harbor) starts at Sonoita, 62 miles away. This shrimping port along the gulf is fast becoming a tourist town, but the beach-camping settlements of Choya Bay and Sandy Beach nearby are more primitive. Their sun and empty beaches, as well as good clamming, tidepool exploring, and shell hunting, appeal to beachcombers.

Hotels, motels, and restaurants are more plentiful in Puerto Penasco than in Choya Bay. If you want to camp, check the trailer parks in Puerto Penasco, or head to beaches in the area where you can park RVs for a small fee (Puerto Penasco has a grocery store with water and some food but no other facilities). You'll find boats for hire in Puerto Penasco and Choya Bay; launching is better at Choya. Launch permits are required for all Mexican waters.

Hermosillo—Sonora's capital

Well worth a stopover, Hermosillo is a lovely, clean city with wide, tree-lined boulevards and tiled walks. The town offers a variety of places to stay and things to do. Much of the original ornate colonial architecture still lines the plaza, but the old adobes have been replaced with brick structures and many modern public buildings have sprung up. Despite Hermosillo's modern appearance, the "old" Mexico is still there—evening promenades in the plaza, shops filled with a wide selection of Mexican crafts and imported goods, open markets, and plentiful seafood.

The University of Sonora is located on the highway in the north central part of the city. Other points of interest include the cathedral, a handsome regional museum, and the attractively planted Parque Madero. Several hotels offer golfing privileges; excellent hunting and fishing are available nearby.

Kino Bay

Beautiful Kino Bay is one of the few accessible spots for motorists on the long undeveloped coastline stretching from the northern end of the Sea of Cortez down to the resort center of Guaymas. Kino Bay and the little town of Kino are 66 miles from Hermosillo by good paved road.

The residents of the original tiny village make their living chiefly by fishing from small boats or dugout canoes. South of the village some luxury condominiums have sprouted, but most of the development is north of town in the more urban shoreline community of "New" Kino, a modern development with motels, RV facilities, and a few restaurants.

· Large Tiburon Island in Kino Bay is the homeland of the Seri Indians and a developing wildlife refuge. You'll need a special permit to visit the island; check with local boatmen.

Guaymas

Guaymas is really three communities: a city and two resort areas. The original city and its port face the Bay of Guaymas; 2 miles northwest, over a mountainous peninsula, is Miramar Beach on Bacochibampo Bay; and another 12 miles up the coast is the resort community of San Carlos Bay.

The city, a major seaport hub of the Mexican shrimp industry and a world fishing capital, is encircled by a range of steep cliffs and mountains. Visitors enjoy the variety of stores, an attractive church, and a landlocked harbor. Native families bring their children to Las Playitas, a small public beach facing shallow water. Guaymas is also the terminus of a popular car-ferry route from Santa Rosalia in Baja California. It's a good idea to have reservations; you can arrange for your passage at the terminal building. A daily train connects Guaymas with Hermosillo and Nogales.

To reach Bacochibampo Bay, you'll drive through a line of private beach homes. Where's the water? It is well hidden by the congested arrangements of hotels, trailer parks, and houses. But remember—all Mexican beaches are public and you'll soon find an access to the rocky shore. Several resort hotels and motels offer accommodations.

San Carlos Bay, north of Guaymas and about 8 miles west of Highway 15, is popular with American tourists. This multimillion-dollar complex includes a luxury hotel, several motels, a yacht club and marina, restaurants, tennis courts, an 18-hole golf course, an RV village, a small trailer park, and a subdivision of seaside homes and cottages. Nearby is an airstrip for private planes and a Club Med enclave.

The waters are filled with an abundant and bewildering variety of game fish. Summer offers the most spectacular fishing, though after May the weather is sometimes oppressively hot. The big runs of marlin and sailfish come in July and August, but game fishing will satisfy the soul of the average angler during autumn and winter months. The most exciting (and most crowded) time is during the annual midsummer Deep Sea Fishing Rodeo.

The transparent blue waters of Guaymas are made to order for those who enjoy skin diving and snorkeling: Very few hazards exist, water temperature and visibility are nearly ideal, and lobsters and turtles are plentiful. Lobsters can be caught most easily on moonless, windless nights; they feed in shallow water.

Besides fishing, Guaymas offers ideal conditions for relaxing and soaking up the sun. If you want to exercise rather than take a siesta, try the tennis courts or golf course. The swimming, good horseback riding, and shopping should also keep you occupied.

The West Coast 27

Guaymas to Mazatlan

South from Guaymas, Highway 15 threads its way through expansive desert scrubland, with the foothills of the Sierra Madre Occidental always visible to the east and the Sea of Cortez coastline barely discernible to the west.

The highway is generally good, but you'll encounter occasional detours around road-widening and improvement projects. Principal cities along this coastal route are Ciudad Obregon, Navojoa, Alamos (a short side trip from Highway 15), Los Mochis, and Culiacan.

Ciudad Obregon

Ciudad Obregon is edged by cotton gins, mills, and granaries. Planned before the argicultural boom began, Obregon reflects the disorder and incongruities typical of rapid growth. Yet its streets are well lighted, and some are creatively landscaped. In the spirit of modern urban planning, Obregon's power lines are underground. An impressive church and a brewery highlight sightseeing in town. Alvaro Obregon Dam, 35 miles north of town, represents the first step in a huge federal irrigation program for this area.

Hunters come to this region (especially from October through February) to shoot wild ducks, doves, and quail that flock together at sunset over the rice fields near town. Deer, wild turkeys, bears, and wild pigs live in the mountains within 50 miles of the city. Arrangements for hunting trips can be made at motels.

Navojoa

An old town dating back to 1614, Navojoa was devastated by a flood in 1914 and subsequently relocated on higher ground. It is a departure point for trips to nearby Alamos, to the Mayo Indian village of Yavaros, to isolated Huatabampito Beach and other west-coast cities. Off the road to Alamos you'll find a good fishing lake.

Alamos—a rewarding detour

The colonial heritage of Alamos, a fascinating town 34 miles east of Navojoa, pervades the town's architecture and the activities of its inhabitants. Declared a colonial monument by the state government, the town has made an effort to preserve reminders of its past as a Spanish silver-mining center in the late 1700s. Though some of the buildings are little more than a century old, they blend to convey an image of colonial antiquity.

Founded in 1540 as a camp for one of Coronado's expeditions, Alamos later became the capital of both Sonora and what is now the neighboring state of Sinaloa. In the 18th century, Alamos and its suburbs were the world's richest source of silver.

Moorish arches, delicately fashioned iron grillwork, and *portales* (covered walks) are indispensable elements of the Spanish personality of Alamos. Don't miss the graceful fountains, splashy gardens, and elegant mansions that once belonged to silver barons. Art galleries, cantinas, courtyards, leather shops, and the Plaza Mayor are some highlights of this treasure of Mexico's past.

Alamos has two excellent inns (Casa de los Tesoros, a converted 18th-century convent, and Mansion de la Condesa Magdalena, a former 17th-century noblewoman's home), restaurants, motels, and a trailer park.

Places to explore near Alamos

Once you've poked around the town of Alamos, you may want to look at the surrounding countryside—the tropical forest on nearby Alamos Mountain, the foothill oasis of the great Sierra Madre to the east, old mines and silver smelters, scattered ruins, and bays and beaches along the coast. Aduana, once the site of a great smelting works where Alamos silver was cast into ingots, is little more than a country village today. The tall cactus growing from the church wall has a special significance. According to legend, the cactus was on the site before the church was built; an image of the Virgin appeared atop the plant and pointed out a rich silver lode. On November 20, a festival commemorates the event.

To Los Mochis and Topolobampo

Intriguingly, Los Mochis was founded by an American, Benjamin Johnston, who came from Virginia to build a sugar refinery and stayed to lay out a township with the wide streets and square blocks of a North American city. Johnston also built a magnificent mansion with an indoor swimming pool, an elevator, a huge banquet kitchen, and elegant formal gardens. After Johnston died in 1938, the family moved back to the U.S. The estate house was later torn down, but the botanical gardens, now called Sinaloa Park, are delightful to visit.

From Los Mochis you can take a rail trip through some of the most spectacular mountain and canyon land in the world—Copper Canyon (see page 112).

Topolobampo, a deepwater port on the Sea of Cortez, is also close to Los Mochis. A boat is helpful for touring the numerous coves, estuaries, beaches, and islands. Sportfishing is excellent if you can go with one of the local commercial fishermen. Topolobampo is also the eastern terminus for a passenger and auto ferry from La Paz across the Sea of Cortez.

DETAILS AT A GLANCE

Mexicali to Mazatlan

How to get there

Most travelers pick one resort and find the fastest way to get there, allowing themselves maximum time on sunny beaches.

By air. Several international airlines, including Mexicana, reach resort areas directly from the U.S. and Mexico. Mexican carriers also supply connecting service between major Mexican cities and coastal resorts. Since flight schedules change frequently, check with a travel agent. Private pilots should obtain a copy of *Airports of Mexico* by Arnold Senterfitt.

By road. Westerners often drive to the northern coast. Highway 2 from Tijuana and Mexicali joins Highway 15 from Nogales, the route to Hermosillo, Kino Bay, San Carlos Bay, Guaymas, Mazatlan, and San Blas. At Tepic, take Highway 200 along the coast to reach southern resorts. Bus travel is not recommended except for short distances.

By boat. Ferry service connects Baja California and the west coast between Guaymas and Santa Rosalia, Topolobampo/Los Mochis and La Paz, Mazatlan and La Paz, and Puerto Vallarta and Cabo San Lucas. Cruise ships often include a stop at Mazatlan.

Tours

You can save money with a package tour. The price usually includes transportation and accommodations; bonuses such as city tours or discounts for local events may be offered.

Accommodations

"Varied" best describes resorts, hotels, motels, campgrounds, and RV parks along the coast. Your choice of suitable accommodations is limited only by the season and your budget. (See the "Essentials" section on page 150 for more information.)

Climate & clothes

The farther south you travel, the warmer it becomes. The "in" season is winter and spring. Summer, a rainy time, brings a decrease in room rates (Guaymas may be an exception) to compensate for heat.

In northerly areas, you may need a jacket and scarf during windy weather; otherwise, take cool, casual clothing for beach or street. Good buys in local beach attire make it wise to wait and add to your wardrobe on the spot.

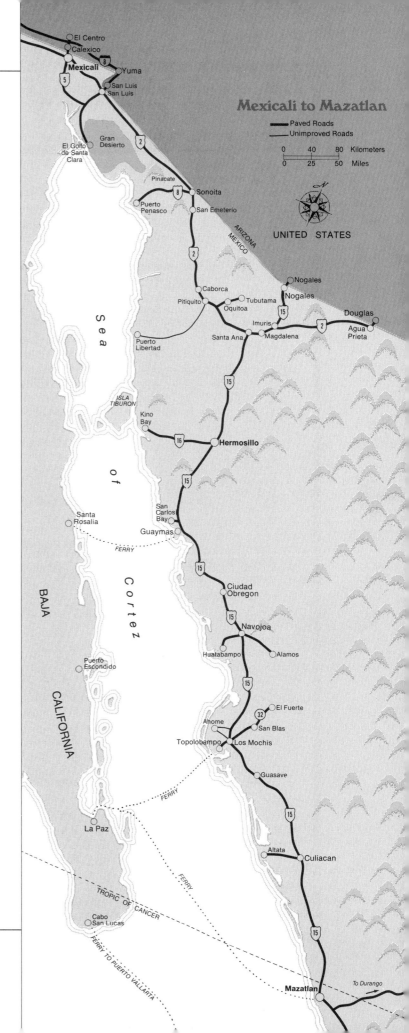

Fireworks, snapping fingers and swirling skirts, the aroma of cooking food, music and dancing—it's fiesta time in Mexico! Just about any event, happy or sad, becomes an excuse for a celebration. So many events crowd the calendar that the book published by the tourism authority, *Fiestas in Mexico*, has around 200 pages.

Below is a list of some of the colorful celebrations to enjoy during your visit.

January 1: New Year's Day celebrations, much like those in the U.S. A carnival-like atmosphere with games, events, and fireworks throughout Mexico.

January 6: Three Kings Day. All over Mexico, children set out shoes to be filled with gifts.

January 17: St. Anthony's Day. Household pets and barnyard animals are decorated and taken to churches to be blessed.

January 18: Taxco fiesta in honor of Santa Prisca, the town's patron saint.

February 2: Feast of the Candles. A colorful fiesta with dances, bullfights, and processions, especially interesting in Tlacotlapan.

February 5: This national holiday commemorates Mexico's present government under the Constitutions of 1857 and 1917.

February 19: Cuautla celebrates the city's defeat of Spanish troops during the War of Independence.

March 1–4: Religious festival held in Taxco.

March 10–21: Strawberry Fair takes place in Irapuato.

March 21: Birthday of Benito Juarez, the "Abraham Lincoln of Mexico."

March–April: Holy Week (variable date). An especially intense and passionate religious fete observed throughout Mexico, particularly inspiring in Taxco, Patzcuaro, and San Cristobal de las Casas. On the Saturday before Easter, papier-mâché figures representing Judas are burned.

April 15–May 5: Fair of St. Mark. One of the most important festivals in Mexico features native dances and bullfights; Aguascalientes has a noted fair.

May 1: Mexico's Labor Day is celebrated with parades, dances, and civic exercises.

May 3: Holy Cross Day. Construction workers mount decorated crosses atop unfinished buildings. Fireworks and picnics take place at the sites.

May 5: *Cinco de Mayo* celebrates liberation from the French; try to see it in Puebla.

May–June: Corpus Christi Day (variable date). In Mexico City, children and babies are dressed in native costumes and taken to the cathedral for blessing.

June 24: St. John the Baptist Day is celebrated with fairs, religious festivities, and practical jokes.

July 7–15: Festival of St. Fermin. Also known as the Festival of Lights because offerings of candles are placed in churches.

July 15–31: Festival in honor of Our Lady of Carmen. Regional dances, fireworks, and bullfights in the state of Campeche.

Late July: Colorful night processions to a hill outside Oaxaca; usually held the last two Mondays.

August 8: Traditional fiesta in Paracho.

August 25: Feast of patron saint of San Luis Potosi.

September 6–9: Festival of Our Lady of the Remedies. Native dances are featured in the atrium atop a large pyramid in Cholula.

September 16: Independence Day. Begins the night of September 15 when *El Grito*—Father Hidalgo's original cry for independence—is shouted by public officials. Impressive celebrations are held at the Zocalo in Mexico City and in Dolores Hidalgo.

September 29: Date variable. Special festival honoring San Miguel de Allende's patron saint.

September 30: Festival in Morelos commemorates birth of Mexican independence hero Jose Maria Morelos and the lifting of the siege of Cuautla.

October 1–31: Month-long cultural festival takes place in Guadalajara.

October 4: Day of St. Francis brings particularly good celebrations to Pachuca, Uruapan, and Puebla.

October 7–15: Village of Alvarado, near Veracruz, honors Our Lady of the Rosary with a week-long fiesta.

October 12: Columbus Day. A national holiday commemorating the discovery of America by Christopher Columbus.

Reverent pilgrim at shrine to Guadalupe, Mexico's patron saint

November 1–2: All Souls' Day, also known as Day of the Dead. All-night candlelight vigils at cemeteries, especially impressive at Janitzio.

November 20: Anniversary of the Mexican Revolution of 1910.

November 25: Fair of St. Catherine is held in Rio Verde area of San Luis Potosi.

Late November: Taxco honors its founding industry with a silver fair.

December 8: Festival of our Lady of Health in Patzcuaro features dancing and fireworks.

December 12: *Dia de Guadalupe* (Day of our Lady of Guadalupe).

Celebrations of Mexico's patron saint take place throughout the country. Mexico City's Guadalupe Basilica is thronged with worshipers.

December 16: Beginning of Christmas festivities. Especially colorful time of year with celebrations all over Mexico; particularly elaborate posadas in Taxco, Queretaro, Oaxaca, and Patzcuaro.

December 23: Night of the Radishes. A yearly competition of imaginative displays made from radishes held in Oaxaca. Festival includes parades, dances, and fireworks.

December 28: All Fool's Day. Like April Fools' Day in the U.S.

Oaxaca's brightly lighted zocalo at Christmas

Mazatlan to Manzanillo

When you reach Mazatlan you've crossed the Tropic of Cancer, where you expect glistening sands, leaning palms, and tropical beach resorts. You aren't disappointed. The region's resort towns are varied: Fishing is the focus in Mazatlan; people-watching is the favorite sport in Puerto Vallarta (with shopping a close second). Paved Highway 200 starts just north of Puerto Vallarta and continues south to the Mexico–Guatemala border; you'll want to take along a current map to check distances and road conditions.

Mazatlan

Long ago, Mazatlan outgrew the small peninsula on which it was originally founded and spread northward along a series of crescent-shaped beaches that extend for miles. Though some of the best restaurants and older hotels are located in the downtown area, major shopping centers and hotel developments are strung out along the beaches to the north.

The boulevard along the sea wall connects old and new Mazatlan; it starts at Playa Olas Altas and runs north for several miles—with several name changes. In other Mexican cities the evening promenade takes place in the park or plaza; in Mazatlan, it saunters along the malecon. The pace of living in the city has picked up as its popularity has increased. But quaint, horse-drawn 2-wheel carts called *aranas* can still be hired for sightseeing trips and 3-passenger, 3-wheel *pulmonias* (open-air taxis) are still popular modes of transportation.

Landmarks include the usual town plaza with old-fashioned bandstand, a yellow-towered cathedral, and some majestic hills. Around town, palms, bananas, papayas, mangoes, and flowers lend a tropical air. At the southern tip of town El Faro, the world's second-tallest lighthouse (Gibraltar's is higher), beams its light some 30 miles out to sea; underneath, grottoes entice visitors in small boats. A harbor cruise departs from El Faro each morning. Farther north stands Cerro la Neveria (Icebox Hill); its tunnels were once repositories for blocks of ice brought by boat from San Francisco and delivered by mule cart to stores and homes.

For a few pesos, daredevil divers leap from the 40-foot El Mirador view tower on the malecon. To the north, the gigantic Fisherman's Monument attests to the force of the sea. A fine aquarium sits back a block from the beachfront on Avenida de los Deportes. You'll see over 250 species of fish as well as sharks, alligators, and seals.

Shopping centers around Playa Olas Altas, the produce market between Avenidas Serdan and Benito Juarez, and an area north of town called the Zona Dorada (Golden Zone). At the city market you can visit seemingly endless rows of fruit and vegetable stalls with appetizing displays of pineapples, mangoes, bananas, and other tropical delights. Buy curios, try on *huaraches*, toss a lacy shawl over your shoulders, and bargain to your heart's content.

The Mazatlan Arts & Crafts Center in the Golden Zone started life as a place for artisans to practice their crafts; today it's a shopping complex displaying a variety of wares from all over Mexico. Sea Shell City, across from Los Sabalos Hotel, sells items made with shells from around the world. Galerias Indio is an upscale shop with fine handicrafts and gift items. Most tourist boutiques, restaurants, shops, and offices are concentrated in these several blocks.

Vaulted dome, gilded altar, and ornate tile mark the interior of Mazatlan's cathedral.

Two ways to get there: Modern railway crosses the upper trestle while burro train plods along below.

An extemporaneous barbecue, fish-on-a-stick are sold by many beach vendors.

The West Coast 33

Filigree-crowned church tower stands sentinel over passing boats at Puerto Vallarta's popular waterfront.

Resembling a Moorish fantasy, gleaming Las Hadas hotel complex lies on a bay near Manzanillo.

34   The West Coast

... Mazatlan to Manzanillo

Big-game fishing developed Mazatlan. Marlin and sailfish swarm in the waters year-round, and their pursuit is both expert and businesslike. Fleets of sleek cruisers cluster at neighboring piers along the docks. Normally as many as four people fish from a boat fully manned and equipped with everything needed for billfishing, except muscle. All you need to carry aboard is your camera and a box lunch from your hotel. Make fishing reservations well in advance during spring.

Mazatlan's harbor is termed the best along Mexico's west coast. From here, the country's largest shrimp fleet sets out to pull in catches often destined for U.S. consumption. The colorful harbor is where you can catch the daily ferry to La Paz, a 17-hour trip. Also located here are docks for cruise ships, freighters, and tankers.

Other outdoor activities take place on the beaches from Playa Olas Altas north to the district of on-the-beach hotels, condominiums, and RV facilities. Opportunities for parasailing, water-skiing, swimming, and sunning abound. You can rent "bilingual" horses (they take commands in both Spanish and English).

Cruises head out to several islands in the bay: Palmito de la Virgen is a bird watchers' retreat and the waters off Deer Island are good for snorkeling and shell collecting. Isla de la Piedra (Stone Island), only a 10-minute boat trip away, offers one of the most beautiful beaches on the entire west coast.

Tennis and golf are available all year; check with your hotel for locations and other details. Bullfights usually take place from December through March. The bullring is right downtown. Charreadas are held on Sunday afternoon in summer at a ring near the train station.

Your hotel can also arrange a tour to some of Mazatlan's outlying areas. A daylong excursion to Copala, a picturesque former silver-mining village, gives you a look at the green, forested back country. Along the way you might stop at tidy Concordia to view the richly sculptured small church and to see furniture makers and other craftsmen at work. Many woodworkers offer product books from which you can order and have the item shipped home.

Mazatlan's largest annual event is the pre-Lent Mardi Gras celebration. During Carnival you'll see parades, official receptions, colorful floats, dances accompanied by exuberant mariachis, and fireworks.

South of Mazatlan

As the coastal route winds southward, the vegetation becomes more varied and lush, characterized by ebony, rosewood, lignum vitae, mahogany, and brazilwood. Palm trees, bedecked with yellow-, purple-, and pink-flowered tropical vines, resemble overdecorated Christmas trees.

When the coastal lagoons come close to the highway south of Mazatlan, you'll see bright pink flamingos standing resolutely in the mud flats. Bananas, papayas, pineapples, mangoes, and citruses grow in jungle clearings. Farms become smaller, and the sophisticated tractors of the north are replaced by simpler farm equipment. Many farmers still till their fields with ox-drawn plows.

About 17 miles south of Mazatlan, Highway 40 branches inland across the mountains to Durango, and Highway 15 swings away from the coast. Your only access to beaches from there south to Tepic is on side roads that lead off to the west.

The island city of Mexcaltitan, beyond Acaponeta, is thought by some archaeologists to be the original home of the Aztecs. All of its streets, which radiate from the center of the circular island, become canals during the rainy season. You reach the island by shore-based launches or on an aerial tour from Mazatlan. During the Feast of St. Peter and St. Paul (June 29), canoes with images of the two saints race around the island. If St. Peter wins, it's thought that fishing will be blessed for the coming year.

Sleepy San Blas is a peaceful, quiet, and beautiful destination for travelers who shun the luxuries of more tourist-oriented towns. Tropical jungles surround the village. Beaches near Mantanchen Bay make ideal spots for sunning and beachcombing; offshore islands abound with colorful tropical birds and rewarding finds for shell collectors. You can charter a boat for fishing or sightseeing, or take an excursion boat to several remote beaches accessible only by water.

From Highway 15, it takes about half an hour to negotiate the 22-mile paved road past thatched huts, small streams, and dense jungle. Streams flow near the roadside; you'll probably see people bathing and doing laundry along the banks. Marshy flats replace coquito palms, and dark estuaries wind through low vegetation, their banks solidly lined with mangroves too thick to walk through. Exposed roots are encrusted with oysters.

Life in San Blas drifts slowly and languorously along. A few small shops selling crafts, dresses, and jewelry are scattered among adobe-and-wattle huts clustered around the church and the rose-scented central plaza. Neat cobblestone streets lined with coconut palms lend a South Seas atmosphere to the area.

During colonial days San Blas was a bustling port; now, the impressive customs house near the end of the main street remains as a decaying relic of a bygone era. On the crest of a small hill overlooking the newer section of town is old San Blas, built during the reign of the Spaniards. Hike or drive up here for a look at the crumbling remains of the fort, church, and other buildings overgrown with vegetation. You may see some iguanas—scaly lizards sometimes growing to more than 2 feet long—inhabiting the ruins.

Mazatlan to Acapulco

Map labels:

TROPIC OF CANCER
FERRY TO LA PAZ
To Culiacan
15
Mazatlan
40
To Durango
Escuinapa
15
Acaponeta
LAS TRES ISLAS MARIAS
FERRY TO CABO SAN LUCAS
San Blas
Playa Miramar
Tepic
200
Sayulita
15
Ixtlan del Rio
Puerto Vallarta
Yelapa
Tequila
To Aguascalientes
200
Ameca
Zapopan
54
Costa de Careyes
Autlan
80
Guadalajara
To San Luis Potosi
Ajijic
Chapala
Tepatitlan
80
Barra de Navidad
Lake Chapala
Ocotlan
Manzanillo
110
La Barca
Cuyutlan
Colima
Ciudad Guzman
Jiquilpan
Sahuayo
Tecoman
Zamora
15
PACIFIC OCEAN
Uruapan
To Morelia
37
Playa Azul
To Mexico City
Ixtapa
134
Zihuatanejo
200
To Mexico City
95
Acapulco

Mazatlan to Acapulco

—— Paved Roads

| 0 | 40 | 80 | Kilometers |
| 0 | 25 | 50 | Miles |

N

Mazatlan to Acapulco

How to get there

Flying to any of the west coast resort cities is easy and fast, and the best way to spend the maximum time in the sun.

By air. Several international airlines, including Mexicana, have direct service to major resorts—Mazatlan, Puerto Vallarta, Manzanillo, Ixtapa, and Acapulco. Connecting service for Puerto Escondido, Puerto Angel, and Huatulco is available through Mexico City, Guadalajara, and Oaxaca, making it possible to combine coastal resort and city experiences.

By road. It's a long, though interesting, drive down the Pacific coast on Highway 200 to southern resorts. Good highways also connect Guadalajara and Mexico City with the coast. Buses are a slow proposition, but inexpensive.

By boat. Cruise ships often stop at Puerto Vallarta, Manzanillo, Ixtapa/Zihuatanejo, and Acapulco, with time for on-shore excursions. For additional information on coastal cruises, see the special feature on page 39.

Tours

Package tours to a resort usually include air fare and accommodations, plus some meals and sightseeing. Check with a travel agency for the best packages. At Huatulco, the newest government-planned resort, you can expect promotional low-cost packages.

Accommodations

Prices of hotels and campgrounds vary with the location. Rates are cheapest during the summer. Deluxe accommodations are found at such resorts as Puerto Vallarta, Manzanillo, Ixtapa, and Acapulco. Huatulco is still developing.

More inexpensive lodging is available along Costa de Careyes north of Manzanillo. For further information, see the "Essentials" section on page 150.

Climate & clothes

The southern coast gets hot in summer; best time of year to visit is in winter and early spring. Take your bathing suit, shorts, and casual clothing for evening. You may want to add a sweater for air-conditioned dining rooms. Designers in Puerto Vallarta and Acapulco offer one-of-a-kind fashions, so it's worth waiting until you arrive to buy resort attire.

... Mazatlan to Manzanillo

At the main beach, a wide, sandy strip about a mile from the center of town, swimming is good all year. Along the beach, you'll find bathhouses, hotels, and stands selling tantalizing sweets. Accommodations are adequate, if not luxurious.

One popular excursion is a jungle boat trip up La Tobara tributary. The 2½-hour journey begins at the bridge over the San Cristobal River and passes through mangrove swamps and crystal-clear jungle pools, giving visitors a chance to see orchids and other tropical vegetation. The boat stops off at coffee and banana plantations. Colorful birds such as egrets, herons, and ibises abound.

The best time to visit San Blas is between November and May. Strong winds usually blow across the beach in the afternoon. Summers are hot and humid, though it's sometimes cool enough for a blanket at night. One warning: Take some insect repellent. Though insect control has improved, small gnats called *jejenes* often swarm around the estuaries and beaches from late afternoon to early morning.

Tepic, an old colonial city with a solid, prosperous look, is the capital of the small state of Nayarit. The main streets have been widened, a process that added modern façades that contrast sharply with the old walled cemetery and the arcaded buildings around the plaza.

Soccer games in the stadium at the edge of town, and promenades and concerts in the attractive city park, provide entertainment for visiting spectators. Points of interest include the main plaza's cathedral, which was built in 1750 and has two perfect Gothic-type towers, and the Iglesia de la Cruz, a church that was once part of the Franciscan Convento de la Cruz (founded in 1744). Also pay a visit to the state museum, rich in past treasures.

The town, situated 3,186 feet above sea level at the base of an extinct volcano, is noticeably cooler than the nearby coast. The broad valley south of Tepic produces sugar cane, corn, and tobacco. A large cigarette factory in town employs many of Tepic's residents. Small banana and papaya groves surround settlements.

Among Tepic's natural attractions are two waterfalls: Ingenio de Jala falls, which flow with full force during the rainy season, and El Salto, west of the city. About 20 miles southeast of Tepic lies Laguna Santa Maria, a crater lake.

Puerto Vallarta

Its cobblestone streets are still rough, uneven, and jolting: The perilous descents from hillside *casas, casitas,* and condos are rugged and scary; and the number of shops, restaurants, and resorts keeps on growing. By some strange grace, though, Puerto Vallarta retains the charm that has made it world famous.

Described in superlatives by most visitors, Puerto Vallarta's environs look more tropical and tidier than those of Mazatlan or Acapulco. Though you'll glimpse much of the native life, the presence of the U.S. tourist is often more obvious because the town is still small, under 150,000 people.

Occasional donkey carts rattle along the street among the taxis, autos, and jeeps. Flaming bougainvillea and blue jacaranda hug stucco walls; sweet jasmine perfumes the night. Even if it's no longer a quiet retreat, "PV" is certainly one of Mexico's fun spots and a highly picturesque town in a perfect away-from-it-all setting.

The town is crowded between the foot of the mountains and lovely Banderas Bay. To get acquainted, locate the Cuale River, the *zocalo* (plaza), the malecon, and the Church of Guadalupe; a 3-hour city bus tour can be booked at your hotel. The river (which runs in an east–west direction) serves as a natural dividing line within the city, separating the business sections from the south beach. The two bridges across the Cuale River provide scenes of constant bedlam rivaling the confusion of any large city freeway. Cuale Island has a pleasant mixture of open stalls catering to the tourist, several restaurants, and a small archeological museum.

The airport, marina, most of the hotels, and the city's business district lie to the north of the river; a few splendid resorts, villas, and some fine restaurants have recently been built in the more secluded southern reaches. Farther up the river loom steep cliffs where luxurious homes cling precariously. One ravine is dubbed "Gringo Gulch" because of the number of Americans maintaining homes there.

Beaches—lovely, wide, and uncluttered—to the north and south of town are ideal for sunbathing, swimming, water-skiing, hiking, tennis, and horseback riding. Although a few beaches run along the malecon, swimming here is not too good. Playa del Sol, downtown, has the action: vendors with goods and fish-on-a-stick, thatch-roofed palapas housing snack shops and cocktail bars, wandering mariachis, and boat and surfboard rentals. Taxis and minibuses run to and fro along the length of the town.

An excellent marina adjoins Playa del Oro, just north of town. It has a number of slips for private yachts and for fishing and excursion boats, a concrete dock for cruise passengers, and a terminal building for the ferry to Cabo San Lucas.

Shopping is a delight in PV's many stylish boutiques, where designers can create a dress or shirt for you within a day or two. The main shopping street is Avenida Juarez, along the river's north bank. For handicrafts, visit the artisans of Cuale Island or the Fonart store (Juarez and Zaragoza). Sergio Bustamente's jungle of papier-mâché, ceramic, and metal animals can be found at Morelos 67.

. . . Mazatlan to Manzanillo

Tours take you to Mismaloya Beach, a jungle hideaway discovered by Hollywood and converted into the setting for the 1964 film *Night of the Iguana*. Foliage has obscured most but not all traces of "el set." The view is worth your time.

For a novel all-day excursion that includes swimming, sunning, hiking, lunching, and shopping, take a boat trip to the sequestered fishing village of Yelapa. If you want to linger, make reservations in advance; accommodations are modest and the choice is limited.

Along Highway 200

Steep hills and indented bays rimmed by scenic sandy crescents mark the Jalisco coast between Puerto Vallarta and Manzanillo. The 140-mile stretch (a 4-hour drive) is scenic enough to warrant a side trip from Puerto Vallarta or Manzanillo, the area's two major destinations. You'll pass through mountain pine and oak forests, rugged high desert, thorn forests, and savannas. Jungles teem with colorful bird life. Inviting detours can easily prolong your trip.

The highway crosses four major rivers flowing from the Sierra Madre Occidental to the Pacific; these rivers are lifelines for inland farming villages and cattle ranches. Bays south of Rio San Nicolas are gradually being developed, with a collection of accommodations ranging from modest to expensive.

Costa de Careyes. Two unlikely resort neighbors share small Playa Blanca 50 miles north of Manzanillo. Early-morning joggers, horseback riders, and hearty swimmers storm the beach at the 600-bed Club Med Playa Blanca, which specializes in riding and fitness programs and has one of the best-organized diving schools in Mexico.

Across the bay at languid 70-room Plaza Careyes, most guests don't stir until midday. Rambling down the long stone driveway, you could be approaching the main house of a coconut plantation instead of a hotel complex.

On a nearby bay, a bougainvillea-draped ziggurat called Fiesta Americana Los Angeles Locos sits alone on a long, sandy beach at Tenacatita.

Barra de Navidad. Fifteen miles north of Manzanillo, a mile-long causeway turnoff from Highway 200 leads to the small fishing village of Barra de Navidad. For an overnight stay, try Hotel Cabo Blanco at the edge of town, or one of the more modest establishments in town. Several open-sided, sand-floored restaurants (noted for oysters and shrimp) face the steep coarse-sand beach with its sometimes turbulent waves. Rental boats along the lagoon can provide access to fishing, birding, and sightseeing.

San Patricio Melaque, larger than Barra, is a long walk or a short taxi ride down the bay. Its shopping is better, and it has a bustling public market.

Manzanillo—regal refuge for the rich

Squeezed onto a slender spine of land that separates two bays, Manzanillo is a resort haven for the world's jet setters. This long-ignored coastal town (now one of Mexico's most important ports for trade with the Orient) has turned into a holiday destination for graduates of Acapulco, the Costa del Sol, and the Greek islands.

The entrepreneur-millionaire Antenor Patino was responsible for the resort complex on the peninsula north of town called Las Hadas, which includes—in addition to a luxury hotel—a marina, a tennis club, a spectacular golf course, swimming pools, restaurants, shops, villas, and a fine beach. The central hotel is a collection of dazzling white buildings that project a Mediterranean air with Moorish overtones.

The area around Manzanillo has everything going for it—vast open beaches, great swimming, excellent fishing (dolphinfish, marlin, sailfish), and a comfortable climate. Good beaches, major hotels, and the area's jetport lie north of Las Hadas.

The city itself is a no-nonsense port. Its paved central streets are narrow, crowded, and often noisy. Action centers around the clean and spacious harbor, a place where families stroll at sunset, and the charming zocalo.

Cuyutlan, south of Manzanillo, is famous for its "green roller"—a miniature tidal wave. At certain times during April or May, the ocean gathers itself into a huge, hurtling force and rushes toward the black-sand beach with a thunderous roar. An awesome sight, the "green roller" reaches heights of up to 30 feet. Cuyutlan is best for daytime sojourns, not for overnight.

Colima, capital of the tiny Mexican state of the same name, is reached easily by following Highway 110 inland from Manzanillo. A balmy metropolis dating back to 1523, Colima lies a short distance from the foot of Volcan Colima, Mexico's second-highest active volcano (it last erupted in 1941).

Colima is an attractive town. Colonial buildings with luxuriant gardens line quiet streets. Life is leisurely. The city's principal attraction is the Museum of Western Cultures on Calle 27 de Septiembre. Antique-car buffs will enjoy the old car museum, 6 blocks south of the city's plaza; on display are more than 300 antique automobiles. Shoppers will find a good selection of pottery. Other notable buildings around Colima include the government palace, the cathedral, and a few churches.

About 9 miles south of town is Agua Caliente, one of the health resorts in this area. Comala, a little town 6 miles north of Colima, is your best bet for handicrafts.

Cruising in Mexican Waters

The warning gong sounds, the band strikes up, the streamers fly—and you're off on a cruise to Mexico. Will it be as glamorous as the *Love Boat* television show promised? Probably not. But for those who enjoy good food, lots of entertainment, and colorful ports of call, cruising to Mexico is a tempting form of transportation.

Few if any of the unpleasant surprises associated with the other modes of travel arise when you take a cruise. Once you're aboard, there's no possibility of mixed-up hotel reservations or lost luggage. Your only decisions during the day will be whether to go ashore, court the sun on board, swim, shop, play cards, see a movie, eat, or sleep. At night you can gamble, dance, or watch the entertainment.

Cruise choices

Cruise lengths usually vary from 3 or 4 days to a week or longer.

Your schedule, budget, and interests will determine your choice of cruise line; depending on the length of the trip, most ports of call are the same for all lines. You will have to decide whether you prefer to visit Mexico's west coast or cruise the Caribbean.

Ports of call for longer cruises usually include large resorts like Acapulco, Cabo San Lucas, Ixtapa/Zihuatanejo, Manzanillo, Mazatlan, and Puerto Vallarta on the west coast; Cancun, Cozumel, and Playa del Carmen on the east coast. (The shorter west coast cruises usually turn around at Ensenada.) Most west coast departures are from Los Angeles and San Diego; on the east coast, Miami and Tampa are the traditional ports of departure.

One exception to the above is Exploration Cruise Lines, the only line sailing completely within Mexican waters. This Seattle-based company operates out of La Paz (Baja California) on 8-day sailings to Acapulco. From January to March, they also operate 3- to 4-day whale-watching cruises to Scammon's Lagoon.

Other cruise lines now operating in Mexico include Admiral Cruises, Bermuda Star Line, Carnival Cruise Lines, Chandris Fantasy Cruises, Norwegian Cruise Line, Princess Cruises, Regency Cruises, Royal Cruise Line, Sitmar Cruises, Society Expeditions, and Special Expeditions.

Cruise details

Most cruise ships operate from autumn to late spring, although some offer trips year-round.

Though prices are lower in the summer months and shipboard temperatures will be pleasant, the cities you visit may be quite hot and humid.

Cruise costs vary, depending on the line, the length of the cruise, and the type of cabin. The price includes all meals (up to eight a day), lodging, shipboard activities, and entertainment. It does not include land tours, tips, and alcoholic beverages. Airfare may or may not be a part of the total price.

In addition to casual clothes, you'll want to include more formal attire for the one or two parties aboard ship.

Contact your travel agent for more details on the delights of visiting Mexico by ship.

Sleek cruise ships ply east and west coasts, with shore stops at major resort cities

Hacked out of surrounding jungle, this thatch-roofed family farm is the tiny state of Nayarit.

For a tropical tan sans sand, take a tip from sun worshipers in Zihuatanejo Bay.

40   The West Coast

Ixtapa/Zihuatanejo

Thirteen years ago, Ixtapa was nothing more than a fine stretch of palm-lined sand and Zihuatanejo simply a rustic fishing village. Then Fonatur, the tourism branch of the federal government, began upgrading the sleepy town and developing a string of hotels on a beautiful bay 6 miles to the north. Today, the planned resort is a popular vacation spot for travelers.

Getting to Ixtapa and Zihuatanejo is easy and convenient. Highway 200 links the area with other Pacific coast resorts and a new road cuts off distance to Mexico City. Daily flights from the U.S. and Mexico City land at the airport serving both communities. Bus service is also available from Acapulco.

Ixtapa

Much smaller than Cancun, its sister resort on the Yucatan Peninsula, Ixtapa is built among 5,263 acres of coconut palms, mangroves, colorful flowers, and foliage. Surprisingly, not even the dozen or so hotels lining the beachfront spoil the region's beauty.

Getting around. Taxis or buses scurry between Ixtapa and Zihuatanejo for shopping and dining; open-air pedicabs connect the hotels, shopping malls, and restaurants. Bicycles can be rented in the hotel zone. Boats offer trips between Playa Quieta (site of Club Med) and Isla Ixtapa, a nature preserve and favored scuba site.

What to do. This is beach and pool life at its casual best. Except during the summer and early autumn rainy season, you'll always find good weather and balmy offshore breezes. When you tire of sitting around a beach or pool, you can play a round of golf at the splendid 18-hole Palma Real Golf Club; take your clubs along or rent them there. The club's lighted tennis courts encourage evening play. Sailboats, water-ski boats, and fishing boats can be rented, and parachute rides arranged, in front of the hotels or from the marina.

Several small shopping malls across the street from the row of hotels contain boutiques, gift stores, and restaurants. Hotel dining rooms, bars, and discos supply nighttime action.

North of Ixtapa. North of the resort lie a Club Med facility on Playa Quieta, and Playa Linda, an inexpensive coastal resort that attracts Mexican vacationers. You'll find trailer hookups, outdoor community cooking areas, a pool, a small store, and boat rentals.

About 90 miles up the coast, near the border of the states of Guerrero and Michoacan, lie the industrial city of Lazaro Cardenas and Playa Azul, an off-the-beaten-path beach retreat.

Golfer sinks his putt for par at Ixtapa's picturesque 18-hole resort course.

Zihuatanejo

The government project at nearby Acapulco also upgraded this once-lazy village. Streets have been paved and cobbled, downtown shops have new facades, and a pedestrian-only shopping mall leads to the beach. You'll find no resorts here, only a few small hotels scattered on hillsides and beaches.

In the village. When every other business is a restaurant or a craft store, you know a town is geared for tourists. Even the lounging cadets at the military garrison near the public pier strike poses right out of a Donizetti opera. But Zihuatanejo is still pleasing, with enough reminders that the town isn't a bogus "Mexicoland."

Around the bay. At Playa Municipal you can charter a fishing boat or take an inexpensive excursion to Playa Las Gatas (superior diving and snorkeling along a coral reef) or to the nature preserve of Isla Ixtapa. Playa Municipal connects to Playa La Madera, a pocket beach at the base of a steep slope dotted with hotels. At the end is Playa La Ropa, a flat crescent with small hotels beneath palms right on the velvet sand. Hail a water taxi along the shore for a bay tour.

The clarity of the water, the abundant variety of underwater life, and the intricate beauty of its reefs make Zihuatanejo Bay popular among skin divers. Even if you've never tried the sport before, take along a snorkel and face mask and begin your underwater adventure by floating quietly over the coral.

Once called an aging beauty, Acapulco's recent facelifts have given the lady new life. At night, she's glamorous and spontaneous.

Relaxed villages south of Acapulco still offer isolated beaches, modest accommodations, friendly service, and some of the best—and least expensive—food along the west coast.

Acapulco & The Southern Coast

The beautiful resort capital of Acapulco has attracted sophisticated tourists since the early 1940s, when it was a haven for Hollywood film stars and European royalty. The beach towns in the state of Oaxaca to the south, by contrast, are small, relatively unknown destinations—for the moment. But hotel construction has started at Bahias de Huatulco, earmarked as an international-scale resort.

You'll have several options for getting to the Southern Coast beaches, depending on your point of departure and method of transportation. Jetting to Acapulco is easy from the U.S.; from Mexico City there's a shuttle service with a dozen flights. You also can get air service to or from Guadalajara, Puerto Vallarta, and other southern cities. Puerto Escondido, Puerto Angel, and Bahias de Huatulco can most easily be reached by air from Oaxaca or Mexico City.

Acapulco

Acapulco is the big city of coastal resorts, with the most visitors and the most hotels (over 400) of any Mexican coastal city. Its visitor attractions are divided between those for foreigners and those for the many Mexicans who swell the winter population. In spite of the heavy tourist traffic and the wealth of diversions that have been introduced for tourists, the area has retained its exotic natural beauty, and steps have been taken to guarantee its preservation.

Winter is probably the best season to visit, but the exciting resort city is popular all year (most hotels lower their rates during the off season, from May through November).

Attractions around town. The city is set at the base of mountains that all but encircle the beautiful blue bay. The main beachside boulevard, Costera Miguel Aleman, runs from the hills north of town to the hills on the south side. It passes along hotel row, a long line of resorts that stretches from the older section of the city to the more glamorous tourist playgrounds. (The exclusive Las Brisas, Pierre Marques, and Princess hotels lie to the south of the city.)

Along palm-lined Costera Miguel Aleman you'll find most of Acapulco's best shops, restaurants, and night clubs. A hilly peninsula to the north of the malecon shelters the harbor; the first big hotels and costly houses were built on its slopes. Here, too, lies Acapulco's one real antiquity—Fort San Diego, built by the Spanish in 1616 to protect the port from Dutch and English pirates. The fort is now an historical museum.

Across the peninsula is La Quebrada, an observation point over the rocky cliffs of the town's seaward side. Acapulco's famous high divers leap from these cliffs to the water 137 feet below; you can get a good view from the observation deck and La Perla restaurant in the El Mirador Hotel.

The Mercado Municipal, a vast public market complex, lies in the old section of Acapulco; to reach it, turn off the Costera onto Hurtado de Mendoza. The market is fun, whether you're shopping for picnic supplies or souvenirs or just looking at what may be the most fascinating place in town. You'll find unfamiliar groceries, fresh breads, bulk seasonings, and produce. Flower vendors brighten the courts between pavilions, and truckloads of bananas and other products crowd the streets.

In the nearby Mercado de Artesanias you'll find a wide display of handicrafts and souvenirs. Also in this area are the city's zocalo and cathedral.

Acapulco Center. A multilevel convention facility on 35 acres of parklike grounds fronted by fountains serves as the city's entertainment complex. This is the site of an annual film festival and the location for special performances of the Ballet Folklorico and Flying Indians of Papantla; check your hotel desk for dates of events. The nearby Acapulco Museum and Cultural Center houses displays of artifacts and contemporary art.

A city of parks. Following a recent beautification program, Acapulco gained parklands throughout the city. Papagayo Park, considered one of Mexico's prettiest, stretches along the beach for 20 blocks. The grounds contain a botanical garden, an aviary, a regional museum, and amusement rides.

Cici Park, on the Costera near Acapulco Center, concentrates on aquatic activities; performing dolphins and seals, water slides, and a pool with artificial waves. An admission fee is charged.

El Veladero Park is Acapulco's national park of the future. The mountainsides surrounding Acapulco are being reforested to prevent erosion, and recreational areas are being created. The 12,500 families who once lived on the mountainsides were relocated to a city 10 minutes away on the other side of the mountain.

Around the bay. Most of the daytime action takes place along Acapulco's grand beaches. Pie de la Cuesta, about 15 minutes north of town, is a broad beach and a popular place to sit and watch the sun set. Fishing, water-skiing, and swimming take place on inland Coyuca Lagoon.

Caletilla and Caleta beaches lie on the bay side of the peninsula that separates the bay and ocean. A small harbor hosts sport-fishing boats, glass-bottom boats, and launches that take visitors to La Roqueta Island to enjoy the beach, have lunch, or indulge the friendly, beer-drinking burros you'll find all over the island.

To the south, between Old Acapulco and the Condesa del Mar hotel, are palm-shaded Hornos and Hornitos beaches, popular with local people. Condesa and Icacos beaches stretch from the Condesa del Mar hotel to the naval base beyond the Hyatt Regency. On the bay side of the hotels, this center for visitor-oriented activity is alive with boats, burros, beach vendors, and bronzed bodies. Palapa-shaded restaurants are only a sandy step away from the water. Parasailing is popular; a parachute, pulled by boat, lifts you from the beach for a brief, bird's-eye view of the bay. Moonlight cruises give good looks at the spectacular city lights.

South of town are quiet Puerto Marques Bay and Revolcadero Beach, site of the Princess and Pierre Marques hotels.

Sporting life. All beaches and beach hotels offer complete water-sports facilities, including power boats, sailboats, pedal boats, surfboards, paddle boards, and water skis. Fishing, especially for sailfish, is exceptionally good; you can rent tackle and boats. You also can rent horses for a gallop over the sand at Pie de la Cuesta and Revolcadero beaches.

Two championship 18-hole golf courses (Princess and Pierre Marques hotels), a 9-hole public course, and more than 80 tennis courts—some indoors and air-conditioned—help you keep fit.

Less athletic visitors may enjoy watching greyhound and horse racing at a track near Las Brisas. Bullfights are held on Sunday afternoons at the bullring in the old part of town; nearby, jai alai takes place Tuesday through Sunday nights (except during June and October) at the Jardin de Caletilla Fronton.

Shopping. Browsing through the multitude of shops in Acapulco is more than a pastime; it's one of the chief activities. Shopping is good—but expensive. You'll find everything you need (or didn't know you needed) in downtown stores, hotel boutiques, and small shopping malls. For handicrafts, take a look at Artesanias Finas Acapulco (Horacio Nelson and James Cook avenues).

The Costera is lined with little boutiques and arcades; some of the best include El Flamboyant, across from the Acapulco Plaza (the hotel also has a fine shopping mall); El Patio, across from the Hyatt Continental; Plaza Condesa, across from the Condesa del Mar; and Fingers Arcade, near Carlos 'n Charlie's restaurant.

South of town, La Vista mall, on a hill across from Las Brisas, is one of the city's best; the Princess also has a variety of boutiques. Near the zocalo in downtown Acapulco, you'll find several good shopping streets, such as Avenida Hidalgo. Samy's Boutique (Calle Hidalgo 7) has long been a favorite with visiting celebrities; Taxco El Viejo (Quebrada 830) is a good choice for handicrafts and silver jewelry.

Night life. Acapulco wakes up when the sun goes down. Hotels, night clubs, and beachfront restaurants vibrate with music and laughter; discos get active around 11 P.M. and go on until dawn.

Night club tour packages, which include stops and sips at three shows, are offered through most hotels. Prices include drinks, cover charges, and tips; English-speaking guides are your escorts. You may not visit the current hot spot, but it's a good way to glimpse the city's entertainment variety.

South of Acapulco

Highway 200 leads south from Acapulco to the border of Guatemala, passing through the area called Costa Chica before reaching the Oaxacan coast towns of Puerto Escondido and Puerto Angel. Though relatively overlooked by most travelers, this southern region is soon to get its own government-developed super resort, Bahias de Huatulco.

Because the area is remote and the road not recommended during the rainy season, visitors usually approach the three beach villages by air or road from Oaxaca and Mexico City. For their location, see the map on page 117.

Cuajinicuilapa, on the border of the states of Guerrero and Oaxaca, is the capital of the country's Afro-Mexican community. The population is descended from Bantu tribespeople who escaped centuries ago from slave ships bound for Acapulco. Most of the area's residents are shy and avoid visitors.

Pinotepa, 40 miles to the south, is a small Indian town noted for its weaving and woodwork. At certain seasons the natives gather sea snails to extract a purple dye, which they use for their fabrics. The Sunday market is very colorful.

Puerto Escondido, a former "hidden port" on Oaxaca's coast, attracts an odd mix of Canadians, retired Americans, Europeans, Brazilians, and surfers. The surf here is the best in Mexico; from April to June, its waves will remind you of Hawaii's famous Pipeline—fast and hollow. Also gaining popularity with Mexican tourists, the town's simple accommodations are well booked through April.

Most of the 20,000 residents live uphill from Highway 200. At the Mercado Viejo, Wednesday and Saturday are especially lively. Tourists congregate along the splendid white beach bordered with palm groves, small hotels, open-air restaurants, and the tourist shops of Alfonso Perez Gasga, the main thoroughfare. For the best espresso, desserts, and *licuados* (blended fresh-fruit drinks), try Bananas or Cafeteria Cappuccino. For seafood, try Los Crotos.

Surrounding beaches, bays, and lagoons abound with bird life. Daylong tours from December through April guide you by bus and boat through the mangrove swamps of Laguna de Chacagua, one of Mexico's national parks and bird sanctuaries, and into a remote fishing village that seems more African than Mexican. Guided tours are also available to Puerto Angel and Bahias de Huatulco (see below). Make reservations at the Hotel Santa Fe or Castel Puerto Escondido. For a few dollars, boat taxis marked "Pto. Es" will take you to nearby Puerto Angelito for snorkeling and swimming.

Thirty small hotels range from tidy to funky. Beachside Hotel Santa Fe has a pool, the town's best craft shop, and a good restaurant. Other good bets: Castel Puerto Escondido (1½ miles northwest of town; tennis, pool), Paraiso Escondido (restaurant, pool, garden, craft shop), Nayar (uphill from the beach; restaurant, garden), Rincon del Pacifico (restaurant, garden). For bungalows with kitchen facilities, look along the surfing beach, Zicatela.

Puerto Angel, some 50 miles to the southeast, lies on a half-moon bay. With beautiful beaches in a rugged rocky setting, the town is 20 years behind Puerto Escondido. Navy boats visit the small station here occasionally, but otherwise fishing is the main action. Restaurants with the beach as a floor serve up oysters and lobsters for which the owners have just dived. Snorkeling and swimming are good; ask about safest spots to avoid undertows.

Most visitors fly from major Mexican airports into Puerto Escondido and rent a car, hire a cab, or catch one of the buses that make the trip hourly. Accommodations are limited to a few beachside, no-frills hotels; Hotel Angel del Mar, atop a hill, is a long hike up from the beach.

Bahias de Huatulco, a gorgeous string of nine bays 70 miles south of Puerto Escondido, is soon to become a resort similar to Cancun and Ixtapa—with 4,000 rooms by the year 2000. At present, an international airport and several hotels (Posada Binniguenda, Veramar, Sheraton, and Club Med) have been completed. The Posada Binniguenda lies on Santa Cruz Bay; the Club Med shares Tangolunda Bay with the other two hotels. A golf course is already taking shape.

The resort sprawls over 52,000 acres, much of it mountainous. It's divided into two distinct areas called the "lowlands" and the "bays." The lowlands contain spacious beaches, long valleys, and wide plains through which small streams race. In the bays area, the beaches are smaller and more secluded. Just inland rise the green mountains.

Water taxis head out from Santa Cruz, a tiny fishing village dating from pre-Spanish days, to the area's wonderful bays. Two of them, La Entrega and El Maguey, are among Pacific Mexico's best snorkeling spots, with coral alive with brightly colored fish.

By the year 2000, Bahias de Huatulco is expected to rival Cancun in size and population. Determined to attract visitors by preserving the beauty of the region, Fonatur's construction codes call for a height limitation of six stories for all buildings. All designs must be in accord with the native Oaxacan architecture.

With a climate much like Acapulco (335 miles to the north), Bahias de Huatulco's temperature averages about 82° F all year. The best time to visit is from November to May.

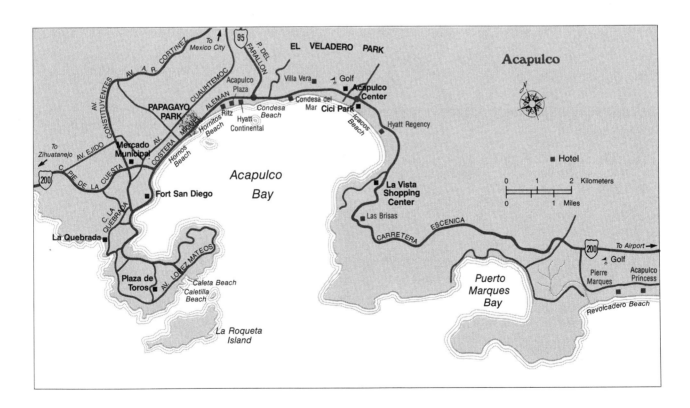

Mexico City

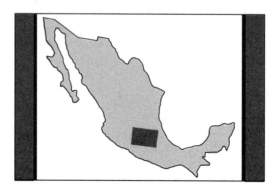

Mexico City is the world's largest metropolitan area, with a population of over 17 million. Despite its big-city problems, it holds its own as a charming foreign capital, alive with color and sound.

Founded by the Aztecs in 1325, Mexico City lies in a mountain-rimmed valley 7,400 feet above sea level. On the rare clear day, you can see the snow-capped volcanic peaks of 17,591-foot Ixtaccihuatl (*ees-tak-SEE-watl*) and majestic 17,893-foot Popocatepetl (*po-po-kah-TEH-petl*), about 35 miles to the southeast.

Mexico City marks the beginning and end of most of the major highways in Mexico. Kilometers to anywhere in the country are measured from the capital. A tour starting there can be telescoped to fit almost any vacation schedule, but the more time you have, the better you can savor and explore this fascinating destination.

Enjoying the city

For greater enjoyment of Mexico City's myriad delights, read about it before you go. If you're the independent type, you may prefer to wander through the city armed with a guidebook, a map, an English–Spanish dictionary, and your own self-inspired itinerary. At your hotel, or through any travel agency, you can engage the services of an official, government-authorized guide (ask to see credentials) who will provide information and transportation to all of the area's attractions. Guides can be hired by the hour or by the day.

To get advice, assistance, and helpful literature, or to register complaints on prices or services, consult the information office of the Department of Tourism at Avenida Juarez 92, a block off the Paseo de la Reforma. English-speaking police in blue uniforms also offer help to tourists. You'll find them along the Reforma, on street corners in the Zona Rosa, around Plaza Garibaldi, and in other areas frequented by tourists.

Around Mexico City

If you're a first-time visitor, you can use the city as a base from which to explore the surrounding countryside on 1- or 2-day trips. Within 50 to 70 miles, you can find a complete cross section of the country—pyramids, colonial towns, restored haciendas now operating as resorts, quaint villages with colorful markets, and dramatic scenery.

To the north lie the pyramids of Teotihuacan and the stone statues of Tula, an ancient Toltec Indian capital. To the south are Cuernavaca, a chic weekend retreat, and the photogenic silver-mining town of Taxco. Toluca, east of Mexico City, hosts a colorful Indian market every Friday; Puebla, 2½ hours east of the capital, is noted for its distinctive tile and piquant *mole* sauce.

Golden Angel atop Monument to Independence appears to direct traffic on Paseo de la Reforma.

*Candy market streetside stall offers a wide array of **dulces** (sweets), many made from fruits.*

Getting around

Mexico City traffic is apt to dampen your enthusiasm for driving in the capital. Public transportation—buses and the Metro system—is inexpensive, and satisfactory once you learn your way around. Taxis vary in type and rates.

Driving—patience and courage

Streets in the older sections of town are narrow, one-way, and congested. On the wider streets, cars move fast, and the traffic circles (*glorietas*) at intersections along many main thoroughfares may give you the sensation of being caught in a revolving door. Taxi drivers, darting in and out of traffic with split-second judgment, are particularly skillful at sizing up the intentions of others. Bicycle and motorcycle riders who weave between cars are a constant menace. As in many European cities, motorists sometimes use only their parking lights when driving at night.

Street signs are black-on-white. Streets often change names every few blocks. Watch for the small blue-and-white *transito* (direction) and green-and-white *preferencia* (right-of-way) signs on the walls of buildings at corners. Traffic at most intersections is regulated by lights; at others, a policeman may be stationed in the center. When he faces you or has his back to you, you must stop; when he turns his side to you, you may proceed.

As you enter the city on a major highway, you may be accosted by individuals who offer to guide you to your destination. Mexican travel authorities strongly recommend that you do not employ these or any other unauthorized guides.

It is important to park your car in a safe place. When you park on the street or in a parking lot—even when an attendant is in charge and you lock the car—don't ever leave clothing, camera equipment, or other valuables exposed inside; lock them in the trunk or, even better, take them with you.

At downtown parking lots (often very crowded) you must leave the key in the ignition or deliver it to the attendant so the car can be moved if necessary. On the street, try to park near a khaki-uniformed car watcher and tip him when you leave. Meters that register up to 4 hours are installed on many streets. Don't leave your car parked on the street overnight. You can always arrange to use your hotel's parking area or a nearby public parking garage.

Taxis—tips on all types

You'll probably find taxis a convenient—and surprisingly inexpensive—way to get around in Mexico City. Though cabs may have meters, they are not often adjusted to keep up with Mexico's rising inflation. Drivers have been supplied with cards showing the current price for the equivalent meter reading. Even so, it's always wise to ask the price of a trip in advance. Tips are not expected unless the driver performs an additional service.

Though plentiful, taxis are sometimes difficult to find outside the main tourist areas. If you call a taxi from a cab stand (listed under *sitios* in the classified phone directory), the fare will depend on the distance the taxi has come in response to the dispatcher's call.

Guides with large, unmarked cars are found outside hotels. They can be hired for a short trip, by the hour, or for the day.

Peseros (so called because their flat rate was once 1 peso) operate up and down the 3-mile main route between Chapultepec Park and the Zocalo (from the park down Reforma, Juarez, and Madero, and returning from the Zocalo via Cinco de Mayo, Juarez, and Reforma). These jitneys are less expensive than cabs because the rides are shared. When the driver has room for more passengers, he holds his left hand aloft. You alight at the stop nearest your destination.

Metro—fast and convenient

Since 1970, Mexico City has had a major transportation system—the Metro or subway. During the excavation, parts of the ancient Aztec city of Tenochtitlan were unearthed. For a glimpse of some of the archeological finds, get off at the Zocalo's Piño Suarez station, where a small, round Aztec pyramid was left in place in the terminal lobby. Unlike many dark and dreary underground tubes, the Metro is well lighted and gaily decorated.

Lines 1, 2, and 3 are most useful to the tourist (see map on page 53). The Metro runs between 6 A.M. and midnight; it's least crowded between 10 A.M. and 4 P.M. Be on the alert for pickpockets.

Buses—bargain travel

Buses are a convenient way to travel through the city—provided you know your way around. They serve almost every section of the capital, but will take at least twice as long as a taxi. Major bus routes for tourists are between Chapultepec Park and the Zocalo, and along Insurgentes Sur to San Angel and the University. Ask at your hotel about direct (*directo*) bus routes. Bus stops are indicated by a small, elevated sign with the word *parada* ("stop").

Native costumes, dances, and music highlight world-renowned Ballet Folklorico performances.

Garlic and chiles—staples of Mexican cuisine

Corn, chiles of varying degrees of heat, tomatoes, tomatillos, and beans—from these Indian-grown basics came the Mexican style of cooking so popular both north and south of the border.

Many of the other foods that we consider staples were cultivated by pre-Columbian Indians of Mexico: avocado, squash, potatoes, yams, and tropical fruits such as papaya, pineapple, guava, and mango.

The Spanish conquistadors introduced rice, nuts, cattle and other livestock, citrus fruits, olives, grapes, cilantro, saffron, and other herbs and spices—and, in return, brought back vanilla and chocolate. During their brief reign, the French added European cheeses and baked goods. Today, each region of the country combines these products and others into a delicious and unique cuisine.

Northern specialties. *Norteña* cooking is a distinct cuisine characterized by ranch-style barbecued meats grilled over charcoal and accompanied by beans traditionally spiced with cumin and cilantro, and often with hot jalapeño or serrano chiles. Salsa (a sauce of chopped chilies, onions, and tomatoes or tomatillos) is poured over the top. On the Gulf of Mexico side, tropical fruits and a variety of seafood contribute freshness to this hotly sauced food.

Central Mexico cuisine. Seafood is also featured along the Pacific coast; the freshwater whitefish from Patzcuaro and Chapala lakes should not be missed. Inland cooking is noted for its exotic combinations of spices, nuts, chiles, and fruits, such as that found in Puebla's *mole* sauce. Candy made from cactus, fruits, seasoned chocolate, and goat's milk are special sweet treats.

Southeastern cooking. Banana leaves replace corn husks for the Yucatecan tamale, and artichokes make an appearance. Food is milder, and sauces are seasoned with sour oranges, garlic, and black pepper.

Libations. Tequila is the nation's drink (see page 96), but the country is also noted for Kahlua liquor and fine *cerveza* (beer). Imported wines are very expensive in Mexico, so try some of the local varieties. *Sangria* (red wine, citrus juices, and tropical fruits) is a refreshing addition to a meal.

Nonalcoholic beverages include mineral waters, *aguas frescas* (fruit-sweetened mineral waters), and *sangrita* (made from tomato and orange juices and powdered chiles).

City diversions

Mexico City offers an astonishing number of attractions for vacationers. You'd need to stay a week to sample the city's offerings, and an additional week to visit some surrounding areas. There's something for everyone—from sightseeing in the Zocalo and shopping in the Zona Rosa (Pink Zone), to mariachis in Garibaldi Plaza and museums in Chapultepec Park.

Because the city is so large, first-time visitors may wish to take a city tour to get oriented. Though similar in content, such tours vary in length, style, and mode of transportation. Most half-day sightseeing excursions include the Zocalo, Chapultepec Park, and University City. A separate half-day tour visits University City and the nearby neighborhoods of Coyoacan, San Angel, and Pedregal. The full-day excursion adds such attractions as the National Pawn Shop, La Merced Market, and local craft centers. A Sunday tour combines a performance of the Ballet Folklorico with a boat ride along the canals of Xochimilco and a tour of the university.

Special attractions

Many colorful local events take place on weekends: Toluca Indian market on Friday (see page 73); Bazaar Sabado in San Angel on Saturday (see page 68); Ballet Folklorico, the floating gardens of Xochimilco, Sullivan Park's Painters' Market, Thieves' Market, bullfights, and charreadas on Sunday. (For details on Sunday events, see pages 56–57.)

Sundays and holidays are also the times when Chapultepec Park (see page 62) is filled to overflowing with family groups; vendors of balloons, soft drinks, candies, and tacos reap their richest harvest then.

Ballet Folklorico. A highlight of Mexico City's entertainment are the beautifully executed and magnificently costumed performances of the Ballet Folklorico at the Palace of Fine Arts. It's one of the liveliest and most satisfying combinations of Mexican music, dancing, costumes, and staging that you'll find anywhere in the country. Buy your tickets for the Sunday morning or Wednesday and Sunday evening performances from your hotel concierge or from a travel agency. Tickets sell out early during tourist seasons.

National Lottery. Every Monday, Wednesday, and Friday night there is a drawing at the National Lottery Building (Juarez and Rosales streets) to determine the day's lottery winners. Prizes range from thousands of pesos to millions. It's fun to watch a part of the lengthy proceedings, in which the most active participants are small, uniformed page boys who call out the winning numbers they draw from revolving cages.

Entertainment at night

The city is as busy at night as it is during the day. Offices close late, cocktail time begins around 7 P.M., and nobody thinks about dinner until 9 or 10. Night-club crowds linger well into the early morning hours. Many of the most elegant night clubs, shows, and restaurants are concentrated in or near the Zona Rosa. Large hotels elsewhere in the city have clubs and bars offering afternoon and evening entertainment. Nighttime tours provide transportation, dinner, one or two shows, and drinks at several popular spots around town.

Sports

Public golf courses and tennis courts are relatively hard to find in Mexico City. Some deluxe hotels have tennis courts and can arrange for golfers to play at private country clubs during the week. Both Chapultepec and Alameda parks are popular with runners. Cyclists can rent bikes in Chapultepec Park.

Jai alai. Jai alai is played every night of the week except Monday and Friday at Fronton Mexico, on Plaza de la Revolution north of the Reforma. Games usually start at 7 P.M. The greatest spectator interest centers on the betting, which is confusing to the novice. On every play the odds change, and "bookies" pace back and forth in front of the stands exchanging money with bettors by means of a cut-open tennis ball attached to a long pole. Those who prefer a less strenuous betting system can use the windows in the lobby.

Bullfights. You'll find a bullfight almost every Sunday afternoon in Plaza Mexico, a bullring off Insurgentes Sur about 2 miles south of the Reforma. Major spectacles take place during the winter; in spring, novice bullfighters develop their skills.

Horse racing. Hipodromo de las Americas on the northern outskirts of the city is the capital's beautiful racetrack. Races are held Tuesday, Thursday, Saturday, and Sunday afternoon year-round except during Christmas and Easter weeks. Hotels can usually arrange for you to get an invitation to the exclusive Jockey Club for lunch.

Futbol. Soccer or *futbol* (a faster, more agile game than U.S. football) is the most popular sport in the world. It's played with verve to capacity crowds. Mexico has soccer comic books, sandlot soccer, and Little League soccer—all indicative of the national preoccupation with the sport. In Mexico City, big-league games are played Thursday evening and Sunday afternoon in the Estadio Azteca (seats 108,000) on the southern edge of the city, the Olympic Stadium in University City, and at the Sports City Stadium near the bullring.

. . . city diversions

Shopping—a Mexican specialty

In Mexico City, you can shop for a wide range of Mexican handicrafts—from exclusive fashion in fine Zona Rosa shops to bright paper products and handloomed serapes in colorful public markets. Mexican women also shop at Perisur, a huge mall on Insurgentes Sur, and at boutiques in the San Angel and Polanco areas of the city.

In most stores, prices are clearly marked and usually not subject to bargaining. But you can haggle in markets and at sidewalk bazaars and street stands. The capital's usual shopping hours are 10 A.M. to 6 P.M. (until 8 P.M. Saturday).

Fonart stores. At government-sponsored stores around the city (Juarez 70, Juarez 92, Londres 136, and six other locations in tourist areas), you'll find a wide selection of handicrafts from all over the country. Prices are set and the quality is very high.

Mercados. The multitude of public markets—particularly colorful on Sunday—offers plenty of opportunities for bargaining and photography. Among the most notable are Centro Artesanal Buenavista, Aldama 187; Mercado La Merced (fascinating food displays), Avenida Anillo de Circumvalacion; Mercado Abelardo Rodriguez, Calle Venezuela (north of the National Palace); San Juan Market (curio market), corner of Ayuntamiento and Aranda; Mercado La Lagunilla, on Ecuador between Allende and Chile; and Mercado Tepito—the Thieves' Market.

Dining options

Like all metropolises, Mexico City has an abundance of excellent restaurants specializing in many different cuisines. But since it's here that you can savor Mexican food on its home ground, sample the local cuisine first. Among the long-time restaurants noted for outstanding native dishes are Fonda del Refugio, Fonda del Recuerdo, Hacienda de los Morales, and the San Angel Inn. Check with your hotel for other suggestions.

Leisurely—and late—mealtimes are the rule. The usual lunch hour is from 1 P.M. on; dinner service starts around 8 P.M., with restaurants filling up from 9 P.M. on.

Price. Meals cost about the same as you would pay at home for equivalent food and service. Ask for *la cuenta* (the check) just before you finish your meal, or you may have to wait for hours. A 15 percent tax is applied to all meals; expect to tip the waiter an additional 15 to 20 percent. (A cover charge is usually added where dancing and entertainment are featured.)

DETAILS AT A GLANCE

Mexico City

How to get there

Most visitors fly directly to Mexico's capital city. It's the country's most accessible location, and often a first stop for further exploration.

By air. Mexico City is reached easily by air in less than 5 hours from most large U.S. cities. Connections to other Mexican cities are usually made through the capital. In addition to Mexican and U.S. carriers, many foreign airlines offer service.

By car. All main roads lead to Mexico City and distances to other parts of Mexico are measured from the city. Direct driving time from the U.S. border is a little more than 20 hours. Highways are good, but don't drive at night and plan your gasoline stops.

By bus and train. Bus travel is cheap—and slow. Border gateway cities for Mexico City service include Tijuana, Mexicali, Nogales, Ciudad Juarez, Matamoros, and Laredo, Texas. One popular bus route is from Acapulco to Mexico City via Taxco and Cuernavaca.

Train travel is even slower; from Laredo the trip takes 24 hours, from Juarez 36 hours, and about 2 days from Nogales and Mexicali. Eight new or refurbished trains have recently been put into service by the national railroad, offering upgraded connections between the capital and such cities as San Miguel de Allende, Veracruz, Nuevo Laredo, and Guadalajara. For information on these trains in the U.S., call a travel agent, or visit Wagon-lits Tourisme Mexicana in Mexico City.

Accommodations

Mexico City hotels come in a wide assortment, from budget motels to deluxe, colonial-style resorts with pool. Most are centered around four locations: downtown around the Zocalo, along the Paseo de la Reforma, at the edge of Chapultepec Park, and in the Zona Rosa. Make (and confirm) reservations in advance. For further information, see the "Essentials" section on page 152.

Climate & clothes

Mexico City's weather is springlike year round. The rainy season—often limited to afternoon showers—extends from May to October.

Dress is sophisticated in cosmopolitan Mexico City. During the day women wear dresses and pants suits, men are attired in suits or in sport jackets and slacks. Leave shorts for resorts. Evenings are dressy and often cool; bring a jacket.

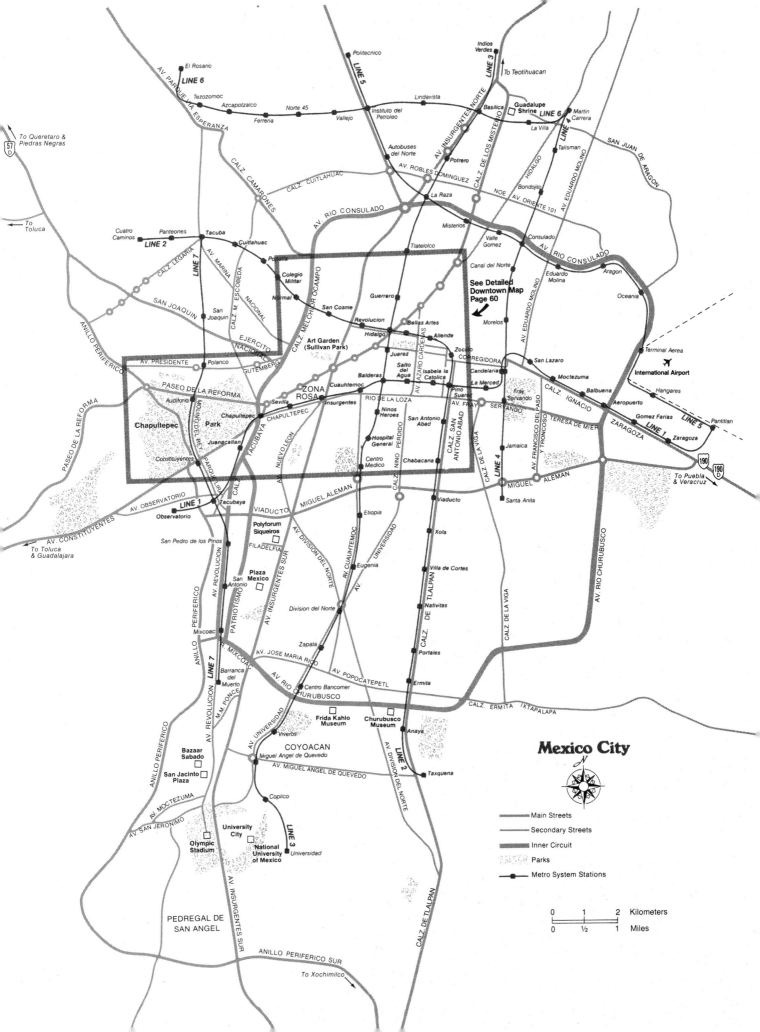

Mexico City

LINE 6 · El Rosario · Tezozomoc · Azcapotzalco · Norte 45 · Ferreria · Vallejo · Instituto del Petroleo · Lindavista

LINE 5 · Politecnico

LINE 3 · Indios Verdes · To Teotihuacan

Basilica · Guadalupe Shrine · LINE 6 · Martin Carrera · La Villa · Talisman

AV. INSURGENTES NORTE · CALZ. DE LOS MISTERIOS · NOE · AV. ORIENTE 101 · HIDALGO · AV. EDUARDO MOLINO · SAN JUAN DE ARAGON

Autobuses del Norte · Potrero · Bondojito · LINE 4

AV. ROBLES DOMINGUEZ · Consulado · AV. RIO CONSULADO · Aragon · Oceania

Cuatro Caminos · Panteones · Tacuba · LINE 2 · Cuitlahuac · Popotla · Colegio Militar · Normal · San Cosme · Guerrero · Bellas Artes · Allende · Morelos · Eduardo Molina · Canal del Norte

LINE 7 · AV. MARINA · CALZ. M. ESCOBEDO · NACIONAL · CALZ. MELCHOR OCAMPO · Revolucion · Hidalgo · Juarez · Zocalo · CORREGIDORA · San Lazaro · Moctezuma · Balbuena · Terminal Aerea · International Airport

Cuatro Caminos · San Joaquin · EJERCITO NACIONAL · Art Garden (Sullivan Park) · Balderas · Salto del Agua · Isabela la Catolica · La Merced · Candelaria · CALZ. IGNACIO · Aeropuerto · Hangares · LINE 5 · Pantitlan

AV. PRESIDENTE · Polanco · Auditorio · PASEO DE LA REFORMA · ZONA ROSA · Cuauhtemoc · Insurgentes · Rio de la Loza · Pino Suarez · AV. FRAY SERVANDO · Gomez Farias · LINE 1 · Zaragoza

Chapultepec · Chapultepec Park · Sevilla · Chapultepec · Ninos Heroes · San Antonio Abad · CALZ. SAN ANTONIO ABAD · Fray Servando · CALZ. DE LA VIGA · ZARAGOZA · To Puebla & Veracruz

Constituyentes · Juanacatlan · AV. NUEVO LEON · Hospital General · Centro Medico · Chabacana · Jamaica · LINE 4 · MIGUEL ALEMAN · Santa Anita

AV. OBSERVATORIO · LINE 1 · Tacubaya · VIADUCTO · MIGUEL ALEMAN · Viaducto · AV. FRANCISCO DEL PASO Y TRONCOSO

Observatorio · San Pedro de los Pinos · Etiopia

Polyforum Siqueiros · FILADELFIA · AV. DIVISION DEL NORTE · Xola · Villa de Cortes

San Antonio · Plaza Mexico · Eugenia · AV. UNIVERSIDAD · Nativitas

Division del Norte · Portales · Ermita

AV. JOSE MARIA RICO · Zapata · AV. POPOCATEPETL · CALZ. ERMITA IXTAPALAPA

Centro Bancomer · CHURUBUSCO

Frida Kahlo Museum · Churubusco Museum · Anaya

COYOACAN · Viveros · Miguel Angel de Quevedo · AV. MIGUEL ANGEL DE QUEVEDO · Taxquena · LINE 2

Bazaar Sabado · San Jacinto Plaza · Coplico

University City · Olympic Stadium · National University of Mexico · LINE 3 · Universidad

PEDREGAL DE SAN ANGEL

ANILLO PERIFERICO SUR · To Xochimilco

To Queretaro & Piedras Negras · 57 D

To Toluca

To Toluca & Guadalajara

To Puebla & Veracruz · 190 D

See Detailed Downtown Map Page 60

Mexico City

N

	Main Streets
	Secondary Streets
	Inner Circuit
	Parks
	Metro System Stations

| 0 | 1 | 2 | Kilometers |
| 0 | ½ | 1 | Miles |

Around the Zocalo

Since the 14th century, when the Aztecs established their capital of Tenochtitlan on an island in Lake Texcoco, the area around the Zocalo, Mexico City's huge downtown plaza, has been the seat of government and religion for the entire country. When the Spaniards arrived in 1519, this 165-square-block area was linked to the mainland by broad causeways and an aqueduct that brought fresh water from the western shore of the lake. At that time, Tenochtitlan had an estimated 80,000 inhabitants.

The conquerors were amazed at the beauty of the palaces, the luxury of their furnishings, and the impressive grandeur of the great ceremonial center immediately north of today's Zocalo. But during their 80-day siege of the capital in 1521, they systematically razed the Aztec structures and, upon the rubble, built a Spanish town.

Your visit to Mexico City, therefore, might well begin where the post-Conquest history of Mexico began.

Historic Center

On April 11, 1980, some 668 square blocks of the downtown area were declared a Historic Center; the city planners' goal was to preserve, maintain, and restore artifacts of the region's Aztec heritage as well as of its colonial period and struggle for independence.

Great Temple. On a 2-square-block area at the northeast corner of the plaza, near the National Palace, the National Institute of Anthropology is slowly uncovering an archeological treasure. In 1978, a chance discovery of a huge monolith dating from the late 1400s led to further excavations that revealed the complete foundations of the Great Temple (Templo Mayor) of the Aztec city of Tenochtitlan. Finds also included a small, still-intact temple and a number of stone chambers containing offerings to the gods.

The temple grounds are open from 10 A.M. to 1 P.M. every day except Monday. To understand the excavations, it's best to go with a guide. A museum nearby displays an imposing mock-up of the present city and its Aztec forerunner.

Zocalo. Measuring 790 feet on each side and bordered by four broad streets, the Zocalo itself has a colorful career. After the Conquest it became the very center of colonial life. Market stalls selling wares of every description filled it until 1789. A gallows stood in front of the National Palace; at one time, fountains marked the four corners of the plaza. The Zocalo has also been the site of a bullring and a park; until about 40 years ago it was the terminus for bus and streetcar lines. Now, because large crowds frequently assemble there, it is a grand expanse of concrete blocks broken only by a flagpole, mobile planters, and a subway entrance.

Coming into the plaza from Avenida Madero, you'll see the Hotel Majestic on the southwest corner. Its roof-garden restaurant is a good place to eat or drink while you enjoy the panoramic view of the Zocalo and the historic buildings that face it. For the night of September 15—the eve of Independence Day—the hotel is booked far in advance by those wanting a box seat for the spectacle staged in the plaza: as many as 300,000 people gather to hear Mexico's president repeat the *Grito* (call to arms) given by Miguel Hidalgo in 1810. Spectacular fireworks and the pealing of the cathedral bells follow the ceremony.

Turning right on the west side of the square, you pass through the Portales, a broad arcade in which merchants maintained permanent stalls from 1524 until some time after Mexico won its independence from Spain in 1821. Small shops now operate there, opening onto the square.

Municipal Palaces. Two Municipal Palaces stand on the plaza's south side. The Old Palace, built in 1532, was almost destroyed by rioters in 1692. In addition to the city office and archives, this building also housed the Royal Mint (established in 1536, the first in the Americas). The New Palace, between 20 de Noviembre and Piño Suarez, was dedicated in 1948. Both buildings are now devoted to administrative functions.

Supreme Court. The building at the southeast corner of the square was completed in 1940. Be sure to go inside for a look at Jose Clemente Orozco's powerful mural, a satirical critique of the judiciary.

National Palace. This squat, three-story building occupies the entire east side of the Zocalo, on the site of the former Palace of Moctezuma. Cortes erected his official headquarters here; in 1562, the Spanish government purchased the building as a residence for the viceroys. Some 300 years later, Emperor Maximilian made improvements, and the building was enlarged when Porfirio Diaz became president in 1876. The third story was added in 1927.

The central balcony and the niche above it together form the focal point of the façade. In the niche hangs Mexico's Liberty Bell, rung by the president at 11 P.M. each September 15. Below the balcony, the main entrance gives access to the great stairway where, in 1929, Diego Rivera painted one of his finest murals—*Mexico: Yesterday, Today, and Tomorrow*. The Benito Juarez Museum, also in the palace, is worth a visit. Inside are displayed objects associated with the life of this Mexican patriot. It's open weekdays from 10 A.M. to 2 P.M. and 5 to 7 P.M., weekends from 10 A.M. to 3 P.M.

Behind the palace, at Calle Moneda 13, is the Museum of the Cultures, where you'll see exhibits depicting the history of cultures throughout the world.

Mexico City's Metropolitan Cathedral is illuminated for special occasions. The magnificent structure dominates the downtown Zocalo.

Diego Rivera's striking mural on the staircase wall of the National Palace depicts Mexico's turbulent history.

Any visit to Mexico City should include at least one Sunday, for certain activities of special interest can be enjoyed only on that day. The questions are, where does one begin, and how does one fit all of these activities into the trip? The only answer is to schedule more weekends into your visit to Mexico's capital.

The three major attractions are the Ballet Folklorico, the bullfights, and the floating gardens of Xochimilco.

Ballet Folklorico performances take place at the Palacio de Bellas Artes on Sunday morning and Sunday evening (though you can also see the show on Wednesday evening). This beautifully executed and wonderfully costumed spectacle is a 2-hour series of regional folk songs and dances. It should rank high on anyone's list of "must sees."

Travel agencies run group tours; the price includes transportation to and from your hotel. Be sure to request tickets when you arrive in Mexico City; the show sells out quickly.

Bullfights are, for many, one of the chief reasons for coming to Mexico. In the capital they take place in the world's largest bullring, Plaza Mexico on Insurgentes Sur, which seats 50,000 fans. The formal season begins in late November and lasts 3 to 4 months. That's when top matadors fight feisty bulls weighing in the neighborhood of 1,000 pounds. During the rest of the year, younger, less experienced *novilleros* fight smaller animals.

When you buy your tickets—which you should do in advance through a travel agency, but can do at the bullring—specify whether you want to sit on the *sombra* (shady side) or on the sunny side. Sombra seats are more expensive. Shun the ticket scalpers! The exciting spectacle begins promptly at 4:30 P.M.

Xochimilco gardens, perhaps the second most popular Sunday destination, is about 15 miles southeast of the downtown area. Several hundred years before the Conquest, the Xochimilco Indians who lived around Lake Texcoco established floating gardens on the lake aboard rafts of varying sizes. They developed a thriving trade in fresh produce with the island capital of the Aztecs. Though there is no longer a lake, a few canals still divide the gardens, long since anchored by plant and tree roots.

You can float along the waterways on canoes and gondolas. Until recent years, each gondola proudly wore its name emblazoned in fresh flowers across the front of its canopy; unfortunately, plastic flowers are used now.

Xochimilco is open every day, but it's at its most colorful on Sunday. Go early; Mexican family groups gather in the afternoon and the traffic is terrible. Along the banks are a number of restaurants where the pilot of your boat can put in, but we recommend taking a picnic. Authorized rates for boat rides are posted at the dock. Agree on the charges before you set off.

You'll save time and money by visiting Xochimilco on an or-

Gaily decorated boat at Xochimilco's floating gardens

Fancy ropework and riding at local charreada

display their works—paintings in all media, etchings, sketches, and sculpture. A plus: you don't pay customs fees for original art!

Broad, winding pathways serve as their exhibition halls. There are splashing fountains, large cages with a variety of colorful and musical birds, landscaped gardens, shade trees, and many benches where you can sit and watch the passers-by.

Charreadas are the progenitors of the Western-style rodeos. Neither cattle nor horses were known in Mexico until after the Conquest in 1521. At that time, those who had won the land for Spain were rewarded with immense haciendas, which they stocked with imported cattle. The tasks of everyday ranch life, as well as all the maneuvers required to herd cattle—rounding up, cutting out, and so on—were new and complicated skills to early Mexican

cowboys. Gradually, however, their abilities were refined into what became known as *charreria,* the art and showmanship of the man on horseback.

Charreadas are usually held on Sunday morning for several hours. They may take place in Chapultepec Park or in the Pedregal or San Angel areas of the city. Check with your hotel's concierge for exact time and place.

Mercado Tepito, long known as the Thieves' Market, is an open-air mecca for bargain hunters, and particularly colorful on Sunday. Located on Calle de Aztecas, between Allende and Brazil streets, the colorful market is a confusion of people and junk. Take a cab or guide with a car. If there's a crowd, beware of pickpockets.

You may find good buys, but it takes sharp eyes, patience, and knowledge of Mexican artifacts to separate copies from originals.

ganized tour; check with the travel desk at your hotel. Some companies offer an all-day outing, with a visit to the gardens and a performance of the Ballet Folklorico or a seat at the bullring.

Art buffs will enjoy a stroll through the Art Garden in Sullivan Park, 1 block west of Insurgentes and 2 short blocks north of Paseo de la Reforma. Between the hours of 9 A.M. and 3 P.M. every Sunday, some 250 artists struggling for recognition

Paintings line Sullivan Park's walkways for Sunday art market

Practical rebozos carry tiny passengers and groceries, leaving shoppers' arms free.

Intricate colors and patterns distinguish the façade of House of Tiles—once a palace, now a restaurant.

. . . around the Zocalo

Metropolitan Cathedral. The magnificent cathedral on the north side of the plaza has detractors who claim that it suffers from an overabundance of architectural styles—a result of its 200-year construction period. Be that as it may, it is one of the most important Catholic churches in the New World, housing a multitude of religious art treasures including two Murillo paintings. It was recently totally renovated, from foundation to bell towers. The adjoining cathedral, El Sagrario (built in 1750), is an excellent example of the ornate churrigueresque architectural style.

Cortes began erection of the first cathedral here in 1524, three years after the Conquest. Foundations for the present cathedral were laid in 1573, and work continued as funds permitted; the awe-inspiring Altar of the Kings was not completed until 1737.

First-time visitors should take special notice of the cathedral crypts (entrance on the west); the Altar of Forgiveness and the choir, almost destroyed by fire in 1967 and later restored with painstaking care; the four huge oval paintings by Miguel Cabrera above the two side entrances; and the 85-foot-high Altar of the Kings, a glory in gold leaf, at the intersection of the nave and transepts. Chapels of artistic merit line the two transepts.

The cathedral is always open for worshippers; the best time for a sightseeing tour is in midmorning.

National Pawnshop. Mexico's state-run pawnshop, Monte de Piedad, stands at the northwest corner of the Zocalo, on the site of the palace where Hernan Cortes and his men were housed upon their arrival in 1519. The present mansion was constructed in the early 18th century and, in 1836, became this hemisphere's oldest credit institution.

Anything except perishable goods may be pawned; if not redeemed within a specific time, articles are offered for sale here or at one of the numerous branches throughout the country. The huge complex, though interesting, offers little shopping value for tourists.

Museum of the City of Mexico. On the northeast corner of Piño Suarez and Republica del Salvador, midway between the Zocalo and the Piño Suarez subway station, stands the magnificent town house of the Counts of Santiago de Calimaya. Its foundations were laid in the 1530s, but the mansion's recorded history begins in 1775, when it was totally restored by the count of that epoch. The building is impressive because of its elegant simplicity and the excellence of its stone carving.

In 1960 the mansion was declared a national monument and, after restoration and adaptation, it became the Museum of the City of Mexico. Ground-floor salons depict the pre-Hispanic history of the Valley of Mexico, from man's appearance there until the defeat and destruction of Tenochtitlan in 1521. Second-floor exhibits transport the visitor through the colonial and independence periods to present-day Mexico City. The third floor houses an art gallery. The museum is open Tuesday through Sunday from 9:30 A.M. to 7:30 P.M.

Church and Hospital of Jesus. Diagonally across the street, on the southwest corner of the intersection, stands the oldest hospital in the Americas. Cortes founded it in 1524, on the spot where Emperor Moctezuma had greeted him upon his arrival five years earlier. In continuous operation since its founding, the hospital now occupies a square block; newer facilities surround the colonial core, which is still in use.

Under the terms of his will, which provided financial support for the institution, Cortes stipulated that the hospital be directed by his descendants. This stipulation was respected until the 1930s, when the government took over the hospital's administration from an unworthy scion of the family. An inexpensive health-care plan for the medically needy now operates at the facility.

Cortes's remains lie in the Church of Jesus Nazareno, a chapel in the complex. When the conquerer died in Spain in 1547, he left instructions that his body be returned to Mexico after 10 years. After being moved from place to place, the remains were finally interred in the church in 1794. But hatred of the Spaniards reached such a pitch during the War for Independence in 1810 that the remains were removed and hidden elsewhere in the church. Historical investigators discovered them in 1946, and they are now entombed in the north wall of the sacristy. The church is open to visitors.

Along Avenida Madero

When a number of Franciscan friars arrived from Spain in 1524, Cortes granted them four square blocks of land on the western shore of the island capital. Then he ordered a narrow street to be cut through from the Zocalo so that the friars might have easy access to church and government offices. The street was called San Francisco in the 16th century when members of the Spanish aristocracy built mansions along its 6-block length. The estates stood proudly for years before they were turned into stores and apartments.

Eventually, as in all large cities, commerce began to move out to the less congested suburbs, leaving the downtown area to decay. In 1970, the government rejuvenated all streets heading into the Zocalo from the west. Unsightly signs and cables were eliminated, building façades were repaired, streets were paved with red tile and sidewalks with pink stone, trees and shrubbery were planted, and colonial-type street lighting was installed.

Today, a stroll down Avenida Madero—renamed to honor the leader of the Revolution of 1910—is a delightful journey into the past and offers a good chance to peek into many former colonial palaces.

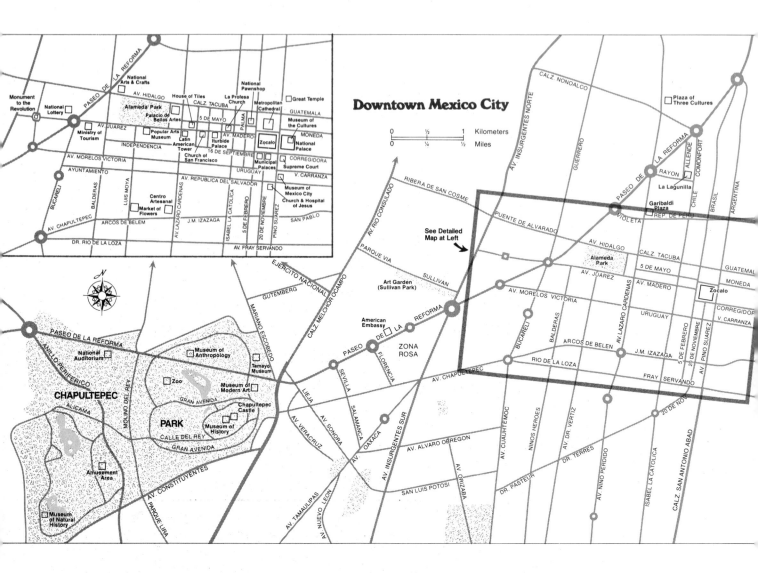

. . . around the Zocalo

The Church of La Profesa, corner of Isabel la Catolica, was built by Jesuits in the 16th century. Here, in 1820, members of the clergy and other Spaniards plotted to foil Mexico's bid for independence by bringing in a Spanish prince to rule the country. Among the plotters was Agustin de Iturbide, who proclaimed himself emperor.

The Palace of Iturbide, just 2 blocks east at Madero 17, is an elegant building. Completely restored in 1972, it now houses the offices of a bank. Visitors are welcome during banking hours. Its construction as a private dwelling was begun in 1779 by the Count of San Mateo. When Iturbide entered the city in triumph on September 27, 1821, the building's owner invited him to make the palace his home. His stay was short—10 months after having himself crowned emperor, in July 1822, he was forced to abdicate and flee into exile. When he attempted to return the following year, he was captured and executed.

The Church and Monastery of San Francisco, nestled behind the Latin American Tower, played a dominant role in the spiritual and social life of the people from 1524 until the 1850s. Today's streets of Madero, Lazaro Cardenas, Venustiano Carranza, and Bolivar form the approximate boundaries of the four square blocks Cortes ceded to the Franciscans. The city's first church was built there in 1525; the present church, the third to stand on the site, dates from 1716. Excavations permit a complete view of the lovely façade and reveal that the heavy structure has sunk 12 feet into the spongy subsoil.

The House of Tiles, directly across the street at Madero 4, is one of the city's downtown showplaces. Another palatial residence, the building was erected prior to 1708 as the town house of the Counts of Orizaba. Its facing of decorative blue and white Puebla tiles was added in 1737. The bronze balustrade came from China. For many years the exclusive Jockey Club occupied the building; then, in 1919, the first Sanborn's restaurant was installed in the spacious patio, where it continues to operate today.

The **Numismatic Museum** is just west of Sanborn's across narrow Condesa Street, on the second floor of the Guardiola Building. The 20,000-piece collection includes duck quills filled with gold dust, cacao beans, and jade beads used as media of exchange before the Conquest; coins brought in by the Spaniards and those they minted in Mexico during the colonial period; and money coined by insurgents during the War for Independence and, a century later, the Revolution of 1910.

The **44-story Latin American Tower** rises at the corner of Madero and Lazaro Cardenas. Despite its enormous height and weight, the tower has suffered no damage from sinking or earthquakes since it was erected in 1956. This extraordinary stability is a result of the building's extra-sturdy construction; it's built on a concrete slab resting on pilings anchored in solid rock 100 feet below ground. Water injected around the pilings helps to keep the tower level. The 42nd floor is a *mirador* (scenic outlook) commanding a superb view of the entire valley. You pay an admission to go there, but the elevator ride to the Muralto restaurant and cocktail lounge on the floor below is free.

Garibaldi Plaza. If you're addicted to mariachi music, the louder the better, Garibaldi Plaza is the place to find it. The plaza is 6 blocks north of Madero and 1 block east of Santa Maria La Redonda (northward extension of Lazaro Cardenas), between Honduras and Peru streets. The plaza and the numerous restaurants and night spots on its perimeter were completely refurbished in 1973 (but are still not good places for unescorted women to visit at night). Groups of musicians begin to gather about 10 P.M.; the later it gets the more music there will be, as mariachi bands that have been performing elsewhere join in the fun. Remember—you pay if you ask them to play.

Avenida Juarez

Continuing westward, Madero turns into Avenida Juarez, which runs for 15 blocks before reaching a 200-foot-high domed monolith. This Monument to the Revolution is just north of the Paseo de la Reforma. A Museum of the Revolution is housed underneath the imposing copper dome.

San Carlos Art Museum. A fine collection of European art (by El Greco, Titian, Brueghel, Van Dyke, and others) is housed in the Buena Vista Palace, Puente de Alvarado 50, two blocks behind the Monument to the Revolution. Prior to its move here in 1968, the museum was located near the Zocalo for over 100 years. It is closed Monday; admission is free.

Palace of Fine Arts. After you cross Lazaro Cardenas, the first building on the right is the Palacio de Bellas Artes, home of the world-famous Ballet Folklorico, the National Symphony orchestra, and classical and modern ballet companies. It also serves as the opera house. Information on all events appears in *The News*, Mexico City's English-language daily.

The building's museum of art contains some of the best murals ever painted by Orozco, Rivera, Siqueiros, and Tamayo as well as exhibitions of Mexican art. The gallery is open daily except Monday, from 11 A.M. to 7 P.M. Your eye will be caught by the 22-ton glass mosaic curtain by Tiffany, installed in the theater in 1910; the curtain is illuminated during a half-hour show before performances of the Ballet Folklorico.

Begun in 1904 and built on land reclaimed from Lake Texcoco, the massive marble structure has sunk 6 feet below street level. Over the years, the sinking caused some of the theater seats to tilt forward, making spectators feel they had to hold on to keep from falling out of their chairs. The remedy was to pump thousands of tons of concrete underneath the building to level it.

National Art Museum. Just east of the Palace of Fine Arts is a collection of Mexican art from pre-hispanic days to the present. The equestrian statue outside, *El Caballito,* stood for many years at the intersection of Juarez and Paseo de la Reforma. The museum, closed Monday, charges a small admission fee.

Alameda Park. Immediately west of the palace is the largest green area in downtown Mexico City, 2 blocks wide and 4 blocks long. Alameda Park, established in 1572, was built over a one-time lake bed. Early in the colonial era, the stake at which victims of the Holy Inquisition were burned was set up on the west side of the park. Throughout the 19th century, the park was enclosed by a wall and reserved for the upper classes, who promenaded there on Sunday.

Midway along the Juarez side of the park stands the imposing monument, Juarez Hemicycle, dedicated in 1910 to Benito Juarez, president of Mexico during the War of Reform and the empire of Maximilian.

Around the park. The Museum of Colonial Paintings, facing the west side of Alameda Park at Mora 7, is housed in the 16th-century Church of San Diego. Hidalgo Street borders the park on the north, and at number 85 is the Hotel de Cortes, dating from 1780. It was built by the Augustinians as an inn for pilgrims along one of the causeways that linked the capital to the mainland. One block east, two 18th-century churches, San Juan de Dios and Santa Veracruz, face each other across a small sunken plaza.

National Museum of Popular Arts. At Juarez 44, crafts are showcased in a charmingly restored colonial building that started life in 1724 as a convent for Indian noblewomen. Two spacious floors are filled with an array of popular arts chosen for their authenticity and superb workmanship. Most crafts are for sale.

Around Chapultepec Park

Stately Paseo de la Reforma was laid out by Maximilian, who reigned as emperor of Mexico from 1864 to 1867. Having established his royal residence in Chapultepec Castle, Maximilian laid out a direct route to the National Palace. From their castle high up on the hill, his wife, Carlotta, could watch the progress of his ornate carriage drawn by six buff-colored mules all the way to the Zocalo.

To get your best view of the entire Paseo de la Reforma, follow Carlotta's example: visit the terrace of the Chapultepec Castle. From this vantage point even the frenzied traffic around the glorietas appears to have a sense of direction.

Paseo de la Reforma

From its intersection with Juarez westward to the park, the Reforma is punctuated by several impressive monuments. On the traffic circle in front of the Crowne Plaza Hotel is a splendid monument to Christopher Columbus, placed there in 1877. Cuauhtemoc, last emperor of the Aztecs, keeps his vigil at the Reforma–Insurgentes intersection from a complex pyramidal monument, completed in 1887. Surmounting it is the heroic figure of 22-year-old Cuauhtemoc in full battle dress.

Most beloved of all the Reforma monuments is the Independence shaft on the traffic circle where the Hotel Maria Isabel Sheraton and the U.S. Embassy stand. Begun in 1902 but torn down in 1906 because of a faulty foundation, the monument was completed in 1909 on pilings driven 70 feet through the spongy subsoil to solid rock. Among the revolutionary figures at the monument's base stands Father Hidalgo, the revered Mexican priest who helped overcome Spanish rule. Aside from the weight of the 150-foot column, the foundation supports an 8-ton gilded angel poised on the shaft's tip. After a severe earthquake in 1957 hurled the angel to the marble pedestal below, and during the many months required for repairs, the benches around the traffic circle were occupied continuously by the statue's devoted admirers.

At the next glorieta, a series of fountains form a graceful canopy of water. For the best look at this comparatively new adornment, visit the intersection at night, when the fountains are illuminated.

The lovely fountain of Diana the Huntress once graced a traffic circle at the entrance to Chapultepec Park, but the fountain and circle were forced to give way to the march of progress and construction of the vital inner-city expressway. Diana now presides over her fountain in a small park nearby.

Zona Rosa

The "Pink Zone," about halfway between Alameda and Chapultepec parks, is to Mexico City what the central plaza is to a provincial town. Bounded by the Reforma, Insurgentes Sur, Chapultepec, and Florencia, the Zona Rosa covers an area of roughly 24 square blocks. Within its confines are a majority of the amenities for tourists—restaurants of all types, night clubs, hotels, travel agencies, art galleries, and shops and boutiques of infinite variety—selling everything from colorful paper flowers to designer clothes. This area abounds with local shoppers as well as tourists.

Though one of the area's hotels was destroyed in an earthquake in 1985, today's visitors will see no other remnants of the disaster in this tourist zone. Recent refurbishing of the swank setting included resurfacing walkways and streets with pink stones (very difficult for walking on in high heels), painting and remodeling shops, and installing colonial-style street lamps. Niza is the zone's main street. Copenhague and Genova streets, now closed to traffic, invite strollers; sidewalk cafes encourage open-air dining.

This is the ideal area to window shop, to meet new friends, to see and be seen. High fashion prevails on these streets; even the trees, trimmed to perfection, have carefully painted trunks.

Park attractions

If you entertain the notion of "doing" Chapultepec Park in a day, forget it! This vast cultural and recreational center covers more than 2,000 acres. It is bounded by Avenida Constituyentes on the south-southwest, extends westward in an irregular form beyond Calle Molino del Rey and the peripheral highway, and in some places overflows Paseo de la Reforma on the north. On the east side (location of most museums), the Melchor Ocampo section of the inner-city expressway has gobbled up a portion of the park land.

Located within these boundaries are five of the country's finest museums, two lakes with boating facilities, a zoo with pandas, a Coney Island–type amusement park with the usual rides plus one of the largest roller coasters anywhere, and several miniature railways. In addition, you'll find restaurants, botanical gardens, polo grounds, handsome fountains and sculptures, bridle paths, and miles of quiet walkways shaded by centuries-old cypress trees (*ahuehuetes*). Los Piños, the president's official residence, is located on the southwest side of the park. Armed guards line the avenue approaching the mansion.

At the park's eastern entrance stands the imposing Monument of the Boy Heroes, dedicated to a small group of military students who defended Chapultepec Castle against American troops in 1847.

Glistening floral bouquets, washed by afternoon shower, sell for only pennies.

For those who shudder at the prospect of traversing so much ground on foot, first-class buses operate out of a terminal at the rear of the Museum of Modern Art. After winding through the old section of the park, the buses emerge onto Constituyentes, go into the new section by its main entrance, work their way north to the Reforma, and then return to the terminal. There are scheduled stops all along the route.

Zoological Gardens. The zoo houses some 2,000 birds and several hundred species of animals. Giant pandas—a gift from the People's Republic of China—attract a lot of attention. The zoo is closed Monday.

Museum of Modern Art. This two-building complex set among sculpture-filled gardens was built in 1964, to the south of Paseo de la Reforma on the east side of the park. Permanently displayed are the works of Jose Marie Velasco, Mexico's talented and prolific landscape painter, along with canvases by Orozco, Rivera, Tamayo,

Siqueiros, Dr. Atl, and more contemporary artists. The museum is open daily except Monday; there's an admission fee.

Tamayo Museum. The park's newest museum sits to the north of the Paseo, and is accessible from the street by a mall (which also leads to the Museum of Modern Art) or by another mall at the end of Calle Ghandi. At the convergence of the two malls, an open-air sculpture court leads to the Museum of Anthropology's entrance.

Mexican artist, Rufino Tamayo donated his personal collection of international contemporary art for display in this dramatic building. Open daily except Monday, the museum charges admission.

National Museum of Anthropology. A miracle of architecture and museum planning, this grand building is easily identified by the 168-ton figure of Tlaloc, the Aztec rain god, standing at the entrance to a tunnel leading to the parking area. Pedro Ramirez Vasquez was the archi-

. . . around Chapultepec Park

tect of this splendid structure, perhaps the most modern and functional museum in the world—and certainly the most spectacular.

A Rufino Tamayo mural and various cultural exhibits occupy most of the main lobby; a fine gift shop is located at the side. At the center of the museum, a patio sports a 5,300-square-yard "umbrella" on a sculptured bronze column. From it falls a refreshing cascade of water that is also a cooling medium for the museum's mechanical systems. Radiating from the patio on the ground floor are 12 exhibition halls devoted to the country's earliest civilizations. Easily the most dramatic is the Aztec Hall with its famed 22-ton calendar, the replica of Moctezuma's feathered headdress, and the scale model of the pre-Conquest capital of Tenochtitlan.

In the garden outside the museum are reproductions of artifacts found at archaeological sites throughout the country. Upstairs, dioramas and exhibits trace the development of Mexico's contemporary cultures. In the basement, an orientation theater presents a 23-minute capsulized history of Mexico's ancient cultures. Though in Spanish, the program is easily understood.

The museum's treasures occupy 100,000 square feet of floor space; a complete view of the interior entails a 3-mile hike. For your convenience, stone benches around the patio provide resting places. A stairway to the left of the patio leads down to a restaurant.

The museum is open Tuesday through Sunday. There's an admission fee, with additional charges for the theater and for a guided tour; fees are reduced on Sunday and holidays.

Massive Tlaloc, Aztec god of rain, welcomes visitors to National Museum of Anthropology.

Chapultepec Castle. A roadway opposite the Museum of Anthropology leads to Chapultepec Hill and the castle that crowns it. Begun in 1783, the castle was originally intended as a weekend resort for the Spanish viceroys. But the War for Independence intervened and it was not completed until 1841, when it was designated as a military academy. It was the last bastion to fall to the invaders during the U.S.–Mexican War of 1847. Then came Maximilian and Carlotta, who made the castle their private residence, adding many of the beautiful features it possesses today. Subsequent heads of state, with the exception of Benito Juarez, resided there. In 1934, the castle became part of the National Museum of History.

The eastern portion of the building displays the rich furnishings left behind by the emperor and empress. Notice Carlotta's exquisite bathtub. In the museum proper, Mexican history is depicted in various salons, several of which are adorned with murals by O'Gorman, Reyes Meza, Gonzalez Camarena, and Siqueiros.

The castle is open daily except Tuesday; a small admission fee is charged. An elevator is available.

National Museum of History. This newer historical museum lies at the bottom of the Chapultepec Hill, below the castle. The multilevel structure offers colorful dioramas and recorded lectures on Mexico's colonial life. Through the large windows, you'll get striking views. The museum is open daily.

Museum of Natural History. To reach this museum, head west on Constituyentes and take the roadway to the right, just before you reach Dolores Cemetery. Spectacularly modernistic in architecture, it houses specimens from around the world. Note especially the Rotunda of Illustrious Men (and women). The museum is open every day but Monday; there's an admission fee.

National Auditorium. West on the Reforma (south side), shortly before its intersection with the peripheral highway, is the scene of classical ballet performances, jazz concerts, and other cultural programs. International sports events are also staged here. Check *The News* (Mexico City's English-language daily) for details.

Awesome 22-ton Aztec Calendar Stone is only one of the impressive exhibits in Mexico City's stunning museum of pre-Columbian artifacts.

Sweeping staircase dramatizes entrance to the Museum of Modern Art in Chapultepec Park.

*Monumental mosaics like Juan O'Gorman's gives
Mexico's National University a unique appearance.*

Avenida Insurgentes

Mexico's longest street runs for over 15 miles, connecting central Mexico City with the Shrine of Guadalupe and Teotihuacan's pyramids to the north and with University City, Coyoacan, San Angel, and the exclusive Pedregal residential area to the south. Just south of Paseo de la Reforma, Avenida Insurgentes passes by the Polyforum Siqueiros, Hotel de Mexico (tallest building in Latin America), and one of the country's largest shopping malls.

Polyforum Siqueiros

On the western side of Insurgentes Sur, on the grounds of the towering Hotel de Mexico, stands the Polyforum Siqueiros, a four-story, 12-sided exposition hall covered with dramatic acrylic murals by David Alfaro Siqueiros. Each of the 12 panels illustrates one phase of the artist's theme, "Humanity's Progress on Earth and in the Universe."

The underground level offers a display of traditional and modern handicrafts for sale, including furniture, ceramics, crystal, and textiles. Also on this floor is a theater-in-the-round and a snack bar. A glass elevator and a winding stairway lead to the ground floor and cupola. At ground level, changing exhibits of Mexican and foreign art catch the eye. The cupola above is adorned with a continuous relief painting by Siqueiros that can be viewed from a revolving platform accommodating up to 1,000 persons.

The Polyforum is open daily; a light-and-sound show is presented in English at 6 P.M. There is a small charge to view the mural; you can look at the handicrafts without paying admission.

Along Insurgentes stretches an 80-foot wall on which Siqueiros paid tribute to the most important figures in Mexican art: Rivera, Orozco, Posada, Mendez, Dr. Atl, and himself.

Southern suburbs

On the outskirts to the south of the metropolis, three suburbs and University City form a section of particular interest. Two of these areas, Coyoacan and San Angel, are very old; the other two, the campus of the National University and the Pedregal residential section, are ultra-modern. All four can be covered in a day by car; more time is needed for a leisurely exploration. Half-day bus tours are also available.

Coyoacan. Once an Indian kingdom, Coyoacan means "Place of the Coyotes." After the Spanish conquerors razed the Aztec capital, they withdrew to Coyoacan until the island city could again be made habitable. Almost overnight, Coyoacan became a Spanish town. Many buildings from the 16th and 17th centuries not only remain standing but are still used, a typical practice in older sections of Mexico City.

Plaza Hidalgo and the Centenario Garden together form the main plaza of Coyoacan. Facing this shady, flower-filled area is a house which supposedly belonged to Cortes—a doubtful claim, since the building dates from the 17th century. On the walls of a chapel in an adjoining patio are modern murals depicting the Conquest.

Across the plaza from the so-called Cortes house stands *La Parroquia* (Parish Church), constructed in the 16th century. To the right of its facade, an arch gives access to the monastery of which it was a part. Two other Moorish-style 17th-century homes bear the names of Pedro de Alvarado and Diego de Oraz, two of Cortes's top lieutenants. But if either Alvarado or Oraz ever lived in the houses originally erected on the sites, it was only briefly; they were both fully occupied elsewhere in consummating the Conquest.

Several museums in the area are well worth a visit:

Frida Kahlo Museum. On the northeast corner of Allende and Londres streets, a museum is established in the home this artist shared for 25 years with her husband, Diego Rivera, until her death in 1954. Open daily except Monday from 10 A.M. to 6 P.M., the museum contains works and personal effects of both artists.

Diego Rivera Museum. Don't miss a visit to Rivera's Anahuacalli Museum in southern San Pablo Tepetlapa (Calle de Museo off Calzado Tlalpan). The stunning lava-rock structure, built in the style of a Maya pyramid, contains Rivera's collection of over 50,000 archeological treasures, in addition to examples of his work and a replica of his studio. The museum is open Tuesday through Saturday, 10 A.M. to 1 P.M. and 3 to 6 P.M. and Sunday from 10 to 2.

Trotsky Museum. A few blocks from the Kahlo museum, at Viena 45, is the house where Leon Trotsky lived after he fled to Mexico from the Soviet Union. Trotsky was assassinated here in 1940; his tomb lies in the garden. To have the caretaker let you in, ring the bell.

Churubusco Historical Museum. Installed in a monastery at the corner of General Anaya and 20 de Agosto, this museum is located in the first building raised by the Franciscans in 1524. It was rebuilt and enlarged in the 17th century and again in the 19th century. During the U.S.–Mexican War of 1847, the monastery became a fortress, falling to the invaders on August 20, 1847. Devoted chiefly to relics of that war, it is open daily except Monday, from 10 A.M. to 5 P.M. There is a small admission charge.

University City. Inaugurated in 1953, the modernistic campus of Mexico's National University extends east and west of the highway over an immense lava flow—the result of the volcano Ixtle's eruption in about 200 B.C. The campus is an outdoor gallery of art expressed in every medium by leading Mexican muralists.

Clearly visible even before you enter the campus is the 10-story, wraparound mosaic adorning the Central Library. Juan O'Gorman was both architect and artist. On the west side of the highway, you'll see a daring stone mosaic carved and painted on the stadium; it was designed by Diego Rivera. Facing the stadium is the rectory, adorned with paintings on three sides by Siqueiros; the central mural is unique for its three-dimensional massiveness.

Of special appeal to those interested in Mexican flora are the university's botanical gardens, where exotic plants from all regions of the country are on view in two greenhouses and three acres of exterior plantings. The orchid and cactus collections are south of the stadium, over a clearly marked roadway. Cacti are arranged in a natural lava-rock setting; the orchids grow in a ground-hugging conservatory. Plants of the tropical rain forest thrive under simulated natural conditions in a conservatory southeast of the swimming pool used during the Olympics. In all, more than 2,000 species are displayed, each tagged with its botanical name.

The National University was founded in 1551 by royal decree in a building on the Zocalo just north of the National Palace. As the number of students increased, each professional school moved to quarters of its own. When the present campus was inaugurated, it drew together students from schools by then scattered all over the city. In 1975, enrollment stood at 245,000 and dispersal was once again the practice, with branch universities established in other areas of the capital.

In front of the Olympic Village section of the university lie the Cuicuilco Pyramids, reportedly the oldest manmade structures in the Western Hemisphere. Buried by lava from the volcano, the pyramids were rediscovered around 1917, although the smaller pyramid was not uncovered until 1968. A small admission fee includes entrance to the museum at the large round pyramid.

Jardines del Pedregal. West of the university stadium are the *Jardines del Pedregal* (Gardens of the Lava Flow), an extension of the same flow upon which the campus is built. To reach this unusual residential area, return north on Insurgentes Sur to San Jeronimo, taking off to the left just beyond Avenida Universidad.

The Pedregal must be seen to be believed. Its modernistic architecture incorporates black lava stone into homes and landscaping with dramatic results. The weird, beautiful trees and flowers that flourish on their rocky beds complete the otherworldly atmosphere. You won't be looking at pre-Hispanic or cultural monuments here; you'll see only the uncommon beauty that sprang from the fertile imagination of a group of architects in the late 1940s.

San Angel. Exploring San Angel on foot through winding, cobblestone streets is a thoroughly enjoyable experience, if you are comfortably shod. The area was "discovered" in the 18th century by viceroys, members of the nobility, and high churchmen. Since it is higher and somewhat cooler than downtown Mexico City, San Angel became a fashionable spot for rest and recreation, especially in the summer. Many of the homes built by aristocrats still stand, mostly behind high walls.

Your eyes will be drawn first to the enormous pile of El Carmen Church and Convent on Avenida de la Revolucion. It was built by the Carmelites from 1615 to 1617. Services are still held in this church, which is resplendent with gold leaf, Puebla tile, and oil paintings. In the thick-walled convent, the National Institute of Anthropology and History maintains a museum of colonial art, as well as workshops where exact replicas of pre-Hispanic ceramic figures and jewelry are manufactured and offered for sale. In the cellar, a crypt holds mummies of nuns and priests, remarkably preserved and still robed in their funeral garb.

San Jacinto Plaza, a long block west of Revolucion, is surrounded by some of San Angel's oldest buildings. The 18th-century Casa del Risco on the east side, for example, was a private residence until it became a museum displaying furnishings of a bygone era—furniture, paintings, chandeliers, and chinaware. Set in one wall of the patio is the huge fountain that gives the house its name; it forms a fantastic *risco* ("cliff") of multicolored tiles and fine porcelain pieces.

On the front of a building on the west side of the plaza is a bronze plaque unveiled in 1959, which reads: "In memory of the Irish soldiers of the heroic St. Patrick's Brigade, martyrs who gave their lives for the Mexican cause during the unjust North American invasion of 1847." The names of 68 officers and enlisted men follow.

Archives of the Library of Congress reveal, though, that these "martyred heroes" were actually deserters from the U.S. Army who, in July 1847, signed agreements to serve in the Mexican army in exchange for land grants. Many of them came from San Patricio, Texas—hence the name. After their capture and court-martial by U.S. forces, 23 were hanged and 24 were lashed, branded, and dishonorably discharged. The fate of the rest is unknown.

Also on the west side of San Jacinto Plaza is the site for Bazaar Sabado ("Saturday Bazaar"). It occupies a 17th-century mansion, from which the sleeping Santa Ana barely escaped with his life on the day U.S. troops took San Angel. On Saturday only, from 10 A.M. to 8 P.M., more than 100 Mexican and foreign artisans display their creations. These run the gamut from exquisite silverware and jewelry to clothing, textiles, and furniture, often of contemporary rather than traditional design. A mariachi band performs for luncheon on the central patio. The Saturday Bazaar is augmented by an art show on the patio and an Indian market on its southwest corner.

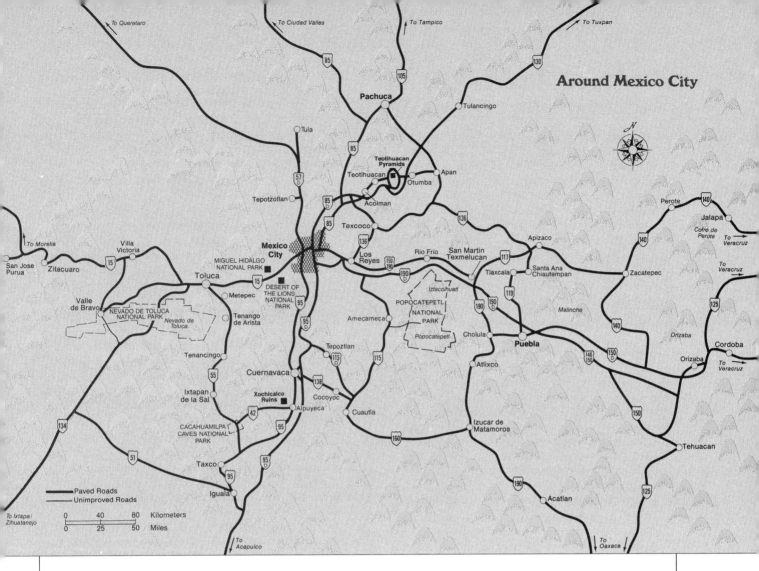

DETAILS AT A GLANCE

Around Mexico City

How to get there

Mexico City makes a good base for short forays into the surrounding area. Driving is the best way to reach most of the small villages.

Cars can be hired in the larger towns—Cuernavaca, Taxco, and Puebla. Roads are good to most destinations. Though traffic is terrible in the capital, it's not a problem elsewhere. Government-licensed guides with cars are also available in Mexico City. Ask your hotel for recommendations. To get the most out of your tour, hire a guide who speaks English fluently.

Tours

If you want to see as much as possible in a short time, package tours are often your best bet. Gray Line Tours (and others) offer a wide variety of excursions.

Accommodations

You'll have your choice of accommodations in most of the towns surrounding Mexico City. Gracious haciendas and charming small hotels with flower-filled gardens await you near Cuernavaca, Taxco, Puebla, and Cholula. Spas provide comfortable lodging at Ixtapan de la Sal, San Jose Purua, and Cuautla. Valle de Bravo offers everything from country clubs to rustic inns. (For more information, see the "Essentials" section on page 153.)

Climate & clothes

"Land of eternal spring" is one name given to the area around Mexico City. Shed your more dressy Mexico City attire; replace it with casual, comfortable clothes to explore surrounding attractions. You'll need flat, rubber-soled shoes for climbing pyramids and Taxco's steep streets.

North of Mexico City

The northern part of Mexico City has several major attractions, including the shrine of the country's patron saint and vast archeological ruins. You can make excursions to the north on your own, via bus tour, or with a car and driver-guide. Though none of the destinations is very far, you should allow at least a half day for visiting Guadalupe Shrine and Teotihuacan, a full day for exploring the area in-depth. Guided tours to the pyramids of Teotihuacan may include visits to the Plaza of Three Cultures, Guadalupe Basilica, and Acolman.

Plaza of Three Cultures

About 16 blocks beyond the intersection of Juarez and Paseo de la Reforma lies the Plaza of the Three Cultures. You can't miss it; from the time you start the drive north on Reforma, the high-rise buildings of the Tlateloco housing project (severely damaged in the 1985 earthquake) dominate the horizon. Turn left around the traffic circle, and then west onto Calzada Nonoalco, the southern boundary of the project. Turn right at the first corner and the plaza is on your right.

The plaza gets its name from the juxtaposition of buildings from three different periods. Below street level are the excavated remains of pyramids and platforms—a small portion of pre-Columbian Tlatelolco's ceremonial center. Beyond the plaza is the attractive 16th-century Church of Santiago Tlatelolco; adjoining it is the Church of the Holy Cross, completed in 1536 for the sons of Indian nobles. It was in this college that Fray Bernardino de Sahagun, aided by survivors of the Conquest, recorded in Nahuatl the history and customs of the Aztecs.

It was in this spot that the last battle of the Conquest took place. A marble plaque on the church states "The 13th of August of 1521, heroically defended by Cuauhtemoc, Tlatelolco fell under the power of Hernan Cortes. It was not a triumph nor a defeat, it was the painful birth of the mixed race that is the Mexico of today."

Guadalupe Shrine

A short distance inside the northern city limits is the Basilica of Our Lady of Guadalupe, Mexico's patron saint. As you approach the enormous plaza in front of the basilica, you'll note the new basilica on the left; it now houses the image of the Virgin. The new structure was designed by Pedro Ramirez Vasquez, who also designed the National Museum of Anthropology. The old basilica, dating from 1709, is now a museum.

The story of the Virgin of Guadalupe is etched in the national consciousness. It is said that on December 9,

1531, a young Indian convert named Juan Diego was on his way to Mass in Tlatelolco when a vision appeared in his path—the Virgin Mary, dark-skinned and clad in the robes of an Indian princess. She told him to go to the bishop, relate his experience, and express her wish that a chapel be erected there on Tepeyac Hill, where she might minister to her Indians.

The bishop was understandably skeptical. On the following day, the Virgin again appeared to Juan and repeated her instructions. Still unconvinced, the bishop requested that Juan bring him proof of the Virgin's identity. Reluctant to embarrass both the Virgin and himself, Juan remained at home on December 11. On the 12th though, he set out in haste for Tlatelolco to fetch a priest, for his uncle was gravely ill. As he had feared, he again encountered the Virgin and had to tell her of the bishop's demand for tangible evidence.

Unperturbed, she instructed Juan to gather roses she said he would find growing on the desolate hillside, and to take them to the bishop immediately. She assured him that there was no need to worry about his uncle, who had recovered his health. When Juan unrolled his serape in the prelate's presence, its inner side contained a portrait of the Virgin. Satisfied at last that a miracle had occurred, the bishop ordered a chapel constructed on Tepeyac Hill; the sacred image was placed above its altar.

The Virgin of Guadalupe became Mexico's patron saint. The Indian's mantle, in a heavy gold frame, now hangs over the altar of the basilica. Skeptics continue to assail its authenticity, but experts have confirmed that the "canvas" is genuinely of 16th-century Mexican manufacture, and that in 1531 there was no one in Mexico capable of painting such a portrait. The paints have so far defied analysis.

In 1787, the Convent of the Capuchin Sisters was built near the basilica over springs said to have miraculous healing powers. The faithful come here to fill bottles with its water; outside, small bottles are sold to tourists.

Mexico City's Christmas season begins with midnight Mass in the basilica December 11, when thousands of the faithful crowd the church and atrium. After an all-night vigil, they sing *Las Mañanitas* (Happy Birthday) to the Virgin at dawn on the 12th.

Teotihuacan

Teotihuacan, 25 miles northeast of Mexico City via a toll road that takes off from the Laredo Highway on the outskirts of the capital, is an archeological site so majestic that the Aztecs, who came upon it several centuries after it was abandoned, named it the "City of the Gods." Its urban area covers 9 square miles; at the height of its glory (A.D. 200–600), its inhabitants numbered between 100,000 and 200,000. The magnificent ceremonial center and some of the outlying palaces and priestly dwellings have been restored, and the zone is open every day.

The largest and oldest monument is the Pyramid of the Sun. It was constructed in about 100 B.C. over a long, sinuous, sacred cave. Relics found there prove that the site had been populated for 200 years or more before the pyramid was built. Including the sanctuary that once stood on its summit, the pyramid is 230 feet high, the tallest so far discovered on the North American continent.

The broad Avenue of the Dead, 1½ miles long, runs precisely parallel to the Pyramid of the Sun. On the north it terminates at the Plaza and Pyramid of the Moon (considerably smaller than the Pyramid of the Sun and erected after the larger structure was completed). To the south it passes in front of the huge enclosure called the Citadel, and there it ends. The patio of the Citadel was used as a ceremonial complex.

On the eastern side of the square court stands the Temple of Quetzalcoatl ("Plumed Serpent"), its façade covered with superbly carved stone heads of feathered serpents and of the rain god Tlaloc.

Facing the Plaza of the Moon and along both sides of the Avenue of the Dead are numerous small, flat-topped pyramids and temples. At the southwest corner of the plaza stands the Palace of Quetzalpapalotl. Completely reconstructed, it exemplifies the sumptuousness of that era's palaces. On the walls of some chambers are traces of the mural paintings that once covered all pre-Hispanic buildings.

In its heyday, Teotihuacan drew religious pilgrims from as far away as Yucatan Peninsula and Central America. During that same period, it was the most important trading center in the Mexican highlands.

Several restaurants operate in the archeological zone, including one installed over 50 years ago in a mammoth grotto. There is also a small, good museum. From October to May, every night except Monday, a light-and-sound spectacle in English is presented at 7 P.M. The script incorporates the legends that sprang up with respect to Teotihuacan, place of mystery. Warm clothing and a lap robe are essential. Reserved tickets are available from travel agencies. Tour packages from Mexico City include transportation; bus service is also available.

Acolman

Just off the toll road, about 6 miles south of Teotihuacan, stands the handsome, fortress-type Church and Monastery of Acolman, established by the Augustinians in 1539. Probably its most interesting feature is its severely simple, beautifully executed plateresque façade—the purest example of that style in Mexico. In the interior of the church, under many layers of paint, colossal 16th-century frescoes in red, black, and yellow were discovered during renovation. They resemble those found in more ancient Italian churches. A collection of religious art is exhibited in the monastery (donations requested).

Staggering the legs as well as the imagination, Teotihuacan's Pyramid of the Sun rises 230 feet.

Texcoco and Chiconcuac

The route to Texcoco heads across a vast lake bed northeast of Mexico City. The salty soil of the old lake bed, dry during the winter months, is being reconditioned to permit farming and reforestation; part of the 66-square-mile area is a planned recreational center. Although this will not put an end to the dust storms that plague the capital during the dry months, it will avert the threat of flooding.

It was in Texcoco (then on the eastern shore of the lake) that Cortes, after being ignominiously routed from the Aztec capital in 1520, assembled 13 brigantines for another assault. Timbers were cut in Tlaxcala and carried across the mountains to Texcoco by 8,000 Indian bearers; by April, 1521, the warships were ready for launching. Four months later, the Conquest had been accomplished.

Texcoco now has more than 75,000 inhabitants. Sunday and Monday are market days; the market is famous for *barbacoa* (pit-barbecued lamb), ceramics and textiles of distinctive style and design, and blown glass.

Chiconcuac is less than 10 minutes north of Texcoco over a narrow dirt road. Before the Conquest, Chiconcuac was also on the lake shore—a tiny village that even then specialized in weaving, delivering its goods to market by canoe. Today, it is a town of over 10,000, and the

Stoic warriors guard Temple of Quetzalcoatl at Tula. Two of the 15-foot-tall figures in this view are original; lighter-gray one at far left is a reproduction.

. . . north of Mexico City

volume and variety of its textile products in wool and acrylic fibers are unsurpassed anywhere.

In more than 50 shops along the main street, you'll find blankets, wall hangings, serapes, handmade hooked or shag rugs, sweaters in any style or color, and *jorongos*—serapes with a slit in the center to put your head through—as well as shawls, overblouses, stoles, and *rebozos* (long scarves). For anything knitted or woven, Chiconuac is the place.

Tepotzotlan

Amid the wealth of religious art and architecture that is Mexico's heritage, the Church of San Francisco Javier in Tepotzotlan is outstanding, a masterpiece of ultrabaroque magnificence. Drive 25 miles north of Mexico City on the highway to Queretaro; the church tower is visible on your left. A museum devoted to the Spanish viceregal era was installed in the monastery after renovation in 1959. Church and museum are open from 11 A.M. to 6 P.M.; the museum is closed Monday.

Every year from mid- to late December, *pastorelas* are presented nightly. An ingenuous version of events surrounding the birth of Christ, these plays were conceived by Spanish nuns during the Middle Ages. Tickets, secured from travel agencies in Mexico City, include dinner, piñatas, village bands, and a *posada*, the reenactment of the Holy Family's search for shelter. Dress warmly!

Tula—former Toltec capital

From about A.D. 950 to 1150, the militaristic Toltecs controlled the Valley of Mexico. About 25 miles north of Tepotzotlan are the remains of Tula, their capital. Distinguished by 15-foot stone idols atop the Temple of Quetzalcoatl, the ruins are extremely photogenic. The restored ball court is Mexico's largest. Though most of the area's best sculptures have been moved to Mexico City's Museum of Anthropology, a small museum (open daily) contains finds from the site, including Choc Mool, the Toltecan rain god.

West of Mexico City

Friday is market day in Toluca. The drive from the capital is well worthwhile, even if you only absorb the local color. The countryside en route is beautiful, and by venturing a little farther you can enjoy the nearby baths, spas, and resort.

One way to get to Toluca is on Highway 15, through the Desert of Lions National Park (neither a desert nor filled with lions) and scenic Miguel Hidalgo–La Marquesa National Park (lake and fish hatchery). On walks through both parks you'll discover ruins, secluded trails, and cool pine forests in which to picnic.

Toluca

Nestled in the center of green Valley of Toluca is the bustling commercial city of Toluca, about an hour's drive from Mexico City. The invigorating, brisk weather typical of this flat valley is the result of its high altitude (almost 9,000 feet). Nevada de Toluca, an extinct, sometimes snow-shrouded volcano, towers over the city. Within its walls, the crater of the 15,000-foot volcano holds two lakes filled with rainbow trout. With a car and guide you can drive to the summit and down to the crater floor. Views are spectacular.

Most visitors spend hours in the alfresco section of Toluca's market. Just south of the city off the peripheral highway, the market operates every day. But it's best on Friday, when additional merchandise floods the adjoining plaza. Also worth a visit are the Museum of Popular Arts on Highway 15 at the eastern entrance to Toluca, the Fine Arts Museum downtown behind the Governor's Palace, and the nearby Charro Museum. Casart (Paseo Tollocan 700 Ote) showcases contemporary crafts from the state of Mexico in a charming two-story building.

Around Toluca

Just west of the city stands the Church of Our Lady of Tecajic, a popular Indian shrine with a much-venerated image. Uetepec, a few miles south of Toluca, is a charming old town with buildings the color of its fine pottery. Plan to visit the Monday market.

Also nearby are the Indian villages of Metepec, noted for its beautiful pottery; Tianguistengo, famous for serapes; Tenancingo, where they make *rebozos* (shawls) so fine they can be drawn through a wedding band; and Almoloya, known for its finely decorated tablecloths.

North of Toluca off Highway 55, a dirt road leads to the Calixtlahuaca Archeological Zone, with an unusual round pyramid among the uncovered buildings. The museum at Teotenango, 11 miles south of Toluca on Highway 55, displays archeological treasures.

Ixtapan de la Sal, a popular spa and resort noted for its luxurious mineral baths, lies south of Toluca on Highway 55. The busiest season is winter, when tourists from colder climes flock here for relaxing sessions at the thermal baths.

There are two towns—the old town, purely Mexican, rustic, and bright with tropical vegetation; and Nuevo Ixtapan, beautifully landscaped, with a luxury hotel and other, more modest accommodations.

West of Toluca on the road to Morelia is the turnoff to San Jose Purua, one of Mexico's most celebrated spas. (Don't attempt to take a trailer down the 4½-mile road between the highway and the town.) The spa hotel at San Jose Purua perches on the edge of a canyon in a lush, tropical setting of flowering trees, bubbling streams, waterfalls, and quiet ponds.

Roughly 80 miles southwest of Toluca, or 2½ hours from Mexico City, Valle de Bravo is reached by a mountainous, paved road. The town slopes down to the shores of a lake constructed as part of a huge hydroelectric project to benefit the surrounding area. The town is an arts-and-crafts center noted for its pottery.

Toluca shopper at outdoor market can be sure her turkey is fresh.

Poinsettias add splash of bright color to the courtyard of Cuernavaca's cathedral. Often called Mexico's garden spot, the city is popular with visitors for its springlike weather, luxuriant walled gardens, fine hotels, and good restaurants.

Taxco's tangled buildings cling to a mountainside halfway between Mexico City and Acapulco. Formerly a silver mining center, picturesque city is now a national colonial monument.

South of Mexico City

The Mexico City–Cuernavaca–Taxco route, called the "Golden Triangle," is one of the most popular package tours sold in the U.S. From Taxco you can continue on to Acapulco (see page 43) on the fast superhighway and return to the capital by air. The toll road (95-D) between Mexico City and Acapulco by-passes Taxco, but you can easily turn off to reach this intriguing colonial town. You can also get to Taxco by taking the older, more winding Highway 95 all the way from Mexico City. Maintained as a toll-free route, it is about 20 miles longer than the toll road and much slower. The two highways join near Iguala.

Taxco is a popular overnight stop. Since most tourists going to Acapulco include this charming town on their itineraries, you'd be wise to have confirmed reservations. (See page 153 for hotel information.) Cuernavaca also has excellent overnight accommodations.

Cuernavaca

Capital of the state of Morelos, beautiful Cuernavaca impresses visitors more with its lush, gardenlike personality than with its bustling, metropolitan character. Travelers who don't have much time to spend in the various regions of Mexico will appreciate the colorful town of Cuernavaca—it's a mixture of all the best Mexico has to offer. But you'll have to peer over walls to discover its charm; on the surface, it appears to be a community in need of cleaning and repair.

Cuernavaca provides a large number of North Americans and wealthy Mexico City residents with a popular weekend and holiday retreat. Rainbows of flowering vines, an intoxicating melange of scents drifting over the walls of hidden gardens, and trees bedecked with splashes of red, orange, blue, and yellow—all create the delightful experience that awaits the visitor to Cuernavaca.

The city was a favorite getaway for Cortes as well as Maximilian and Carlotta. At an altitude of 5,000 feet, it is noted for a balmy climate all year around. House and garden tours in early spring give travelers a chance to see some of the magnificent mansions. Barbara Hutton's former home on the outskirts of town is now a popular Japanese restaurant called Sumiya.

The Borda Gardens on Avenida Morelos (small entrance fee) were once the epitome of the town's elegance. Here you'll find a grand old villa, a mirror pool, fountains, and the exotic, recently refurbished gardens. The villa, summer home to Maximilian and Carlotta from 1864 to 1867, was built as a retreat by Taxco silver king Jose de la Borda in the 1700s; today it houses arts and crafts and a small museum.

The simple Church of Guadalupe, once the Borda family chapel, adjoins the gardens; the cathedral is across the street.

San Francisco Cathedral, Hidalgo and Morelos, has a beautifully restored modern interior; the exterior reflects the bold architectural style of Cortes Palace (see below). During colonial years, missionaries used the cathedral, then a monastery, as a departure point for their work in Asia; when the church was modernized in the late 1950s, a mural depicting the martyrdom of 16th-century missionaries was uncovered. A chapel at the rear of the grounds contains some interesting Indian art.

For a special treat, attend the 11 A.M. Sunday Mass to absorb the unique, spine-tingling experience of hearing inspirational music played by a mariachi band. Come early to get a seat for this very popular event.

Museo de Cauhnahuac, in the former Cortes Palace on the zocalo, houses the exposed Tlahuican pyramid and Diego Rivera's famous mural, The *Conquest of Mexico,* a gift to Cuernavaca from former U.S. Ambassador Dwight Morrow (father of Anne Morrow Lindbergh). In the palace museum, visitors can review the history of the states of Guerrero and Morelos.

Teopanzolco Pyramid, on Calle Rio Balsas near the railroad station, is an Aztec temple built around A.D. 1200. The small pyramid was rediscovered when vegetation surrounding it was blown away by cannon fire during the Revolution of 1910.

The Museum of Herbal Medicine, Matamoros 200, is located in a house supposedly built in 1865 by Maximilian for his Indian mistress. Displays include a variety of plants used for medicinal purposes.

Shopping opportunities are not extensive in Cuernavaca, though the town does boast an unusual store run by monks of the Emaus Monastery. The gift shop, which displays unusual silver jewelry, is located in the courtyard of the cathedral. Note also the fudge made with chartreuse liqueur. Most of the town's boutiques are found along the town's main shopping street, Guerrero; nearby crafts stores include Ceramica Santa Maria, Zapata 900; Tianguis, across from the Cortes Palace; and Artesanias Galeria del Arte, at the corner of Hidalgo and Comfort. Cuernavaca's public market convenes on Sunday; huaraches are a particularly good buy.

Dining in Cuernavaca is a real treat—and one of the best reasons to visit the city. Las Mañanitas, *numero uno* in Mexico, is one of the town's four or five outstanding restaurants.

Little hotels, hidden behind the walls, are all excellent bases from which to visit nearby places of interest—the Caves of Cacahuamilpa, Lake Tequesquitengo, and the ruins at Xochicalco.

...south of Mexico City

Around Cuernavaca

You'll discover some of Mexico's most interesting sightseeing around Cuernavaca. Restored haciendas, ancient Indian villages, and pre-Columbian remains can be investigated on drives of less than an hour.

San Antonio Falls, about 1½ miles from downtown Cuernavaca, cascades over 100 feet into a lagoon below. A walkway has been cut into the rocks behind the falls. At the top of the falls lies the tiny village of San Antonio, noted for its fine pottery.

Xochicalco, a meditative mountaintop site about 25 miles southwest of Cuernavaca, resembles the Toltec capital of Tula and is as extensive as the famous Monte Alban outside Oaxaca. From the ruins, you get a spectacular view of the valley of Morelos.

An important ceremonial and trading center from A.D. 700 to 1000, it was a crossroads for travelers from Teotihuacan and the Mayan realms. Walk around the Temple of the Feathered Serpent; eight images of toothy serpents undulate around priests wearing headdresses of mythical *quetzal* feathers.

Down the hill from the temple lies what many believe is Mesoamerica's only underground astronomical observatory. From 11 A.M. to 1 P.M. daily, you can walk into a cave to reach a chamber where a 2-foot-wide hexagonal shaft runs 20 feet up toward daylight. Around the summer solstice, the sun beams straight down the shaft, creating an image on the cave floor. Take along a good flashlight for your explorations.

Tepoztlan snuggles against spectacular cliffs just north of the junction of highways 95-D and 115-D. This ancient Indian village has only recently become a stop on many travelers' itineraries. The Aztec tongue of Nahuatl is as widely spoken here as Spanish.

The town's fortresslike structure is a Dominican convent, built between 1559 and 1588. An archeological museum behind the convent contains a collection of pre-Hispanic Indian art. On the steep, rocky hill above town, a pre-Columbian pyramid rises; it was erected in honor of the god of *pulque* (a potent drink made from maguey cactus).

The best time to visit Tepoztlan is Sunday, the market day. Two colorful celebrations take place during the year; a carnival a few days before Lent and, in early September, a celebration of the town's conversion to Christianity.

Cocoyoc, one of the country's top vacation spots, lies only 12 miles from Tepoztlan. Once part of a sugar plantation, restored Hacienda Cocoyoc is a green oasis in the surrounding brown countryside. Though little known outside Mexico, the resort is crowded on weekends with Mexico City residents. (For more information, see page 80.)

Vista Hermosa, once part of Cortes's vast estates, is another restored hacienda open to the public. A visually delightful spot, it offers an attractive dining area and a truly lovely pool. (See page 80.)

Cuautla, 45 minutes east of Cuernavaca, is a relaxed hot-springs resort that has been popular with vacationers since the early 17th century. It's a good place to have lunch during a drive around the area.

Tequesquitengo lies about 25 miles south of Cuernavaca on the eastern edge of a crater lake popular with Mexican families for a variety of water sports. Around the lake you'll find a collection of modest hotels and restaurants.

Taxco

With its twisting streets and red-tiled roofs, Taxco hangs onto a steep mountaintop as if part of a movie set. It's one of Mexico's most picturesque towns, a favorite subject for artists and photographers. The Mexican government has designated Taxco as a national colonial monument.

Taxco is immersed in a heritage of silver. The town has been molded by silver mines, silver barons, and the silver industry of modern times. Silver was first discovered in the area by Cortes in 1522, paving the way for the arrival of a French miner, Jose de la Borda, who created his own silver empire in the 18th century. A few crumbling, ghostly mines testify to his good fortune and subsequent wealth.

The silver industry evolved to its present status about 60 years ago after being revitalized by an American, the late William Spratling. Today, you'll find silver showrooms and workshops all over town—though little silver is actually mined around Taxco anymore.

Getting around. Taxco's streets, hills, buildings, and shops are best explored on foot. You'll need rubber-soled shoes to avoid slipping on the steep, cobblestoned streets. These are mostly one-way and change names frequently. Maps and information are available at the Department of Tourism office on Avenida John F. Kennedy at the northern entrance to the town. The tourist office also licenses guides; if you hire someone to show you the area, make sure he has a permit from the tourist office.

Taxis and minibuses (called *burritos*) transport visitors from hotels in outlying areas to Taxco's downtown zocalo (Plaza Borda), shops, hotels, and restaurants.

Sights around town. In Taxco, as in most Mexican towns, the zocalo is the center of activity. Shaded by tall

Exploring Cacahuamilpa Caves

 The great caves of the world embody the same characteristics—like mountains and glaciers they are ageless, yet everchanging. Trickling, seeping water dissolves the rock in such a way that spelunkers are never sure they've found every passage or palatial chamber.

In their dazzling complexity, the Caves (*Grutas*) of Cacahuamilpa, though not well known outside of Mexico, rank right along with Mammoth Caves of Kentucky and Carlsbad Caverns in New Mexico.

The Mexican government has now made them easier than ever to see. As you stroll the 1¼ miles of concrete walkways, electric lighting illuminates great rooms (more than 100 feet high and 200 feet long) and clusters of long stalactites and stalagmites.

Cacahuamilpa is 95 miles south of Mexico City via Highway 55 from Toluca, or 20 miles northeast of Taxco on a side road branching off the main highway between that city and Cuernavaca. At 3,360-foot altitude, the caves are close to springs, rivers, and falls. Nearby are a swimming pool, a parking area, and restaurants.

An Englishman discovered the caves about 140 years ago, long after the Indians who originally inhabited them had left. Lured on by curiosity, he ventured deep into the caverns and never returned; a cross inside is his memorial.

Official national park guides lead scheduled tours daily (10 A.M. to 3 P.M. Monday through Saturday, until 4 P.M. Sunday). For large groups of visitors, special tours at other times can be arranged for a slightly higher admission charge. Tours take about 1½ hours.

Outside the entrance, local people sell canes with forked tops and attractive containers shaped like water birds, all carved from native woods.

---

trees and graced with a bandstand and benches, it's a good place to sit, listen to music, and watch life swirl around you. Several restaurants around the zocalo also offer people-watching opportunities.

Lovely Santa Prisca Church's graceful twin towers and tiled dome are a photographic delight. The church, built by Borda in 1751, is an outstanding museum of ecclesiastical art. Casa Borda, once the silver magnate's private residence, now houses a silver shop. Casa Figueroa, built by a friend of Borda's, was known as "The House of Tears" because it was erected with forced labor; today it houses an artists' gallery (admission charge). Casa Humboldt, now a government-sponsored crafts store, was formerly an inn for travelers between Acapulco and Mexico City.

The Spratling Museum, just downhill from the church, was built by William Spratling, the American who revived the town's silver industry. On display are his collection of pre-Columbian artifacts, paintings, and silver ore samples, and historical exhibits from Taxco and other areas in Mexico. The museum is open daily except Monday; there is a small admission charge.

Shopping. Silver shopping is fun, but be sure to shop carefully, since a great quantity of cheaply produced merchandise is mixed in with fine handcrafted pieces. Most good silver shops are found in the old section of town: Spratling, Castillo, and Antonio Pineda are long-time shops with good reputations. La Mina de Plata, on Kennedy, sits at the entrance to a real mine.

In addition to jewelry and flatware, there is also a good selection of embroidered clothing, serapes, and ceramics. A colorful Sunday market in the zocalo brings Indians from the surrounding area with handcarved furniture, bark paintings, and other craft items.

All types of stores cluster around the plaza, with old shopping streets radiating from all sides of it. Other shops extend north around Posada de la Mision. Some shops close for a few hours in the afternoon; others are not open on Sunday.

Festivities. Fireworks illuminate the zocalo on the nights of the city's numerous fiestas. Among the many celebrations are the Fiesta de Santa Prisca on January 18, Fiesta de San Felipe de Jesus (the silversmiths' patron saint) on February 5, Fiesta de las Flores (Flowers) at the end of May, and the National Silver Fair in late November.

Taxco has one of Mexico's richest Holy Week pageants; almost everyone in town participates in the events. Candlelight processions take place nightly, the Last Supper is reenacted on Holy Thursday, and the Crucifixion is dramatized at the Convent of San Bernardino on Good Friday. From midnight Friday, when a Procession of Silence weaves through town, church bells are muffled, pealing only for the grand Easter Sunday processional. You'll need hotel reservations far in advance to attend these celebrations.

Hotels. Taxco's hotels, for the most part, cling to the hills around town, providing spectacular views of fireworks in the square below. La Ventana de Taxco (The Window of Taxco) offers grand dining views and excellent cuisine.

East of Mexico City

A visit to Puebla and Cholula east of Mexico City can easily be made in a day, but an overnight (or longer) trip gives you a chance to visit a national park dominated by the country's highest volcanoes, a zoo where you are caged and the animals roam freely, and the resort town of Tehuacan, from whose springs come most of Mexico's bottled water.

Many travelers combine a visit to this area with a loop trip to Veracruz on the Gulf of Mexico—east by way of Puebla, Orizaba, and Cordoba, and back by way of Jalapa, Perote, Apizaco, and Texcoco. This drive will immerse you in a rich variety of landscapes and climates—green valleys, high desert, pine forests, and tropics. One rewarding feature of this loop drive is the opportunity to see five of Mexico's most famous mountains—Popocatepetl, Iztaccihuatl, Malinche, Pico de Orizaba, and Cofre de Perote.

Tlaxcala

Capital of Mexico's smallest state, Tlaxcala is set in the hills of an area steeped in history. A crossroads of Indian trade routes and cultures, this region was named for the Tlaxcaltecas, allies of Hernan Cortes in confronting their common enemy, the Aztecs. The Tlaxcaltecas gave him their constant support—particularly during the battle of Lake Texcoco in 1521, when the final Spanish victory over the Aztec empire was achieved.

Weaving is an important craft in this region; vibrantly colored serapes and woolen fabrics are produced here. The area around Tlaxcala and nearby Santa Ana Chiautempan is one of Mexico's most prolific wool centers. Top-quality tweeds, handwoven serapes, woolen bedspreads, and rugs are sold in San Martin Texmelucan, Huejotzingo, and at a government market along the toll road at Rio Frio.

Cholula

Cholula, just off Highway 190 about 18 miles beyond San Martin Texmelucan, is a town of churches. Here, as elsewhere, the Spaniards built churches over structures sacred to the Indians. You can visit some 39 chapels in close proximity to each other; many more are not far away. This ancient city has been under study and restoration for many years.

Most notable is the Sanctuary of Los Remedios, a climb of some 200 steps atop Tepanapa Pyramid, a mile in circumference at its base. Not a true pyramid, this structure is actually a citadel composed of numerous substructures fashioned over a period of several centu-

ries, beginning about A.D. 100. Tunnels allow you to explore some sections. A museum near the entrance houses a collection of Choluteca pottery, a polychrome lacquer-type ware decorated with intricate designs.

In nearby Huamantla, a running of the bulls (said to predate Pamplona's) takes place in August on the Sunday following the Feast Day of the Assumption. You watch the 4-hour event from the town's rooftops.

Puebla

Puebla is one Mexican city that has retained much of its Spanish heritage. Its modern architecture seems incongrous amid the many colonial buildings, some of which are among the oldest in the Northern Hemisphere. The city's plazas, especially its main plaza, are ideal vantage points from which to absorb the beauty of the multicolored tilework adorning many town buildings.

Sights. Ornate and intricately decorated churches abound in Puebla. Two you shouldn't miss are the Cathedral of Immaculate Conception on the zocalo, with its carved marble doorways, 14 chapels, and two large bell towers, and the elaborately gilded Chapel of the Rosary in the Church of Santo Domingo, at 5 de Mayo and Avenida 4 Poniente.

Visit the Puebla Regional Museum in the ornate 17th-century Casa de Alfenique at Avenida 4 Oriente and Calle 6 Norte. The second floor is furnished in the style of the colonial period. A small admission fee is charged. When the Reform Laws of 1857 outlawed convents, religious communities hid their activities. One of these religious orders, the Secret Convent of Santa Monica, at Avenida 18 Poniente 203, is now an art museum (admission fee). You enter a secret passageway from a house to discover a maze of rooms, cell blocks, and winding staircases.

The Palafox Library in the House of Culture, Avenida 5 Oriente 5, is a priceless collection of 50,000 volumes that date back to the museum's founding in 1646. Water casks in the elegant room hang above the cedar shelves to protect the precious books from fire.

For a fine city view, tour the Forts of Guadalupe and Loreto, 2 miles northeast of the zocalo. The latter fort contains a historical museum commemorating the 1862 Battle of Puebla against the French. A 15-minute drive south of Puebla brings you to Africam, a 200-acre game preserve housing African wildlife in natural settings.

Foods. If you have a sweet tooth, try Puebla's regional specialty—*camote*, candy made from sweet potatoes. This is also the city that invented *mole* sauce, a mixture of chocolate, chili, tomato, avocado, nuts, butter, and spices, served over meat or tortillas. The Convent of Santa Rosa, Calle 3 Norte near Avenida 12 Poniente, boasts that mole was invented on its premises; you can tour the restored convent's 18th-century kitchen.

Tiled dome of Sanctuary of Los Remedios sparkles in the sunlight. Cholula is noted for the number of its churches.

Hilltop Cholula church was constructed over old Indian pyramid. Tunnels allow visitors a chance to explore the interior.

Shops. Puebla has always been an important ceramics center. Even before the Spaniards arrived in Mexico, Indians of the area were accomplished potters, using nearby clay deposits to manufacture earthen kitchenware. After the Conquest, potters from Toledo, Spain, brought their famous Talavera pottery techniques to the newly founded city. The three best-known tile factories are La Purisma, La Trinidad, and Uriarte, but you'll discover other, smaller shops around town.

Another fine Puebla product is onyx. At the Barrio de los Artistas, a complex of artists' studios in old tile-clad buildings, streetside stalls are filled with onyx fruit, ashtrays, paperweights, and other attractive items.

Tehuacan

This mineral-springs resort is the source of much of Mexico's bottled water. You can visit four of the bottling plants to drink your fill of plain, carbonated, or fruit-flavored waters. Tehuacan's invigorating climate is enhanced by its luxuriant atmosphere—jacaranda, bougainvillea, and *casahuate* trees, and myriad birds whose chattering awakes you with the rising sun.

Several spa resorts offer choices of accommodations. Good bus service connects Tehuacan with Puebla, about 80 miles to the north.

En route to Tehuacan, you'll see Mt. Malinche off to your left. Unlike Popocatepetl and Iztaccihuatl, Malinche (named for Cortes's Indian mistress) is snowless all year.

Activities in town. Saturday is market day in Tehuacan. Some of the area's specialties include custom-made leather jackets, woven handbags, sombreros, and baskets. Onyx items are good buys. You'll find the stone comes in a variety of natural colors; only the turquoise or green colors are dyes.

The Museum of the Valley of Tehuacan, at Avenida Reforma 200, is housed in a former 16th-century convent. Most of the regional exhibits relate to the archeology and botany of the area. A small admission fee is charged.

Around the Valley of Tehuacan. Caves in the valley unearthed ears of wild corn that dated back to 15,000 B.C., proving that it was the staff of Indian life for centuries before the Conquest. Arrangements to visit Coxcatlan, one of the larger caverns, can be made through your hotel. You'll need a car and driver as the caves lie about an hour's drive south of Tehuacan on the road to Teotitlan.

Other discoveries in the Valley of Tehuacan include deposits of fossilized sea life that appear to date back some 120 million years. To find out the details on visiting this area, inquire at the city hall.

Just as the Germans put up castles, the French erected chateaus, and the British constructed manor houses, the Mexicans built haciendas. Today many of these beautiful, luxurious resorts double as inns for travelers.

A night spent in one of these Mexican monuments to a more gracious age can actually be less expensive than the price of a standard hotel room. Even if you can't stay overnight, you can often stop by for a meal, or just browse through the property.

Many of these haciendas date back several hundred years, some tracing their origins to the time of the Spanish Conquest. Most offer huge rooms, substantial grounds, picturesque restaurants, and a variety of sporting facilities—tennis courts, golf courses, riding stables, and fantastic pools.

Many lie only a few miles from Mexico City, making it possible to enjoy both the cosmopolitan pleasures of the capital and the charms of the surrounding countryside. The only catch: To reach some of the haciendas you'll need to hire a car and driver or take a taxi. Both can be expensive.

We've stretched our list beyond vintage haciendas to include a restaurant (no rooms), an ex-convent, and a spa in Ixtapan de la Sal; though the latter facility was built in the 20th century, it lies in an area favored by Aztec emperor Moctezuma.

Hacienda hotels are popular with locals. They're very active on weekends; you'll have a better chance of getting a room midweek. It's best to make reservations through a U.S. travel agent.

Hacienda de los Morales (Vazquez de Mella 525, Polanco District, Mexico City). An elegant 16th-century mansion, now a res-

Elegant dining room at Casa de Sierra Nevada

taurant with beautiful gardens, exquisite service, and delicious food. Reservations for lunch and dinner are a must—phone 540-3225.

Hacienda Cocoyoc (20 miles east of Cuernavaca). Aztec emperors and, later, Cortes vacationed in the area around this grand site. Formerly a 16th-century sugarcane manor, it's the largest of the hacienda hotels (around 300 rooms, some with private pools) and spread out over 70 acres of well-tended grounds with aqueducts rising above the swimming pools; among its amenities are several restaurants, a night club, a 9-hole golf course, tennis courts, and stables.

Hacienda de Cortes (in Altacamulco near Cuernavaca). Cortes built this small gem of a hacienda in the 16th century. Rebuilt and refurbished after its burning during the Revolution of 1910, it is now a 21-room hotel. Swim, play tennis, and stroll over to the fine Sumiya restaurant.

Hacienda Vista Hermosa (15 miles south of Cuernavaca in San Jose de Vista Hermosa). A 16th-century sugar mill and hacienda, the property was owned by Cortes. The original aqueduct surrounds a huge swimming pool. A picturesque restaurant and bar, tennis courts, golfing, water-skiing, and fishing are nearby.

La Mansion Galindo (about 75 miles north of Mexico City on Highway 57 to Queretaro). Luxuriously restored, this 16th-century mansion boasts 160 suites, three restaurants, an Olympic-size pool, six tennis courts, riding stables, and an 18-hole golf course. It borders a lake.

La Estancia de San Juan (6 miles from Galindo). Slightly smaller and a little less posh, the 110-room resort has tennis and golf facilities, stables, and boutiques. Warm up on chilly nights beside the fireplace in your room.

Hacienda Jurica (beyond Queretaro about 120 miles from Mexico City). Built in 1557 and now managed by Westin Hotels, this is one of the country's most charming haciendas. Set in 25 acres of beautiful landscape, it offers swimming, golf, tennis, stables, evening entertainment, and a disco.

Hacienda San Gabriel Barrera (just off the highway between Guanajuato and Irapuato). This well-restored hacienda with its exquisite chapel is part museum. It has a single tennis court, a small pool, a good restaurant, and a crafts shop.

Casa de Sierra Nevada (San Miguel de Allende). Three former 18th-century buildings have been transformed into one tiny and elegant inn with antique furnishings; most rooms have fireplaces.

It's a member of Relais et Chateaux (an international association of fine hotels), one of the country's most expensive hotels, and well worth it. Stop by for dinner, at least.

Hotel Ixtapan (75 miles southwest of Mexico City on Highway 55). Moctezuma came to Ixtapan to relax in the sunshine, fresh air, and 105° thermal waters. Over the years, others found it equally healthful, and in 1939 a hotel, now a complete spa resort, was opened. The emphasis is low-key, based on relaxation and beautification—massages, facials, mud baths, swimming, tennis, golf, and horseback riding. The hotel has 250 suites and 58 private chalets. You can stay overnight or sign on for the week-long spa program.

Hacienda del Solar (Taxco). A romantic and intimate colonial hotel also contains the city's finest restaurant, La Ventana de Taxco. Well-furnished rooms in the main hacienda and villas are scattered around the historic five-acre property. Swimming, tennis, horseback riding, and golf are available. You're a taxi ride away from the town.

Ex-Convento de Santa Catalina (Oaxaca). A few blocks from the zocalo, this rambling 1576 convent has been restored and furnished with colonial antiques. You'll have a choice of 91 rooms; enjoy the small gardens, pool, and patio. The restaurant is one of the city's best. This Oaxacan gem makes a good base for exploring the archeological treasures and craft-filled Indian villages nearby.

Young swimmers at Hacienda Vista Hermosa's pool

Four expansive plazas surround the cathedral in downtown Guadalajara.

Guadalajara & The Colonial Circle

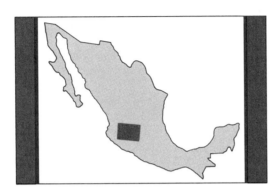

Capital of the state of Jalisco, Guadalajara is Mexico's second-largest city. It's a favorite of many American tourists, who enjoy the gracious city's unique blend of modern and traditional architecture, tree-shaded residential streets, temperate climate, and cosmopolitan atmosphere.

Guadalajara also makes an attractive base from which to explore the country's colonial past. To the east is the heartland of the 1810 Revolution of Independence —Guanajuato, San Miguel de Allende, and Queretaro. To the south lie Morelia, a living museum of Mexican history, and the enchanting towns of Uruapan and Patzcuaro. In between stand colonial villages packed with historical monuments, buildings, and legends. Several of these towns have diligently maintained their colonial ambience and historical authenticity in spite of years of renovation and growth.

Guadalajara

Plan a long stay in Guadalajara to completely explore its delights. But you're not likely to grow bored too quickly in a place where horse-drawn carriages and caravans of laden burros share the right of way with the latest model cars, where graceful colonial buildings mingle pleasantly with modern structures, and where the siesta is a jealously cherished ritual that shuts down businesses for two hours every working day.

Guadalajara's partial conversion to a sleek metropolis has been attained at some sacrifice of Mexican mellowness, and there may be moments on Avenidas 16 de Septiembre or Juarez when you'll have to remind yourself that you're a thousand miles below the border. But Guadalajara retains much that is "old" Mexico.

A colonial route

Mexico's heartland, called the Bajio region, can be visited easily on a loop trip from Guadalajara. You'll cover around 500 miles and go back in time about five centuries when you explore this rich area, which lies between Guadalajara and Mexico City.

Good road connections, beautiful scenery, and a wealth of colonial architecture and history highlight any journey into this countryside. You'll find fine accommodations and restaurants in many picturesque towns and a splendid array of handicrafts along the route. Guided bus trips are available from Guadalajara, or you can hire a car and driver and do it on your own.

Exploring Guadalajara

A slight handicap in learning your way around Guadalajara (and many other Mexican towns) is that the city is divided into sectors, whose streets change names as they pass from one sector to another.

Guadalajara has four sectors; the boundaries are Avenida Morelos, Calzada Independencia, and Avenida Gigantes. Thus Avenida 16 de Septiembre suddenly becomes Avenida Alcalde as it crosses Avenida Morelos near the cathedral; Avenida Juarez has two other names—Avenida Javier Mina east of Calzada Independencia, and Avenida Vallarta west of the university.

Getting around

Even if you're self-reliant, it's a good idea to take a preview tour of the city, or to hire a guide either through a travel agency or from the government tourist offices. These are located in the former Convento del Carmen (Juarez 638) and facing Plaza Tapatia (Morelos 102).

Daily city tours (4½ hours) usually include the famous pottery suburb of Tlaquepaque in the southern part of the city; check with your hotel desk for details. Organized day tours are also available to nearby Lake Chapala and the distillery town of Tequila. If you wish to overnight outside the city, you may want to select a package itinerary with guide, car, meals, and hotels from the choices offered by a travel agency.

Taxicabs are plentiful and inexpensive, though prices tend to go up at night. Always agree on the price before you engage a cab. Buses run between downtown and outlying areas, following Calle Hidalgo and Avenida Lopez Mateos.

You won't find out too much about Guadalajara from the driver of a *calandria* (horse-drawn carriage) as you clip-clop around the downtown area, but you will enjoy the experience. These horse-drawn antiques, complete with black-liveried drivers, were once the private conveyances of well-to-do families. When some vehicles went into public service, their drivers put on yellow arm bands to indicate that their calandrias were for hire. The arm bands must have reminded someone of a yellow-shouldered lark, because residents have long referred to the carriages as "larks" or "buntings." Calandrias are found near the Regional Museum, Mercado Libertad, and San Francisco Church.

Downtown

The heart of the city has recently received a face lift. Pedestrian malls offer grand opportunities for strolling and shopping. Plaza Tapatia (a 7-block mall between the Instituto Cultural Cabañas and Degollado Theater) is a good place to start your downtown walk. Stroll along the block-wide mall (between Hidalgo and Morelos); you'll pass fountains, waterways, and colorful tilework. Colonial monuments are just steps away.

The cathedral. Be sure to explore the interior of the cathedral, especially beautiful when the huge chandeliers are lighted. Begun in 1561, completed in 1618, partially destroyed in 1818, added onto in 1848, and modernized in 1944, the cathedral reflects a potpourri of architectural styles. A painting attributed to Murillo hangs in the sacristy.

Four plazas surround the cathedral, forming a cross: the Plaza de los Laureles fronts the cathedral, the Rotunda de los Hombres Ilustres (with the remains of Jalisco's most famous native sons), the Plaza de los Tres Poderes (Three Powers, formerly called Plaza de la Liberacion), and the Plaza de las Armas (Sunday evening band concerts). Many of the city's most important colonial buildings center around these plazas.

The churches. The Church of Santa Monica (Calle Santa Monica near Calle San Felipe), intricately carved in the Churrigueresque style, was completed around 1720. The churches of San Francisco and Aranzazu both face shady San Francisco Park (16 de Septiembre and Calle Sanchez). San Francisco has the most impressive exterior by far, but the ornate altar of Aranzazu is perhaps a masterpiece of its kind.

Instituto Cultural Cabañas. Once an orphanage and still known locally as Hospicio Cabañas, this impressive building is now a cultural center devoted to art, concerts, and theater presentations. It also houses the best work of the muralist (and native son) Jose Clemente Orozco, among them the powerful *Man of Fire* on the central dome. Wander through 23 flower-filled patios preserved and enhanced by recent remodeling. A small admission fee is charged.

The museums. The State Museum lies near the Government Palace. The original building was constructed in the 17th century as a Jesuit seminary. Here you'll find historical, zoological, and archeological exhibits, as well as art galleries. The collection of contemporary art includes Murillo paintings and a great three-dimensional mural by Gabriel Flores (the mural is on the ceiling of the auditorium).

The Archeological Museum of Western Mexico, on Plaza Juarez at 16 de Septiembre and Independencia, traces western Mexico's cultural development. The Orozco Museum (Aurelio Aceves 27) displays more than 90 works by this well-known artist. The museum, closed Monday, was Orozco's former home and studio.

Government buildings. The Government Palace is the seat of Jalisco's government. You're welcome to go in and look around the 17th-century building and peruse several powerful Orozco murals (located near the stairway), depicting episodes in the building's history. The palace is open weekdays; there is no admission charge.

The Municipal Palace is built in the colonial style to harmonize with neighboring buildings. This is the place you go to buy back your front license plate; if you park illegally, a policeman will remove it from your car. The transaction will cost you an hour (plus the fine), but while you wait, you'll have the chance to see a truly distinguished mural by contemporary painter Gabriel Flores.

Degollado Theater. The theater's classical façade can be seen from the Plaza de los Tres Poderes. To ensure yourself an opportunity to enjoy the elaborate interior, buy tickets to a performance. Home of the famous Guadalajara Symphony, the theater also plays host to a variety of other performing arts. The University of Guadalajara Folkloric Ballet performs here at 10 A.M. Sunday; check with your hotel for ticket information.

To discover what's going on when, buy the *Guadalajara Weekly* or the *Colony Reporter.* They give current information on events for the English-speaking, along with news for the retired community.

Parks & plazas

The Plaza de los Tres Poderes (formerly the Plaza de la Liberacion) and the Plaza Tapatia were major results of Guadalajara's modernization. Blocks of old buildings were removed to create these long rectangular "squares," now rich with fountains and bright flowering *tabachin* trees.

You'll hear the word *tapatio* mentioned frequently around town—it refers to any quality that is particularly Guadalajaran. Very tapatio is the Plaza de los Mariachis (off Independencia), where mariachis gather in the narrow mall to serenade you as you sip sangria or tequila at a parasol-shaded outdoor table. They require a fee for their music; check the price in advance.

The Agua Azul Park (off Independencia near the railroad station and 2 blocks from the Guadalajara Sheraton) is a great place to people-watch each Sunday afternoon. Free performances are often presented in the outdoor theater. Children will appreciate the zoo and rides, and everyone will enjoy the park's many colorful macaws. Though these birds have complete freedom, they usually stay on canopied perches suspended over the walkways.

Another tree-shaded and fountain-cooled escape from the bustle of the city is Alcalde Park, on Jesus Garcia 2 blocks off Calle Alcalde (boating on the lake, fountains, and picnic grounds).

Plaza de las Armas is the site for the Latin dating game, the *paseo,* which usually takes place the first Thursday evening of the month. With all the young

DETAILS AT A GLANCE

The Colonial Circle

How to get there

Guadalajara, a major tourist destination in its own right (see city map and details on page 86), is also a jumping-off spot for visits to Mexico's heartland. Most travelers fly to Guadalajara, then rent a car (with or without a driver) or join a tour to visit the smaller colonial cities.

By air. Guadalajara is easily reached by air from the U.S. and Canada. Domestic carriers offer frequent service from Mexico City, Acapulco, Puerto Vallarta, and other large towns.

By car. A network of roads northeast and southeast of Guadalajara creates a loop trip that allows you to visit most colonial cities in 4 or 5 leisurely days.

By bus. Several companies offer bus tours of the area; it's best to check with a professional travel agent before you go to Mexico.

Accommodations

Hostelries range from modest to deluxe, depending on the city. For more information, see the "Essentials" section on page 155.

Climate & clothes

Temperatures are cool in the mountainous region to the southeast of Guadalajara and warm in the northeast valley. Pants, for both men and women, are acceptable in all towns. Except for an occasional deluxe resort, men need not bother with ties.

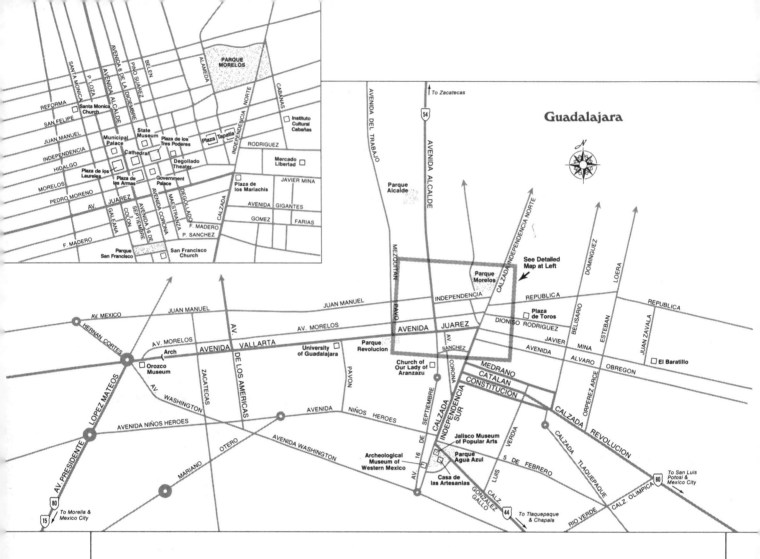

DETAILS AT A GLANCE

Guadalajara

How to get there

Guadalajara is easy to reach from the U.S. and all major Mexican cities. Called the City of Roses for its abundant gardens, this charming colonial city is the capital of the state of Jalisco—and a favorite destination for most visitors.

Day trips are available to scenic villages around Lake Chapala, to the shopping meccas of Tlaquepaque and Tonala, and to factories in the town of Tequila, noted for its local spirits. Several flights a day connect Guadalajara with the coastal resort of Puerto Vallarta.

By air. Mexicana and other international carriers offer direct flights to Guadalajara as well as through service from Mexico City and other large towns. Service is also available on smaller commuter lines.

By car. Highway 15 connects Guadalajara with the Pacific coast and Mexico City (via Morelia). From the northeast, Highway 54 is a direct route from Saltillo.

By bus and train. Numerous buses reach the area from the border cities, Mexico City, and other larger towns. A brightly refurbished train, the *Tapatio,* travels between Guadalajara and Mexico City (in the U.S., travel agents have information).

Accommodations

Guadalajara's hotels range from inexpensive to deluxe; most convenient downtown hotels have been refurbished recently. RV parks and campgrounds are available. For more information, see the "Essentials" section on page 154.

Climate & clothes

Guadalajara, at 5,200 feet above sea level, has clear, bracing weather year-round. Casual attire (not shorts) is appropriate for sightseeing in both the city and in surrounding small towns. Men may need a tie and jacket for evening.

eligibles parading around the plaza, boys in one direction and girls in another, everyone has a chance to meet, greet, or make a date with someone who strikes their fancy.

Sports & sporting events

Jalisco gave birth to the fine tradition of the charro; you'll see lively exhibitions of horsemanship at colorful Sunday charreadas in Agua Azul Park. During the winter, the inevitable bullfights take place at the bullring north of the city, though Guadalajara's younger generation is developing a preference for *futbol* (soccer) and good old *beisbol* (baseball). Three soccer rings and a large baseball field attract thousands of spectators. Cockfights are legal and occur in their own arena near Tlaquepaque.

Visiting golfers associated with a country club in the U.S. can get a guest card for the four golf and country clubs around the city; Santa Anita Golf Club is a public course. Many hotels offer tennis facilities, or you can make arrangements for a court at the Guadalajara Racquet Club.

Places to shop

Make your first stop the large Casa de las Artesanias de Jalisco, located at the entrance to Agua Azul Park. It's an intriguing two-level museum and salesroom where you can examine exquisite products typical of various regions of the state—furniture, pottery, tinware, glass, ceramic sculpture, and fabrics. Everything's for sale.

The prices are generally higher (in some cases, much higher) than elsewhere in Guadalajara and in nearby Tlaquepaque and Tonala—but you'll be sure of top quality, and many items are still only half the price of similar articles sold in the U.S. Larger purchases can be shipped directly home. This state-sponsored center also has branches in Ajijic and Tequila.

You'll find another government store, Jalisco Museum of Popular Arts, at Alcalde 1221. Many of the city's fine shops and good restaurants are concentrated in the Pink Zone along Avenida Chapultepec and on the west side (Avenida Union to Avenida de las Americas). On these and other good shopping streets like Juarez, Vallarta, and Pedro Morena (noted for leather), you'll find everything from designer clothing to handloomed

fabrics. Modern shopping malls include Plaza del Sol (see page 89), Plaza Mexico, and Plaza Patria.

Mercado Libertad. You can haggle over prices at only a few places in Guadalajara, and the mercado, claimed to be the largest open market in Latin America, is one of them. Nearly destroyed by fire quite a few years ago, it was rebuilt in a more modern style. As you work your way through the overwhelming confusion of merchandise, you'll come upon everything you can think of, from renowned Paracho guitars to dried iguanas for witches' brew. Small restaurants line the market's second floor and offer a good overview of the activities below.

El Baratillo. This "bargain counter" on Juan Zavala near the market opens for business every Sunday morning. Though most customers are Guadalajarans, more and more tourists who enjoy garage sales, flea markets,

Magnificent murals by Jose Clemente Orozco, Guadalajara's native son, cover the stone walls and ceilings of the Instituto Cultural Cabañas, a former orphanage and now a center for arts.

The music of the Mexican *mariachis* was born in Jalisco during the days of the grand ranchos. Songs boasted of horsemanship or wailed over lost loves. Just as jazz migrated from New Orleans to Chicago, mariachi music originated in the state of Jalisco and was brought to Mexico City at the time of the revolution. From there it spread, soon becoming recognized as the country's national sound.

Makeup of the band

In the beginning, the orchestra consisted of *vihuelas* (small five-string guitars) and harps. But other variations of this music tradition existed and are still heard today. Veracruz style features a harp accompanied by small regional guitars; *huasteca* style is characterized by wild violins and falseto singing; and *norteño* is a combination of button accordion, *bajo sexto* (large 12-string guitar), and often a saxophone.

Mariachi sound has undergone some transformation during the past 100 years. The first instrument to be added to the original orchestra was a six-string guitar.

As mariachi groups grew more mobile, the cumbersome harp became a liability. Because its principal function had been to provide balance in the lower register—a plucked bass effect—someone devised a giant vihuela. This became the *guitarron* (giant guitar).

Last to be added were the dominant voices of the trumpets. Experts believe the trumpet traveled to Mexico from Europe, arriving in the 1920s.

Costumes of aristocracy

At first, mariachi costumes were similar to those worn by all rural people—white pants and shirts, a

Mexico's wandering minstrels

colorful scarf, and huaraches. But Jalisco's musicians started a new trend when they borrowed attire from the aristocratic charros of their area. Today, these well-fitting riding pants, elaborately embroidered bolero jackets, boots, and wide sombreros are favored by most of Mexico's mariachis.

Where to hear them

Though you'll hear other types of music in Mexico, these strolling troubadors are the ensembles that most often blare forth in the country's cafes and night clubs, pro-

vide background for charreadas and bullfights, and entertain on the plazas.

Guadalajara is often called the "home of the mariachis"; some of the finest sounds are heard in its Mariachi Plaza. A visit to Mexico City's Garibaldi Plaza is like visiting a mariachi supermarket. Hundreds of musicians wait to be hired, for one song or for the evening.

A true mariachi knows about 5,000 songs and plays them from memory. It's also estimated that 98 percent of all mariachis play by ear.

. . . exploring Guadalajara

haggling, and browsing are discovering it. A staggering display of items awaits you in 12 long blocks of merchandise—many new, most used.

Plaza del Sol. One of Latin America's largest shopping centers, this plaza opened in 1969. It has an astounding range of shops and services. The plaza is located in an area of hotels and motels on the southwestern section of the city between Mariano Otero and Lopez Mateos.

Tlaquepaque. Guadalajara has sprawled east to merge with San Pedro Tlaquepaque. Though the town is best known for its ceramics and glass blowing, other arts are practiced here as well. Silver jewelry, leather goods, rugs, and much more can be found in this folk-art center, which is usually included in a day tour of Guadalajara. You'll probably want to go on your own.

The number of shops in Tlaquepaque is overwhelming; at last count there were more than 300 boutiques and jewelry stores. Comparative shoppers may find that prices are lower in downtown Guadalajara's Mercado Libertad, but the tremendous variety of design and pattern is only available here. And the ambience alone makes the trip worthwhile.

Red-brick malls lead the way to shops (many have patios sprinkled with potted plants and flowers). The main street is Avenida Independencia. Weary shoppers will appreciate the bars and cafes along Plaza el Parian; best of the hacienda-style restaurants is "Sin Nombre" ("No-Name"); though it has no sign, you'll find it at Madero 80.

Sergio Bustamente's workshop and gallery (Independencia 238) is a fantasy world of papier-mâché, ceramics, and metal sculpture. The antiques of Antigua de Mexico (Independencia 255) are housed in a restored 17th-century villa. Another colonial villa contains Museo de la Ceramica, a free museum of ceramics at Independencia 237. You can pick up free brochures listing other outstanding shops along the pedestrian mall.

Tonala. Another good spot to shop for ceramics is Tonala, an Indian village a couple of miles from Tlaquepaque, where you can watch the artisans at work. You'll usually find better-quality merchandise in established shops. Plan your visit for Thursday or Sunday, the big market days, to see more color and variety.

The morning markets, which are set up around the handsome cathedral, are great fun, whether you're a shopper or a looker. Walk right past the few stalls with tourist souvenirs to the heart of the market, the place where people from the surrounding area come to do their weekly bargaining and buying. You'll see everything from fresh produce and meat to crockery and fine embroidery.

Unlike Tlaquepaque, Tonala has more factories than stores; some sell directly to tourists. In the courtyards of many houses you can watch local artisans at work. Tonala is also popular for copies of pre-Columbian figures. Their "weathered" look comes from being buried for a few months.

Cascading fountains enliven the entrance to Degollado Theater, home of the Guadalajara Symphony and the university's Folkloric Ballet performances.

Mexico produces a tremendous amount of exuberant folk art—primarily handicrafts designed for household use. Notably rich in handicrafts is the region around Guadalajara.

Artisans in each of the nearby craft towns produce pottery, glassware, baskets, serapes, and toys for sale in local markets; you'll usually buy the item directly from the person who made it. After you've visited several towns, you'll begin to appreciate their distinctly different styles.

Guadalajara

A recognized craft center, Guadalajara's markets gather items from the artisans who work in surrounding communities. On your visit, reserve time to shop at the Casa de las Artesanias de Jalisco. Located at the north end of Agua Azul Park in a state-operated building, this center both displays and sells regional handicrafts. Here you'll find examples of the crafts made in each village; you'll also see some unique articles and learn how to identify high quality and top workmanship.

This combination museum, shop, and trading center showcases almost every type of Mexican handicraft from finely carved furniture to jewelry fashioned from abalone shell, turquoise, gold, and silver.

The center is open daily. You'll also find smaller branch stores in other cities in Jalisco state.

Another craft center featuring displays from all over Mexico is located in a former Capuchin convent at Independencia 684. Particularly good buys are found

Hand-burnished duck from Tonala

Colorful collection of blown glass

on guitars from the Paracho region and traditional white wool serapes from Jocotepec.

For a look at some of the state's best weaving, go to Telas at Hidalgo 1378. You'll have a chance to watch the weavers at work. If you buy any fabric, the shop will ship it to you.

Though state-operated stores have set prices, bargaining is expected at Guadalajara's Mercado Libertad and at public markets in other towns.

You can also bargain at some shops. If you plan to pay with a credit card, do your bargaining before the method of payment is discussed.

Best time to shop or visit a market is in the morning. Shops throughout the area are usually closed from around 1:30 P.M. to 4 or 5 P.M. for siesta.

Tlaquepaque

A few miles southeast of the center of Guadalajara, between Highways 80 and 35, is the well-known craft center with the fun-to-pronounce name of Tlaquepaque (tlockay-pockay). The town was once known only for pottery—not all of it good—but local craftspeople have branched out into furniture, textiles, glass, and other crafts.

The Museo de la Ceramica, located in an elegant colonial house on Avenida Independencia, has a collection of pottery from the Valley of Atemajac, including *barro de olor* (odoriferous earthenware) and unique *petatillo* pottery. Typical of this region, petatillo is characterized by its distinctive, almost Oriental designs of stylized animals against a background of tile-red slip with white cross-hatching.

Don't miss the glass factories on Avenida Independencia,

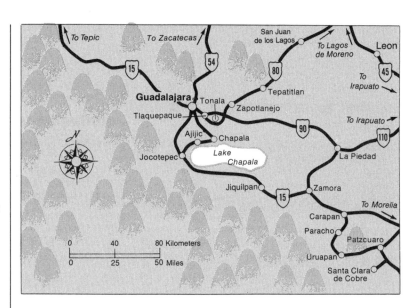

where you can buy glass objects and watch blowers at work. Gift shops line this main street.

Sergio Bustamente's studio, filled with unusual papier-mâché, ceramic, and metal sculptures are worth viewing—even if you don't plan to buy.

Tonala

Drive east from Guadalajara for about 20 minutes to reach Tonala, which produces some of Mexico's most unusual pottery and stoneware. In addition to more practical pieces, its artisans produce many beautifully decorated, hand-burnished birds and animals, and sculptured objects.

Some of the best places to shop for pottery in this small town include Jorge Wilmot at Constitucion 104 (also a noted jewelry designer) and Ken Edwards at Madero 70. Don't miss the Sunday market; you'll find bargains.

Lake Chapala area

If you follow Highway 15 south of Guadalajara for 35 miles, you approach Lake Chapala at Jocotepec.

This lakeside town is noted for handwoven serapes—in traditional styles with geometric designs and small flowers in pastel colors on an off-white background, and in contemporary designs featuring birds and flowers.

Ajijic, about 12 miles farther northeast on the same road, is also known for weaving. Numerous artists and writers, many of them American, have settled in this picturesque village.

Other craft towns

Though most of the towns on the Colonial Circle are filled with an assortment of handicrafts, some are noted for a distinctive type of product. Below is a list of some of these towns and their specialties. You'll make other discoveries.

Zapopan: Huichol Indian yarn paintings. **Paracho:** guitars. **Patzcuaro:** weaving, wood carving, basketry, and henequen rugs. **Santa Clara del Cobre:** copperware. **Uruapan:** lacquerware and weaving. **Guanajuato:** embroidery, unique pottery, and jewelry. **Morelia:** embroideries. **Queretaro:** opals. **Leon:** leather goods.

Suburban attractions

In and around Guadalajara's city limits, you'll discover a fruit-producing region, one of Mexico's largest waterfalls, and a revered relic. Day trips head for tequila-producing country and to Mexico's largest lake.

Zapopan

In the suburb of Zapopan, a brightly-clad, 10-inch-high statue known as the Virgin of Zapopan is credited with defeating the Chimalhuacano Indians in a battle against the Spanish in 1531. Over the years the Virgin has become revered by descendants of those same Indians, who now consider her their patroness.

In 1734 during the midst of an epidemic, the little statue was taken to afflicted towns and villages around Guadalajara. Wherever she appeared, the plague reputedly ceased. As a result, the Virgin was credited with a miracle and given the title of "patroness against thunders, storms, and epidemics." From that time on, the statue of the Virgin, protected by a glass covering, leaves her church on an annual visit to all sections of the city.

From her 17th-century basilica at Avenida 20 de Noviembre and Piño Suarez, the revered Virgin is sent forth each summer to tour all of the city's churches, returning to her own in October. So popular is her homecoming that you'll need to reserve seats for the unusual and emotional procession on October 12. A month-long religious and cultural celebration called Fiestas de Octubre takes place once the Virgin is safely home. If you wish to attend, you'll need reservations well in advance.

The basilica is located on the west side of Zapopan's main square. Fiesta activities take place at the Benito Juarez Auditorium, where Highway 54 crosses the Periferico.

At the Franciscan monastery next to the basilica a small museum displays Huichol Indian crafts (see special feature on the next page). The monastery also provides lodging for the Indians who come to Guadalajara from their northern mountain homes to study catechism, reading, and writing. Huichols can often be seen around town in their colorfully embroidered costumes.

Barranca de los Oblatos

Calzada Independencia Norte extends north 7 miles to the scenic Barranca de los Oblatos (Monks' Canyon). Thermal rivulets plunge down the red walls of this 2,000-foot-deep gorge; the tropical valley below produces much of the fruit marketed in Guadalajara. A cable car descends each morning to take workers to the power plant on the floor of the rugged canyon.

Juanacatlan Falls

Juanacatlan Falls, one of the largest waterfalls in Mexico, is at its best from June to September. The nearby village of Juanacatlan makes handloomed items. From Guadalajara, head southeast toward Lake Chapala for about 14 miles; turn onto a paved and signed road and continue for another 7 miles.

Lake Chapala area

Lake Chapala lies 35 miles southeast of Guadalajara. Surrounded by mountains, it's accessible by several good roads. Stretching alongside Highway 15, this hyacinth-dotted lake is Mexico's largest, measuring 50 miles long and 20 miles wide. It's fed, albeit sluggishly, by the Lerma River and empties into the Grande de Santiago River. An 18-mile paved road connects the villages of Chapala, Ajijic, and Jocotepec on the northwest shore, passing through several residential subdivisions where many of the homes are occupied by retired North Americans. A road from Highway 15 skirts the southern shore.

The climate is temperate and mild all year in the lake region. Fishing for sunfish and Chapala whitefish is popular, as are boating, bird watching, and swimming.

Chapala. Traditionally the destination for Sunday outings by Guadalajarans, Chapala has a large community of retired and foreign residents. It was a favorite with the international set long before any of the other lakeshore resort villages became popular. Two private clubs extend their privileges to visitors; one features a golf course, the other is a yacht club.

On weekends, strolling mariachis serenade patrons in the restaurants around the lake and boats from the pier take sightseers to a nearby island. Band concerts and paseos (where the girls stroll in one direction around the main square and the boys walk in the other direction) are still held on Sunday evenings. You can usually count on spectacular sunsets over the lake; photographers line the waterfront to catch shots of the boats returning to shore. When you find a restaurant serving the local specialty, whitefish, be sure to sample it.

If you continue eastward along the north shore of the lake, you go through the lakeside villages of Ocotlan and La Barca. From La Barca, you can follow the highway south to Sahuayo where it joins Highway 15, or continue south to join it at Zamora, a town noted for strawberries.

Ajijic. Ajijic has long been home to many foreigners, from lively young liberals to quiet, well-known artists and writers. This international atmosphere, along with the town's neat whitewashed buildings and cobblestone streets, makes Ajijic a delightful village to visit. Shopping is a rewarding adventure; you'll discover art galleries, weaving studios, and craft stores of all kinds. The retired community represents a large segment of the population.

Ajijic's streets are full of potholes; it's best to park your car and walk around town or pick a place to sit and watch the passing scene. Posada Ajijic is a good spot for a margarita—or for an overnight stay.

Jocotepec. Founded in 1528, Jocotepec is the largest town on the lake and the most Mexican in feeling. Evidence of the town's age is apparent in a few crumbling walls, and in the old colonial architecture and rough streets. Heavy, handmade white serapes with a colorful central motif are the local specialty item. Fishing is the town's chief livelihood; you'll see fishermen's huts, and yards of fishnets strung out to dry. The most colorful time to visit is on Thursday, the local market day.

Tequila & opals

Tequila, about an hour west of Guadalajara, contains nothing much of interest except large distilleries which produce Mexico's national drink. You can tour a distillery (see page 96), take a look around town, and then continue another 12 miles to the town of Magdalena. Around Magdalena's central plaza lie several shops that sell opals mined from the nearby countryside. Bargain for a stone that catches your eye, but remember that opals can crack when dry.

The Spiritualistic Huichols

 Christianity arrived in Mexico with the Spaniards. For the majority of people, it soon replaced pagan beliefs and practices. In some of the more isolated regions, however, the Indians' religion is still an odd mixture of old and new, with roots reaching far back into the dim past. Religious ceremonies are both unusual and colorful.

The rugged mountains of the Sierra de Nayarit north of Guadalajara is the homeland of the Huichol Indians, among the last tribes to come under Spanish rule. Though numerous efforts have been made to convert the tribe to Christianity, many Huichols still adhere to a religion that centers around agricultural deities.

Three important ceremonies in this ritualistic society combine tenets of Christian faith with their pagan dogma.

Holy Week. During Holy Week, the Huichols' wooden image of Christ (called Tatata Nuitzicame) is removed from the altar and adorned with sacred eagle feathers. (The feathers are believed to be the means through which communication is established with the sun god, since it is thought that the eagle ascends the closest to heaven.)

Then, the image is swathed in fabric and placed on a bed of leaves on the floor. Men and women, led by a native priest, sing and chant to invoke the gods' blessings.

At one point during the Holy Week ceremonies, an outdoor procession, led by the "governor" of the tribe and priests carrying symbols of their power, solemnly circles the church building.

Corn festival. Corn, thought to be the source of all life, is honored at another special religious observance. This is a more joyous time when the Huichols affirm their belief that Nacahue, mother of all gods, gave the tender part of the corn to the first man for planting, and from it was born the first woman.

Corn stalks are often the theme of the beautiful Huichol yarn paintings. For a look at some of the best of this traditional art form, visit the small Huichol museum and crafts store in the monastery adjacent to the basilica housing the Virgin of Zapopan in suburban Guadalajara (see page 92).

Communicating with the gods. The Huichols believe that they can speak directly to their gods with the help of the peyote plant. Those who go in search of the sacred plant make a 600-mile pilgrimage to a legendary mountain known to the Indians as Virikuta.

Tribal members who undertake the grueling journey are regarded as holy ones who seek to rise beyond their mortal state and communicate with the deities. The Indians feel that they have paid a visit to the home of the gods.

The peyote is shared in an elaborate ritual that supposedly brings special favor to those who partake of it.

Colonial Circle

Often called the Colonial Circle or the Colonial Loop, the area between Guadalajara and Mexico City is also known as the Cradle of Independence. It was in these little villages that Mexico's fight for self-rule began. The region contains fine examples of colonial architecture, craft-filled villages, and widely contrasting landscapes, from fertile plains to mountains.

Sights east of Guadalajara will make you more aware of Mexico's history—a wealth of arched aqueducts date from colonial times; small farm plots are still tilled by Indians with ox-drawn plows; huge, crumbling haciendas abound; laden burros plod along the roadsides on their way to market; and small towns are dominated by the reassuring presence of the parish church's ornate tower.

Two main routes head east into the colonial countryside. By combining them you can create a loop trip from Guadalajara (or from Mexico City). Both Morelia and Guanajuato are about 5 hours away from either city.

Southeastern route. Paved Highway 15 heads southeast through Morelia and Toluca to Mexico City; it's two lanes wide from Guadalajara to Toluca, and increases to four lanes en route to Mexico City. You'll find slow going in the mountainous sections east of Morelia and in the shallow, barren canyons and ravines east of Zitacuaro. Lakes Chapala, Camecuaro, and Patzcuaro, the waterfalls near Uruapan, and the heavily forested mountains make the region between Guadalajara and Morelia one of Mexico's most scenic stretches.

East of Zitacuaro, you leave the cool pine forests for high, semiarid plains. The wind sweeps freely across the rolling countryside, hills are covered with sparse grass, and erosion has seriously furrowed the thin, drifting soil. Much of the wide, flat valley around Toluca is divided into small farms, each with its adobe house and adjoining stack of fodder elevated on poles. In the windy late winter and early spring, gossamer clouds of dust hover over the landscape, obscuring the countryside.

Just before reaching the Valley of Mexico, the road climbs to its highest point in the Sierra Madre Occidental (10,000 feet) and you go through another stretch of pine and fir forests. Miniscule farms sit in clearings on the steep mountainsides; as you start the descent into the valley, clusters of attractive, expensive homes come into sight.

Colonial heartland route. You avoid the mountains in the southeast (though you'll miss some of Mexico's most beautiful scenery) by taking a network of roads north and east of Guadalajara through Mexico's heartland. Using Highways 90, 45, and 110 as access roads, you can easily visit three colonial gems—Guanajuato, San Miguel de Allende, and Queretaro.

From Guanajuato, you can cut down to Morelia, about 100 miles south, passing Irapuato, Salamanca (see page 101 for descriptions of both towns), and Yuriria (beautiful 16th-century church) en route. Or you can take Highway 110 east to Dolores Hidalgo and San Miguel de Allende. (A faster road cuts directly east from Guanajuato to San Miguel de Allende, but the scenery is much less spectacular.)

Leon—a leather capital

Generously referred to as the Shoe Capital of Mexico, Leon is a bustling city in the state of Guanajuato. Shoes aren't everything here; Leon is also well known for all types of leather goods. The general atmosphere reflects the city's highly industrial economy. It's a large place with many big-city problems: you'll probably discover that traffic is terrible, and you may have difficulty finding comfortable accommodations.

Nevertheless, the city retains many charming colonial buildings and has a central square surrounded by old archways and flower-filled plazas. The Municipal Palace (City Hall) on the main plaza has an exquisitely carved exterior; Our Lady of the Angels church displays a collection of carvings by native artisans. A spacious, wide boulevard runs the length of the city and trees bordering the plaza are trim and lush.

Noted as a sports center, Leon boasts both a stadium and extensive sports complex with soccer and baseball fields and a gym. A few miles south of Leon and 6 miles east on a blacktop road is the popular health resort of Comanjilla. Here, thermal spring waters are piped into large swimming pools and the bathtubs and miniature pools of guest rooms.

Silao—center of Mexico

The small town of Silao, southeast of Leon at the junction of Highways 45 and 110, is noted for its serapes and handmade tin toys.

Atop a mountain just east of the town is a huge stone statue called *Cristo Rey* ("Christ the King"); it can be seen from the highway for several miles in both directions. The mountain where the statue stands is said to be the exact geographical center of Mexico. A road leads up to the statue from Highway 110 just east of Silao, but it's unpaved and difficult to negotiate. A better, slightly longer road leaves the same highway a few miles east of Guanajuato.

South of Silao, Highway 45 winds into the largest of seven valleys that make up the vast Central Plateau. It's one of Mexico's most fertile agricultural areas, providing metropolitan Mexico City with food and dairy products. Along Highway 45 lie the Mexican food-processing plants of several U.S. companies.

Wrought-iron scrollwork, wooden doors, and plastered walls mark colonial architecture.

Guanajuato—18th-century silver capital

Founded by the Spaniards about 450 years ago, Guanajuato grew into a city of wealth and extravagance during the heyday of its legendary silver mines. It saw some of the fiercest fighting of the War of Independence, then went into a slow decline. Today, it has emerged as a small, stately city with a strangely provocative and slightly Moorish air.

A unique feature of Guanajuato is its subterranean street (Avenida Subterranea Miguel Hidalgo)—a stone-arched tunnel that meanders under the city. Because of lack of space for another roadway through town, a tunnel was built on the dry bed of the Guanajuato River. It follows the river's original course for almost 2 miles. The river was diverted to another channel after one of Mexico's greatest floods occurred in Guanajuato in 1905.

Floodwaters rampaged through the narrow, ravinelike channel of the normally unassuming river, drowning thousands of residents.

Guanajuato is a city made for walking. Built where three ravines meet, the city offers the delight of random strolls along the narrow, cobbled byways that wind up the hillsides, turning into flights of stairs when the going gets too steep. You'll find yourself drawn on by the unusual façades of houses (no two alike), beckoned by the filigree of street lamps and overhanging balconies, and diverted by narrow passageways into unexpected squares. And for all your wandering, you're never really lost—the center of town is always waiting for you down the hill.

Sightseeing. Jardin de la Union—a good place to begin a day's exploration—is a delicate and graceful plaza. Here you can sit on ornate wrought-iron benches and listen to band concerts several nights each week. Facing

Maguey hearts yield Mexico's fiery drink of distinction

The process of making tequila can be a far lengthier one than most imbibers of the Mexican national drink realize. The magic liquid used in producing the renowned drink comes from the *Agave tequilana* plant. Also known as the maguey plant, it's related to the century plant common in the southwestern United States.

Making the drink

How do you make tequila? It involves several time-honored steps. First, the spiky leaves of the blue maguey plant are cut off, leaving only the heart—called a *piña* because of its resemblance to a huge pineapple.

Maguey hearts (some weighing as much as 150 pounds) are then harvested, loaded on trucks, and taken to the factory. Here, they're cut up and placed in giant steam ovens, then roasted until they're soft enough to be shredded easily. After shredding, the pulp is pressed to extract the juice.

The juice is poured into large vats, sugars are added, and the mixture ferments. After four days, the distillation process begins; two distillations are required before the tequila is drinkable.

Tequila can be ready to market within a week after the maguey hearts are harvested, but for a fine, full-bodied tequila, much more time is needed. Longer aging means better—and more expensive—tequila. The highest grade spends up to seven years in wooden casks, achieving a mellow golden color and velvety texture.

Touring tequila plants

The town of Tequila, about 35 miles northwest of Guadalajara, is the center of the tequila industry and the best place to see Mexico's national drink in the making. Though *pulque,* a form of fermented drink made from another species of cactus, was drunk as far back as the time of the Aztecs, the Spanish were the first to distill tequila.

The town of Tequila was founded in 1530 by a Spanish captain, Cristobal de Onate. In 1873 Don Cenobio Sauza founded the tequila industry, using mules to drag the stones that crushed the maguey hearts. Today the Sauza family and several other large growers produce many millions of liters a year.

If you wish to see the various steps in the process, tours are available at several tequila factories around the town of Tequila. To tour the Sauza distillery, make reservations at the Sauza bottling plant at 3273 Avenida Vallarta in Guadalajara. Even if you don't have reservations, you can often join morning tours of the distillery in Tequila. The Sauza family estate, across from the distillery, is also open to visitors. The old Herradura tequila plant (and its newer version) are located in nearby Amatitan.

the plaza is Teatro Juarez, a theater in the classic style of the late 19th century. One of Guanajuato's few examples of postcolonial architecture, it once rivaled Mexico City's opera house in prestige and splendor. Don't miss seeing its opulent, Moorish interior.

Next to the theater is the Franciscan Church of San Diego, built in 1784. Its façade is magnificent, though the interior isn't especially impressive. A block away, Plaza de la Paz is dominated by La Parroquia church; its baptistry and sacristy date back to 1696.

Up a narrow alley from this plaza the comparatively recent building of the University of Guanajuato, designed to blend with the colonial architecture, looms over its neighbors. La Compañia (built in 1747), a part of the university, is a beautiful church inside and out. Its colonnaded dome will serve as a landmark as you stroll around town.

Diego Rivera was born in Guanajuato, next to the university at Calle Positos 47, and his birthplace has been turned into the Diego Rivera Museum. The first floor is furnished with turn-of-the-century antiques; the second and third contain many of his paintings. Expect a small admission fee. The State Museum of Guanajuato, in a restored home just a few doors away at Positos 7, displays paintings from the 18th and 19th centuries.

Three other destinations require longer walks: the marketplace (Mercado Hidalgo) on Avenida Juarez, with both produce and local handicrafts for sale (Sunday is market day); the pleasant parks by the two dams that hold back the Guanajuato River; and the granary, better known as the Alhondiga de Granaditas. The Alhondiga, scene of a bloody battle in revolutionary days, now houses the State Historical Museum (admission charge) and is one of the most informative and well-organized museums in Mexico.

A roundabout drive (or a steep climb) takes you up the hill behind Teatro Juarez to the Statue of Pipila. At the start of the War of Independence of 1810–21, this miner—with a flat stone strapped to his back as a shield—braved enemy bullets and molten lead to set fire to the door of a loyalist stronghold at the granary. Such zeal, commemorated by this statue, was responsible for Guanajuato becoming the first major city to fall to the forces of independence.

One of Guanajuato's premier attractions, and one you may prefer to miss, is the collection of well-

Guanajuato nestles in a valley surrounded by verdant hills, once rich in silver.

San Miguel de Allende, one of Mexico's lovliest colonial towns, celebrates Easter with pageantry and fervor. Colorful religious observances take place during the entire week preceding Easter, but two of the most spectacular processions occur on Good Friday.

Morning procession

Early that Friday morning the faithful from nearby mountainside villages fill the streets of the old city awaiting church services and preparations for the "people's procession."

About 10 A.M., men dressed as Roman soldiers appear, marching in front of a wooden cross and led by a piper playing a haunting Indian melody. Following them are boys painted to resemble lepers, girls carrying dolls, and other children costumed as shepherds, leading their pets.

Life-size images of various saints are collected from churches, dressed in satin and velvet robes for the occasion, and are carried through the streets. (You may even see a replica of an apple tree with a serpent coiled around its trunk.)

Because the procession departs from San Juan de Dios church and stays mainly on the side streets en route to the outskirts of town, it attracts little attention from the downtown population, and business proceeds as usual.

Afternoon pilgrimage

It's a different story for the well-organized late afternoon procession through town. All stores are closed, and the houses along the parade route are draped with purple ribbons; people line the main streets hours ahead of time to ensure themselves a good view.

Three priests bearing candles and crosses lead the pilgrimage.

Little girls dressed as angels pass by with eyes downcast and hands folded in prayer. In striking contrast to the white-gowned girls are long lines of solemn, black-clad señoras carrying flickering lanterns.

Climaxing the street procession is a special honor guard, bearing a large glass coffin with flowers at its base. By now, it's almost dark and the onlookers head for their homes.

Easter Sunday

Easter Sunday begins with morning Mass, the rest of the day being spent in festive celebration. Bands play in the plaza and the citizens wear their finest and most colorful costumes. It's truly a day to see and be seen.

Reserve in advance

Tourists usually outnumber San Miguel's hotel rooms during this period, so be sure to make reservations well in advance. For more information on visitor accommodations, see the "Essentials" section on page 155 and the feature on hacienda hotels on pages 80–81.

If the town's accommodations are exhausted, you can stay in one of the neighboring cities, though you might miss some of the festivities.

San Miguel de Allende, a gem in Mexico's colonial crown

preserved mummies in the catacombs of the Panteon Cemetery (open daily) about 1½ miles southwest of the Jardin de la Union. Doomed to exposure because their descendants fell behind on crypt rental fees, the bodies escaped decomposition because of the dry climate and special soil properties. Some are still dressed and have hair. You'll usually find guides to give you a tour; an admission fee is charged and tips are expected.

Three miles from the midtown plaza, a church and silver mine bear witness to the glories of the past. La Valenciana is considered one of the most perfect and elegant churches in Mexico. Its architecture, the craftsmanship of its intricate façade and carved altars, and the impressive view from the property all merit a visit.

Across the highway you'll find the crumbling ruins of La Valenciana Mine, which for a half-century poured millions of pesos annually into the treasury of the Spanish viceroyalty and financed the construction of the elegant homes and churches of Guanajuato and its suburbs.

To get your bearings in Guanajuato, you may want to take a guided tour. A travel agency at Juarez and 5 de Mayo (also the location of the state tourism office) offers a variety of sightseeing jaunts. English-speaking guides can also be hired from your hotel for a private look around.

Shopping. Guanajuato offers many fine shops within walking distance of the central plaza. Quality is generally good; prices are reasonable. Look for silver, brass, crystal, mirrors, and jewelry. Casas de las Artesanias, the government-sponsored handicrafts store, is located in the former home of the Spanish Conde de Rul on Plaza de la Paz. Shops around the plaza are also the best place to look for antiques.

Culture. Guanajuato state is regarded as one of Mexico's most culturally oriented—and every autumn the city of Guanajuato lives up to this reputation with an International Cervantes Festival. From the last part of October through the first part of November, Guanajuato is host to an impressive international array of performing artists. Many events take place in churches and other historical buildings around the city.

Dolores Hidalgo—birthplace of El Grito

In this little village, on a Sunday morning in mid-September of 1810, Father Miguel Hidalgo y Costilla spoke to his followers from the front steps of the parish church. Burning with the fire of his conviction that the Mexican people should be freed from their Spanish conquerors, he exhorted his congregation to take arms against their oppressors, a rallying cry known as El Grito. This incident marked the beginning of Mexico's struggle for independence. Statues of Hidalgo, regarded as the father of the movement, appear throughout the land.

Several large commemorative monuments have been erected in Dolores Hidalgo, but it is the quiet reverence for the parish church and the historical significance of its well-worn front steps that make an indelible impression on those who visit the town. Hidalgo's house, a block south of the plaza, is now a museum of the life of this patriot priest.

Atotonilco church

Off the highway between Dolores Hidalgo and San Miguel de Allende is the village of Atotonilco. While on his way to battle the Spanish royalists, Father Hidalgo stopped at the parish church here with his disheveled independence "army." He took from the church an embroidered tapestry showing the image of Mexico's patron saint, the Virgin of Guadalupe, and made it the banner of his cause.

The plain façade of the sanctuary of Atotonilco belies the fact that it's a treasure house of religious paintings, sculptures, and examples of early Christian-Indian art. Literally hundreds of artworks fill the church, including stone carvings, miniature murals, statuary, and manuscripts. Pilgrims come here by the thousands.

Atotonilco means "place of hot water." The church was built in 1784 over hot springs, and mineral baths are available to the public. Just south of Atotonilco is a well-known thermal springs resort, Hacienda Taboada.

San Miguel de Allende— a national monument

Strolling the picturesque streets will be your main pastime in San Miguel de Allende (less than 1 hour east of Guanajuato), for this is an exceptionally fine example of a Spanish colonial town—so outstanding that the Mexican government has made it a national monument. In order to preserve its charm, all new buildings must be in harmony with the existing Spanish-style architecture.

Juan de San Miguel, a Franciscan friar, founded the town in 1542. "Allende" was later added to its name to honor Ignacio Allende, a hero of the struggle for independence. The city's narrow cobblestone streets climb the slopes in gradual stages. During a walk around town you'll see plaques on the walls of fine old colonial houses, telling what famous figure lived there or what important event took place inside. To visit these houses, inquire at the public library (Insurgentes 25) or the Instituto Allende (San Antonio 20) about the Sunday-morning house and garden tour; no tours take place in December.

Buildings of note. Of the dozen churches in San Miguel de Allende, the most unusual is the parish church of San Miguel on the central plaza, which reflects a crazy pot-pourri of architectural styles. Originally this was a rather plain Franciscan building, but in the 19th century it acquired a Gothic appearance—the work of an untrained Indian mason who studied postcards of French Gothic cathedrals, then created his own variation with ornate towers and a stone façade.

West of the church is the house where Ignacio Allende was born in 1779. The Latin inscription over the door reads, "Here was born he who is widely known."

Other buildings worth exploring include the 18th-century Church of San Francisco, which has a 17th-century monastery attached to it, and a group of religious structures on Insurgentes—a photogenic collection of domes, steeples, niches, and scalloped roofs. Inside Los Trasteros Church, examine the "miracle paintings," votive paintings made by pilgrims grateful for miraculous cures.

Culture. The beauty and quiet of San Miguel de Allende has attracted a sizable colony of foreign artists and writers. Instituto Allende, housed in the former hillside estate of the Counts of Canal, was started in 1938 by William Stirling Dickinson as an arts school. Now a part of the University of Guadalajara, the school offers art and Spanish classes. You can register for summer classes lasting a week, a month, or longer. A shop sells students' arts and crafts.

A branch of the National Institute of Fine Arts, the Ignacio Ramirez Cultural Center is located in the Convent of the Conception, which dates back to 1775. A variety of performing arts as well as arts-and-crafts classes take place in these colonial cloisters at Hernandez Macias 75; lunch is served in the central plaza.

Another school, Academia Hispano-Americana, offers intensive Spanish classes and related courses on Mexican history, literature, and folklore. Students usually live with resident families to learn the language more quickly.

Equestrian events are also popular. Several fine riding academies are located just outside of town. You can learn to ride or simply rent a horse.

Visitor amenities. Shopping has been a big part of town life since Father Juan de San Miguel taught crafts to the Indians of his day. The town is noted for its fine tin-smiths. Because Indians of the colonial era were not allowed to work in precious metals, they created similar items in tin. Llamas Brothers (Zacateros 11) and Cerroblanco (Correro 9) are well known for their tinware.

Look, too, for items made from straw, serapes (according to some, they were first created here), and wrought-iron items. As a bonus, San Miguel de Allende has more art galleries than any other city in Mexico. For an overall look at regional handicrafts, visit the Fonart store at Hernandez Macias 95. Sunday is market day on the plaza.

You'll find accommodations in restored haciendas, colonial mansions, and monasteries; prices range from expensive to modest. Several of the more deluxe hotel dining rooms offer some of the area's best food; for more information, see the "Essentials" section on page 155.

The Ignacio Allende Dam, 5 miles south of town, is popular for boating and water-skiing. Here, too, are a 9-hole golf course and tennis courts. A restaurant overlooks the dam.

Queretaro—historical haven

To reach Queretaro from San Miguel de Allende, you first ascend a steep hill at the eastern edge of town, then take a blacktop road at the junction with Highway 57, a few miles north of Queretaro. Or you can travel south on Highway 49 from San Miguel de Allende to Celaya on Highway 45 and then continue to Queretaro on this route (a toll road).

At the northern edge of Queretaro, Highway 57 passes some of the industrial plants that are firmly kept on the outskirts of the town. At Queretaro, the route merges with Highway 45 near the impressive bullring, and together the two routes proceed to Mexico City—138 miles on a high-speed expressway.

Steeped in the past. Much of Queretaro's charm lies in its history. The town site was occupied by the Otomi Indians long before the discovery of the New World. It became a part of the Aztec empire in the 15th century and was overcome by Spanish forces in 1531. (The "conquest" of Queretaro by the Spaniards consisted of a one-day, weaponless confrontation.)

Secret plans for national independence were formulated in this city, and it was here that the Treaty of Guadalupe Hidalgo was ratified, ceding California, New Mexico, and a portion of Texas to the United States. The constitution under which Mexico is now governed was drafted in Queretaro in 1917.

Emperor Maximilian and his two faithful generals were executed in 1867 on the Hill of the Bells at the western edge of town; the spot is marked by a chapel (a gift of the Austrian government), which is dwarfed by the monument to Benito Juarez that stands next to it.

The city today. Queretaro is a fascinating colonial city with intriguing, colorful parks and plazas. The state tourist office (Escobeda 22) has city information and a display of handicrafts. At the heart of town, Plaza Obregon is dominated by the Church of San Francisco, whose colored-tile dome was brought from Spain in 1540. The plaza is the setting for band concerts on Thursday and Sunday evenings.

One downtown building of significance is the Federal Palace on the Plaza de las Armas. It was home to Spanish governors and La Corregidora, heroine of the 1810 revolution. Visitors are welcome to look around. The Regional Museum on Juarez is housed in the former monastery connected to the Church of San Francisco. Crowded with colonial relics and a valuable library, it's worth a look (small admission fee). Next door is an artisans' cooperative with regional handicrafts. Two-hour bus tours of the city depart from the museum.

The Municipal House of Culture lies in a lovely colonial mansion off Plaza de la Independencia. In the plaza a statue commemorates the Marquis who supervised the construction of Queretaro's aqueducts; 400 years ago, they carried water from the mountains to the city.

Queretaro is the center of Mexico's gem industry. Around the well-manicured main plaza you'll find several reputable shops selling opals mined in the nearby mountains, along with stones from other areas. Make your purchases only in a well-established shop—the "gems" sold by itinerant peddlers frequently turn out to be glass.

Celaya—home of Mexico's Michelangelo

Celaya is probably most famous as the hometown of Francisco Eduardo Tresguerras—architect, artist, and poet, often called the "Michelangelo of Mexico." El Carmen Church is considered his greatest architectural work. Tresguerras is buried in a little chapel of his own design in Celaya's ancient San Francisco Church, the newer altars of which he also designed.

Taste the town's favorite sweet, *cajeta*, made from goats' milk boiled down with sugar to a thick, gooey syrup. Many cajeta shops line Lopez Mateos Boulevard.

Juventino Rosas—known for waltzes

The unassuming town of Juventino Rosas lies 15 miles north and west of Celaya. Formerly called Santa Cruz, the town was renamed in honor of one of Mexico's most famous composers, born here in 1868. Rosas wrote the beautiful waltz *"Sobre las Olas"* ("Over the Waves"), also known in English as "The Loveliest Night of the Year." He received only a few pesos for his composition and although he wrote many other pieces, none achieved the fame of this number. He died in poverty at age 26 in a Cuban fishing village.

Irapuato's strawberry harvest

First of several booming cities in the valley of El Bajio (The Depression) is Irapuato, probably most famous as

Mexico's strawberry-growing area. It produces huge quantities of these juicy red berries, many of them sold at roadside stands. In the town, several ultramodern quick-freezing and preserve-making plants efficiently process the berries.

Around the town's ancient cathedral and market plaza is an attractive pedestrian-only mall. A modern hotel, a block-square market building, and innumerable shops were built in keeping with the mall's colonial decor.

West of Irapuato about 30 miles is Rancho Corralejo, birthplace of Father Hidalgo. The ruins of the old hacienda where the "Father of Mexico's Independence" was born, and the adjoining humble ranch chapel, are 4 miles north of Highway 90 on a good, slightly narrow, blacktop road. The turnoff is just beyond a branch of the Lerma River, some 6 miles west of the town of Abasolo—site of another of Mexico's larger thermal spas.

Salamanca—an oil town

If you're in a hurry after leaving Irapuato, you may wish to by-pass Salamanca and neighboring Celaya by taking the modern limited-access Highway 45-D (a toll road). The entrance is 3 miles beyond Irapuato. If you continue past Irapuato on the old Highway 45, the next place of consequence is Salamanca, best known for the huge Pemex oil refinery located just east of town near the Lerma River. Oil for the refinery comes from Poza Rica in the state of Veracruz. After processing in Salamanca, it is distributed to cities throught the highlands.

The ornate Temple of St. Augustine is worth a look, as are some of the craft shops, many of which specialize in Christmas ornaments.

The highway runs south through gently rolling hills from Salamanca to Morelia, at the junction of Highway 15. Two features of this pleasant 65-mile trip are the renovated church and monastery at the lakeside town of Yuriria and, 20 miles farther, the 2-mile-long causeway across Lake Cuitzeo. Dugout canoes dot the lake's mirrorlike surface, enhancing its natural beauty.

Morelia—old-world atmosphere

Morelia lies about halfway between Guadalajara and Mexico City, and makes a good stopover on the 16-hour drive. Highway 15 becomes the main street of the town. At the town's eastern entrance, an aqueduct extends for more than 1 mile; stone benches line a 2-block pedestrian street between the aqueduct and the Sanctuary of Guadalupe. So many of Morelia's elegant old buildings have been preserved that the city is practically a museum of Spanish and Mexican history. Ordinances require that all new construction conform to the style of the early architecture.

Capital of the state of Michoacan, this gracious city—a Tarascan Indian town formerly called Valladolid—takes its present name from native son Jose Maria Morelos, a mule skinner who became a priest and a hero in Mexico's struggle for independence.

Another revered priest and the first bishop of the state, Vasco de Quiroga, was responsible for starting the crafts industry for which the area is famous, and for establishing the College of St. Nicholas, one of the America's oldest state universities.

Sights to see. Morelia is an easy town to explore on foot, as many of its attractions are centered within a few blocks of the cathedral, one of Mexico's most impressive. The most intriguing old buildings are clustered around the central Plaza de los Martires. Lacey detail and ornamental ironwork soften the tall, mosquelike arches of the nostalgic old band pavilion in the beautiful plaza; the delicate foliage of stately jacaranda and other flowering trees casts latticed shade across the broad paseo. The plaza is especially lively on Sunday.

Just a few steps away from this main plaza is the cathedral. Construction of this graceful, twin-spired building took over a century (1640–1744). Take a look at the three-story pipe organ and many fine paintings inside. The Government Palace in front of the cathedral dates back to 1770. The murals in the courtyard were painted by Alfredo Zalce, a famous Morelia artist.

An 18th-century palace houses the Michoacan Museum, at the southwest corner of the plaza. The museum contains an art gallery, archeological exhibits, and colonial relics. Admission is charged. Around the museum lie several blocks of government buildings, including the Municipal Palace and the Palace of Justice, whose courtyard is decorated with murals honoring Morelos.

North of the plaza, the state tourist office is located in the enormous Clavijero Palace, next to the College of St. Nicholas. Once a Carmelite convent, the striking building on Morelos Norte is now the Casa de la Cultura, a restored center for performing arts and the repository of the state's best pre-Columbian art and artifacts.

Three blocks east of the cathedral, the Church of San Francisco was founded in 1531. In the cloister of the adjacent convent you'll find one of Mexico's best crafts displays, Casa de las Artesanias; items overflow into the plaza outside. Note especially the lacquerware for which Morelia is justly famed.

Morelia's Children's Choir is based in the former convent of the Church of Santa Rosa (founded in 1590). Visitors are welcome to attend rehearsals of this famed choir, which has performed in Rome and Carnegie Hall.

Jose Maria Morelos was born in the house at the corner of Corregidora and Garcia Obeso streets, 1 block south of the cathedral; the house he bought later, on the corner of Morelos Sur and Aldama streets, is now a museum. La Iglesia del Niño de la Salud ("The Church of the Child of Health") on the outskirts of town is noted for an image believed to have miraculous healing powers.

Other places of interest: Mercado de Dulces (candy market on Calle Gomez Farias), a planetarium on Calzada Ventura Puente (open in the evening, shows at noon and 6:30 P.M. weekends), and Bosque de Cuauhtemoc, Morelia's largest park with band concerts and a contemporary art museum).

Visitor amenities. Morelia has many delightful little hotels downtown and in the hillside suburb of Santa Maria; for more information, see the "Essentials" section on page 155. A public golf course adds to the city's recreational options.

Patzcuaro—village and lake

Patzcuaro sits in a hilly landscape about 2 miles from vast Lake Patzcuaro. The shallow, 13-mile-long body of water has a profusion of inhabited islands. Transportation between the score or more of tiny shoreline villages is chiefly by boat. Villagers spend most of their time either fishing on the lake or producing handicrafts at home.

Around town. The photogenic 16th-century city of Patzcuaro still uses many of the churches and mansions built in colonial days (1521–1810). Once the political seat of the Tarascan Indian kingdom and later an important Spanish settlement, Patzcuaro blends the best of these two heritages.

At the basilica on the hill, the Colegiata, you can see the Virgin of Health—an entity that bridged the gap between Indian beliefs and church dogma. The Virgin, made of cornstalk pith and orchid mucilage, is revered throughout Mexico and is thought to have great healing powers. The Virgin's feast day on December 8 brings visitors from miles around.

Remarkably, life in the city is much as it was in colonial days. The Tarascan Indians practice a variety of crafts and hold frequent fiestas. *Los Viejitos*—a dance in which men or boys hobble around on canes and wear grotesque masks that make them look old—is a frequent traditional performance.

At its 7,200-foot altitude, Patzcuaro can be cold in the evening; bring along a coat.

Touring. The best place to begin your wanderings around this surprisingly spread-out town is at its zocalo, Plaza Quiroga. A small tourist office is located in the Municipal Palace; another office is at the Casa de los Once Patios ("House of Eleven Patios"), a one-time convent now sheltering artists' studios and handicraft shops. A Museum of Popular Arts (admission fee) is found in the former College of St. Colegio de San Nicolas; within the museum grounds are the remains of a pre-Columbian town and pyramid.

Butterfly nets, once traditional tools of Lake Patzcuaro fisher-
men, appear today primarily to capture photographers' eyes.

... Colonial Circle

The city's commercial center, 1 block north of the main plaza, bustles with merchants and handicraft shops. On Friday a ceramics market takes place on the east side of San Francisco Church (1 block north and 1 block west of Plaza Quiroga).

After you've seen the town, you may want to take one of the local excursions. These include a 15-minute ride to the top of El Estribo ("The Saddle") for a view of the city and lake, and boat trips to some of the islands. Janitzio Island is a classic for photographers; its butterfly-net fishermen provide ideal early-morning subjects.

Boat and automobile trips are available to some of the lakeside villages (Chupicuaro, Erongaricuaro). Santa Clara del Cobre (also known as Villa Escalante), 12 miles south of Patzcuaro on paved Highway 120, has some of the country's finest handcrafted copper products, from striking jewelry to graceful urns, pitchers, and pots—all made on primitive, hand-operated forges.

Shopping. Best buys in this region include lacquerware, silver jewelry, pottery with fish designs, ceramic animals, red-checked wool fabrics, woodenware, and cop-

Woodchoppers and laden burros plod purposefully along country road near the highway to Morelia.

Distinctive designs and hours of painstaking effort are required to create the lustrous lacquerware from Uruapan.

104 Colonial Circle

perware from Santa Clara del Cobre. An excellent place to find everything at bargain prices is Tzintzuntzan, a small village about halfway between Patzcuaro and Quiroga; the market is on both sides of the highway.

Specialties. At restaurants, ask for the delicate and delicious *pescado blanco*, a small, almost transparent whitefish caught in the lake.

Uruapan area

Uruapan, 48 miles from the Highway 15 turnoff at Carapan, exudes an air of drowsy remoteness. The town is set in a verdant, floral landscape—a burgeoning mixture of pine, cedar, oak, and ash, with banana, avocado, mango, and other tropical trees and plants. Uruapan, some 2,000 feet lower in altitude than Patzcuaro and in one of the country's extremely lush areas, is referred to as the Flower Garden of Mexico.

Lacquerware—notably trays and masks—is produced in several small shops in Uruapan and the surrounding area. The best work has engraved designs cut through layers of lacquer. Guitars are made in Paracho, on the highway 15 miles south of the junction town of Carapan. Be on the lookout, too, for beautiful wooden articles, especially those made from cedar.

On the town's central plaza stands La Huatapera, formerly a chapel and hospital and now a crafts museum exhibiting some of the finest Tarascan workmanship, including primitive dolls and statues, lacquerware, and copperware.

Uruapan's pride is its unique park, Parque Nacional Licenciado Eduardo Ruiz. Paths lead along a meandering river up to its headwaters—a series of bubbling springs. Local residents often bathe in Baño Azul, one of the river's pools. The park provides an ideal setting for picnics, photography, and siestas. The Municipal Museum at the park entrance displays and sells native crafts.

For another purely relaxing excursion, ride out about 6 miles to Tzararacua Falls. The waters of the Cupatitzio River gush from many points around a natural stone amphitheater and drop about 90 feet into a pool surrounded by tropical trees, plants, and flowers. Rustic circular houses on a trail to the falls make cool picnic spots; horses are available for those who prefer not to walk.

In 1943, the Paricutin volcano pushed its way 1,700 feet up from the cornfields in the valley floor near Uruapan. After destroying several villages and forcing 4,000 people to flee their homes, the volcano grew quiet. You can drive out to view the weird, blackened landscape; the road ends 4 miles from the volcano. If you're possessed of greater curiosity, you can explore the lava fields on horseback. A guide and horses can be hired from the village of Angahuan. The volcano is 24 miles (round trip) from Uruapan, on a cinder-surfaced road.

Lake Camecuaro

On Highway 15, watch for a small sign pointing out the spur road heading south to Lake Camecuaro, a little-known but idyllic spot where you can stop for a picnic, take a restful boat ride, or walk around and stretch your legs. The ½-mile road from the humble village of Camecuaro is paved, but the road at the lake itself is rough. You can park at the entrance and walk through the grounds.

Lake Camecuaro is narrow and only about a ½-mile long. Giant cypress trees protrude from the clear azure water, white ducks glide among the gnarled roots, and a few bronzed boys may be swimming in the shaded water. If you join them, you'll find that they're a hardy bunch—the water is incredibly cold.

Artist paints a cool vista at Lake Camecuaro Park near the village of Zamora.

Small hotels perch precariously atop vertical walls of rock at Mexico's spectacular Copper Canyon southwest of Chihuahua.

Northern Mexico

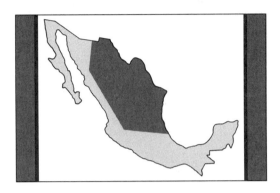

ateway to Mexico's Grand Canyon, backdrop for western movies, and sunny refuge from long winters "up north," Northern Mexico offers a range of attractions to visitors from the central and eastern U.S.

From the Texas border, drivers take any of several highways to Mexico City, or travel to the pleasant towns along the Gulf of Mexico. Even West Coast drivers often go out of their way to take the speedy interior route, Highway 45, to the country's capital. The north central and northeastern sections of Mexico are not exactly filled with tourist destinations, but a few highlights deserve mention.

Interior route

Some consider the north central area of Mexico, traversed by Highway 45, dull and monotonous. Part of it is. At least half the way—between Ciudad Juarez (where the road crosses into Mexico from El Paso, Texas) and Durango—the country is flat and semiarid.

Highway 45 never drops below the 3,752-foot elevation at Ciudad Juarez, where it begins. The road climbs gradually; for much of the way, the uphill grade is almost imperceptible, making this route good for trailers. You may encounter dust storms in the northern reaches between February and April, and occasional winter snows around Chihuahua. Major cities along the route offer good accommodations.

Northeast routes

Three routes take you through northeastern Mexico from the border: the combination of Highways 101 and 180

along the Gulf Coast, and Highways 57 and 85 (the Pan American Highway) through the interior. These roads are all in reasonably good condition. Of the interior routes, Highway 57 is faster, since it doesn't climb and wind through mountains as does Highway 85. Driving time from the border to Mexico City is about 18 hours.

From the border towns of Piedras Negras and Ciudad Acuña, just across the Rio Grande from Eagle Pass and Del Rio respectively, it's a pleasant drive over gently rolling countryside to Monclova, where Mexico's largest steel mill is located. At Monclova, Highway 30 to the southwest goes to Torreon and is an excellent shortcut for motorists heading for Mazatlan on Mexico's west coast.

Motorists on the Gulf Coast Road (Highways 101 and 180) are usually going to Tampico and Veracruz. On their return, they often make a loop through Mexico City, pick up the Pan American Highway, and head north through Ciudad Victoria and Monterrey.

Along Highway 45

About halfway between the border city of Ciudad Juarez and Chihuahua, just below the town of El Sueco, Highway 102 heads west off Highway 45 to Highway 10. Along Highway 10 at Casas Grandes, archeologists are excavating the ruins of a once-large city. Uncovered to date are pyramids, a ball court, and remnants of an irrigation system.

Chihuahua

Chihuahua, one of the largest cities in north central Mexico, still retains a frontier feeling—due, perhaps, to its distance from other major cities. From here it's around 900 miles to Mexico City, 700 miles to Guadalajara, and 500 miles to Monterrey. Founded in 1709, Chihuahua owes its beginnings to the rich silver strikes that were made in the nearby mountains.

The city lies in a high and wide valley ringed by the Sierra Madre mountains. Over the last few decades, modern irrigation and farming methods have transformed the arid desert into a prosperous green land. Many of the city's restaurants specialize in beef from ranches in the area.

Parts of the city are quite modern, but the older sections contain some fine examples of colonial architecture. Among them are the Government Palace on Hidalgo Plaza, where Father Hidalgo was executed in 1811, during the War for Independence; the nearby Federal Palace, where Hidalgo was imprisoned while awaiting execution; and the immense cathedral facing the central Plaza de la Constitucion.

Tree-shaded Calle Bolivar is lined with colonial mansions, among them the Regional Museum, filled with ornate furniture on the first floor and rooms devoted to Tarahumara Indian culture and Mennonite life upstairs. (A Mennonite community moved to the area from Europe over 60 years ago and still lives in nearby Cuauhtemoc).

La Quinta Luz on Calle 10 was the home of Pancho Villa, Mexico's guerrilla-revolutionary. A sort of Mexican Robin Hood, Villa with his band of bandits ranged across the northern states, ostensibly serving the cause of la revolucion. After Villa's widow died in 1981, the government turned his home into the Museum of the Revolution; it houses a collection of his weapons and belongings.

Some souvenir shopping takes place within walking distance of downtown at the Mercado de Artesanias Mexicanos (Victoria 506) and at the Artesanias Mexicanas de Jalisco (Aldama 508). But the best crafts from all over Mexico are sold at the Museo de Artes y Industrias Populares (Reforma 5). An excellent Tarahumara Indian museum adjoins the shop.

From Chihuahua, you can take a spectacular rail trip through the mountains and canyons of the Sierra Madre Occidental to the town of Los Mochis on Highway 15 (see page 112).

Ciudad Camargo

Ciudad Camargo is an old but progressive Mexican town in the heart of cattle country. Operating from a modern headquarters building, the cattlemen's association is central to the town's activities. A large meat-packing plant, located at the southern edge of town, refrigerates and ships meat throughout Mexico and the U.S.

In this bustling and businesslike town, the highlight of the year is the fiesta for its patron saint, Santa Rosalia. Starting on September 4, eight days of celebration include dances, horse races, cockfights, and other boisterous entertainment. An 18th-century parish church named after the saint is 4 blocks east of the highway.

Hidalgo del Parral

Virtually cut off from everyone except intrepid miners until Highway 45 was completed, Hidalgo del Parral has remained somewhat isolated and primitive. (Most travelers still tend to use Highway 49 to Fresnillo via Gomez Palacio, rather than Highway 45.) Rich metallic ores were first discovered here in the mid-16th century, and the mines are still producing.

Six churches are scattered throughout the town—all of them with bullet holes in their stone walls. A large 18th-century church on the plaza has a richly embellished interior and gilded altar screens.

Durango

Durango reflects an openness of design and a provincial atmosphere that are atypical for a city of its size (250,000). The streets are wide and paved; the zocalo is gracious and still well kept. One of the most pleasant cities along the highway, Durango boasts several large parks, a few smaller parks, and a riverside promenade. The massive cathedral has a cheery yellow façade and magnificent vaulted ceilings. Inside the Government Palace (Durango is the state capital), the walls of an entire inner courtyard are decorated with murals. The 17th-century Casa de Conde de Xuchil, 2 blocks east of the main plaza, houses several shops.

From Durango, scenic Highway 40 winds up and over the Sierra Madre Occidental to meet Highway 15 just south of Mazatlan. The 200-mile route is paved, but not particularly fast; it is not recommended for trailers or motor homes, nor for travel at night.

Zacatecas

This colonial silver-mining town lies 8,200 feet above sea level. Parts of the town are so steep that stone steps—not streets—climb the canyon walls. The whole town has a faint pinkish cast, a result of the local sandstone used in the buildings.

Zacatecas centers around its magnificent, intricately carved cathedral; the vaulted interior is supported with stalwart stone columns. The old market to one side of the cathedral has been modernized and now contains fancy shops and restaurants. On the other side, the stairway of the Government Palace glimmers with rich paintings depicting Zacatecan history. Don't miss the Pedro Coronel Museum adjoining the Church of Santo Domingo; it's the private collection of one of the city's artists and includes works by Goya, Picasso, Miro, and Chagall.

For a small charge, a minitrain takes you on a hair-raising tour into the caverns of El Eden Mine (every half-hour from 1 to 8 P.M.); at night the mine becomes a disco. After the tour an elevator whisks you to the top of the mine, where you can take a cable-car ride over the city. The tramway connects two hillsides on the north side of town, Cerro de la Bufa and Cerro Grillo.

A paved road also ascends La Bufa, topped by an ancient chapel (built in 1728) and a demure plaza. A museum details Pancho Villa's capture of Zacatecas in 1914. Several shops display crafts from the area.

South of Zacatecas on Highway 49, take time to meander through the narrow, quiet streets of Guadalupe. The town's handsome convent houses numerous works of art and handprinted books.

Aguascalientes

A colonial city and state capital, Aguascalientes is also a railroad center. Crafts (especially serapes, linens, and hand-embroidered cottons) and winemaking are other important industries in this grape-growing region. The town's name refers to its location near thermal springs. The waters provide an opportunity for visitors to indulge themselves for a languorous afternoon.

Around the renovated central plaza stand many interesting buildings, among them the cathedral (fine religious paintings), State House, Municipal House, and Morelos Theater. Within walking distance are San Antonio Church, the Temple of Guadalupe, and San Marcos Church. The garden in front of this church is the setting for events during the annual San Marcos Fair, in late April and early May.

The arm of the Black Christ within the Temple of El Encino is said to be growing; in the cloisters, an art museum houses the works of Jose Guadalupe Posada, a famous local artist. For shopping, go to Casa de las Artesanias on Avenida Lopez Mateos.

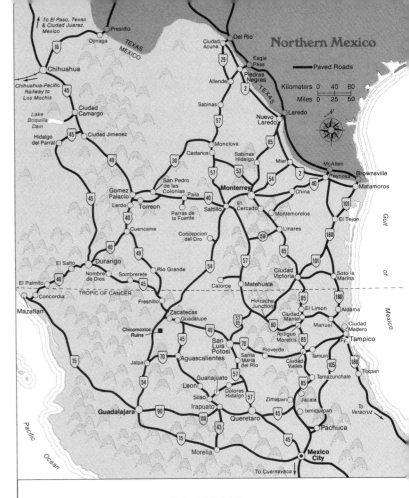

DETAILS AT A GLANCE

Northern Mexico

How to get there

This large stretch of territory is best explored by car, though commuter plane service links Mexico City and the larger cities, and rail travel is upgraded.

By air. Monterrey is connected by flights to and from the U.S. Commuter traffic to small towns is less frequent; you'll usually find just one flight a day.

By road. Highways in northeastern Mexico are paved and clearly marked, making driving the best way to get to—and tour—the area. Buses are only for the adventurous.

Accommodations

Plan to reach a fairly large town for overnight stops. Not much is plush, but clean rooms are available (see the "Essentials" section on page 156).

Climate & clothes

If possible, plan trips for spring or autumn. The northern section is desertlike and sizzles in summer, while the Gulf side can be very humid. Pick your wardrobe for comfort.

Through the Northeast

The border country near the Gulf of Mexico is a winter home for many North Americans, who leave colder climates for the sunny Rio Grande Valley. Others head for Monterrey, Mexico's third-largest city, or venture farther south to try their luck at Gulf fishing.

Saltillo

Covering a vast plain at a mile-high elevation, Saltillo stretches into low hills; higher mountains surround it in every direction. This is the capital of the state of Coahuila and a popular stopping place in summer because of its relatively cool climate.

Founded in 1555, Saltillo retains much of its Spanish character. "Downtown" runs chiefly along the two one-way streets of Victoria and Aldama, from the central plaza west for about 6 blocks to the shady Alameda. The State Capitol faces onto the plaza; across from it is the Cathedral of Santiago with its 200-foot tower and richly-carved façade.

In several small factories you can watch weavers at work on the brightly-colored serapes characteristic of Saltillo. Skilled craftsmen fashion articles of silver, tin, brass, and copper. Look carefully for the market on Allende; the street, lined with small shops, looks like a normal business block.

Highway 40 runs east from Saltillo to Monterrey on a divided expressway, and west from Saltillo to Torreon through large expanses of desert. About midway between the towns, a few miles south of an oasis junction called Paila, is the winemaking town of Parras de la Fuente. Nearby lies Rincon del Montero, a popular resort.

Southwest of Saltillo, Highway 54 heads for the desert past the old mining town of Concepcion del Oro to Zacatecas, beyond which you can continue to Guadalajara. About 10 minutes southwest of Saltillo, along Highway 54, is the almost forgotten site of one of the bloodiest confrontations of the U.S.–Mexican War—the Battle of Buena Vista (called the Battle of Angostura by the Mexicans). A small shaft marks the rocky spot where the battle took place on February 23, 1847.

Matehuala region

In the desert around Matehuala, veritable forests of several species of agave and yucca are the source of various fibers generically known as *ixtle;* these are the basis of Matehuala's all-important industry. Finer-quality fibers are used mainly for sacking and for decorative pieces such as place mats and wall hangings. Coarser fiber is made into packing material, brush bristles, doormats, and upholstery filling.

South of Matehuala you'll start seeing the *nopal* or tuna cactus, the fruit of which is quite delicious. Natives gather the fruits and sell them along the highway. They are also used to make a regional sweet—*queso de tuna* or tuna "cheese."

From the town of Matehuala (food, lodging, and gasoline available), you can drive or take a bus to Real de Catorce, a colonial silver-mining town that has had its ups and downs. Once a prosperous community, it boasted a population of 40,000 in its heyday.

Today, only about 800 residents remain, and the attractive opera house (where Caruso once sang), churches, public buildings, and residences are slowly crumbling. But special events bring the town to life briefly: From September 25 to October 12, pilgrims come to the church from all over Mexico to honor the town's patron saint, San Francisco de Assisi; a fiesta on December 28 includes Indian dancers and fireworks; a fair takes place on January 3.

San Luis Potosi

The largest city along Highway 57 is San Luis Potosi, capital of the state of the same name. The main highway by-passes the city by a mile or so; if you make the side trip into town, you'll consider your time well spent. A rich mining center since the 1600s, San Luis Potosi is also a modern industrial city and a major rail center.

Civic buildings and colonial structures stand around a series of plazas and a garden, all within a few blocks of each other. The local bazaar, Mercado Hidalgo, offers good buys on the prized Santa Maria rebozos, pottery, and cactus candy. A handicrafts market, contained in a 16th-century convent, features popular art from throughout the state; Calle Hidalgo, a pedestrian mall, is lined with the city's finest stores.

Also of interest are the cathedral, the lovely Church of Our Lady of Carmen, the Regional Museum (admission fee), the National Museum of Regional Masks (closed Sunday afternoon and Monday), the Bullfight Museum, and the Casa de la Cultura (art museum, admission charge). South of the city several spas are noted for healing waters: Lourdes (at Santa Maria del Rio) to benefit intestinal problems, Gogorron (at Villa de Reyes) for circulation and arthritic ailments.

Santa Maria del Rio

About 29 miles south of San Luis Potosi, the tidy town of Santa Maria del Rio sits on the banks of a languorous river. The community is noted throughout Mexico for its fine rebozos (shawls). For generations its women have been weaving beautiful silken rebozos. You can purchase handicrafts at the weaving school on the main plaza.

Pink sandstone adds a touch of color to the buildings in Zacatecas, a colonial silver-mining town rich in history.

Monterrey

You can reach Monterrey from many directions, but if you're driving south from the U.S., you'll probably take Highway 85 from Laredo. The first 45 miles south of the border are monotonous. Beyond Vallecillo, though, the road climbs gradually into the foothills of the Sierra Madre, then drops down into the industrial city of Monterrey—capital of the state of Nuevo Leon and Mexico's third-largest city.

Bustling, modern Monterrey has a great deal of charm, making it a good base for travelers. Plenty of fine hotels and restaurants assure a comfortable stay; a variety of scenic attractions around the region invite exploration. It's best to leave the driving to someone else—traffic is congested and confusing, parking almost nonexistent. Book a city tour through your hotel and pick up a guide with a car to see the countryside.

Monterrey also has its share of 17th-century landmarks, fountain-dominated parks, and flower-filled gardens. The city's zocalo is five times the size of Mexico City's; from the State House a Grand Plaza extends 11 blocks to the modernistic City Hall. This plaza leads into smaller Plaza Hidalgo and Avenida Morelos, a pedestrian-only shopping area with some of the city's finest stores, restaurants, and hotels. Many colonial buildings center around Zaragoza Plaza and its cathedral (begun in 1603 and completed in 1753). The plaza is the site of band concerts on Thursday and Sunday evenings.

The Bishop's Palace (El Obispado), on the west side of the city, was built in 1785 as a residence for church dignitaries. It functioned as a fort during the Mexican–American War, was occupied by Pancho Villa during the Revolution of 1910, and now houses a museum (admission fee). Stop by ultramodern La Purisima Church en route to the palace to see the impressionistic statues of the Apostles.

Shopping is good, particularly for leather, glass, and lead crystal (one of the world's largest lead crystal factories is open for weekday tours). On the outskirts of town, Mexico's largest brewery, Cervezeria Cuauhtemoc (Carta Blanca and Bohemia), offers a baseball museum, weekday guided tours, and free samples. A worthwhile trip is to the Alfa Cultural Center (Coatzacoalcos 1000 in the suburb of Garza Garcia). The center has fine arts galleries, an interesting science museum, and a planetarium. It's open daily except Monday from 11 A.M. to 7 P.M.

Around Monterrey

In the area around Monterrey you can picnic beside a gushing waterfall, go boating, tour underground caverns, and buy fresh orange juice along the road.

Garcia Caves. About 30 miles northwest of the city, a labyrinth of spectacular limestone caverns is open daily to visitors. A little funicular railway makes hourly trips from an excursion depot 5 miles northeast of the village

The converging gorges that make up the Grand Canyon of Mexico are known as Barranca del Cobre (Copper Canyon). This great chasm is often compared to Arizona's—but Mexico's is four times bigger and 280 feet deeper.

Access to this rugged part of the Sierra Madre Occidental is by train, a 400-mile rail route that took 76 years to build. The train climbs steep grades, threads through 86 tunnels, and crosses some 40 bridges on its route between Los Mochis on the west coast and Chihuahua in the interior.

Waterfalls slip over rims of red rock into deep ravines where palms and ferns grow in the shade and bush poppies tumble over sunlit slopes. Yet all is not wild in the Sierra Madre. Juxtaposed against the forested ridges are the simple huts of the Tarahumara Indians, who still inhabit this rugged part of the world.

The trip. Passenger trains depart from either Los Mochis or Chihuahua at 7 A.M. daily, making the run in some 15½ hours if there are no delays. You'll get your most spectacular daylight views of the climb by starting in Los Mochis.

Once you reach canyon-rim country—about 7,000 feet—the route levels out to high plateau. A 20-minute stop at Divisadero gives you a chance to take photos and shop for crafts.

With binoculars you can search out their cave homes and farm compounds in the semitropical canyon bottom. Their switchback trails weave a fragile network up the lichen-streaked canyon walls.

Continuing on to Chihuahua, you descend through range and farmland, dotted with Indian villages and small ranches.

How to get there. Going with a tour group usually makes this trip more comfortable. Copper Canyon tour operators are current on where to find the best accommodations and food—services that can easily change from one year to the next.

On some tours, you ride in restored private cars; others book blocks of seats on Mexican National Railways' trains. One operator even brings its own water, food, and chef. On a tour you won't have to worry about when to get on the train or where to get off.

Depending on the type of tour you choose, your trip may include a night or more at the rim with days free for hiking, guided horseback rides, or a jeep trip into the canyon depths. Check with a travel agent for current information. Canyon tour operators include Bananafish Tours, Pan American Tours, Sanborn Tours, and Sierra Madre Express. Or write directly to Mexican National Railway, 1500 Broadway, Suite 810, New York, NY 10031.

A Tarahumara Indian hunkers down for a brief rest during an infrequent trip to the city

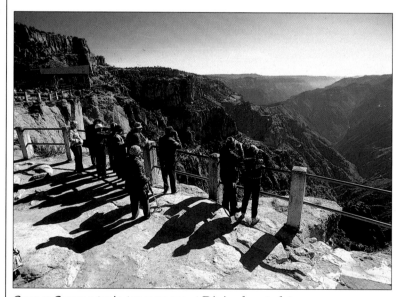

Copper Canyon train tours pause at Divisadero to let passengers stretch, take photos

of Villa de Garcia to the entrance of the state-operated caverns. The round trip and tour take about 2 hours (admission charge includes funicular and guided tour).

Horsetail Falls. Highway 85 enters Huajuco Canyon south of Monterrey and follows it about 20 miles through some of Mexico's most lush and fertile countryside. Some 25 miles south of Monterrey, a rewarding detour off the main highway leads to an idyllic waterfall called Cola de Caballo (Horsetail), which spills in delicate ribbons for 225 feet down a mossy, fern-draped precipice.

Montemorelos. Just off the highway about 50 miles south of Monterrey is Mexico's largest orange-growing district. Fresh oranges and glasses of thick, pulpy orange juice are sold along the road. At Montemorelos, Highway 85 is joined by Highway 35 from China (pronounced *CHEE-nah*), a popular shortcut to Mexico City from the border cities of McAllen (Texas) and Reynosa (Mexico).

South on Highway 85

Ciudad Victoria is the capital of the industrial state of Tamaulipas, which extends in a narrow strip along the Rio Grande and then follows the Gulf of Mexico south as far as the coastal town of Tampico. The growing of natural fibers is the region's most important industry. Colorful hammocks and other decorative objects are sold on the streets and in the markets. Highway 85 is joined at this point by Highway 101 from the Texas towns of McAllen and Brownsville.

Highway 85 crosses the Tropic of Cancer 24 miles south of Ciudad Valles and the country becomes increasingly lush, with dense vegetation, masses of colorful vines, thick forests, and groves of mango, banana, and avocado trees. Fragrant flowers bloom profusely everywhere; beautifully brilliant *flamboyant* (royal poinciana) trees brighten the green vegetation.

The quaint old town of Tamazunchale, at the foot of the Sierra Madre Oriental, is the unofficial capital of the isolated Huasteca Indians, who live for the most part in the nearby mountains. Butterflies and birds are the town's most colorful inhabitants; alert visitors may see some unusual species in this area. Also of interest are the 16th-century church and the unusual market, offering tantalizing tropical novelties.

Some spectacular views are available along Highway 85 between Tamazunchale and Jacala, a mountain mining town. Zimapan, south of Jacala, a colorful mining town established when lead and silver deposits were discovered after the Conquest, is still active. South from Zimapan lies Ixmiquilpan, where you can visit one of Mexico's oldest and grandest churches and convents, built by the Augustinians in 1550.

Tampico—on the Gulf of Mexico

You get your first glimpse of the Gulf of Mexico at Tampico, one of the country's biggest and most dynamic seaports. The port itself is inland on the Panuco River, and the city has grown up on half a dozen hills, amid freshwater lagoons. Tampico's visitors are mostly fishermen; hunting for duck, quail, and turkey is also popular. A museum showcases Huasteca Indian culture.

Serapes brighten a market stall at Saltillo, where you'll have a chance to watch weavers at work.

Verdant forest backs Palenque's 1,300-year-old Temple of the Sun.

Southern Mexico

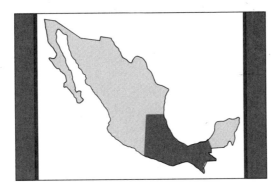

outhern Mexico is often overlooked by tourists. Yet it offers rewarding experiences that are too often missed by those who prefer metropolitan areas to more primitive regions. The area is a delightful mixture of historically interesting cities, quaint villages with colorful markets, small fishing ports, and modern seaports. It's also a diverse geographical region, with cool highlands, hot tropical beaches, lush forests, scrub-covered plains, and groves of tropical fruits.

Southern Mexico is Indian country, home to the Mixtecs, Zapotecs, Lacandons, Chamulas, Zinacantecos, and others. Nowhere else in Mexico have Indians retained their cultural characteristics in such pristine form as they have in the southern states of Oaxaca and Chiapas. And the archeological sites of Palenque, Mitla, La Venta, Monte Alban, and El Tajin leave you with lasting impressions of much earlier civilizations.

The oldest colonial city on the Gulf of Mexico, Veracruz was founded by Hernan Cortes in 1519. Today it's the republic's largest seaport and a good place to overnight if visiting the archeological zone of Zempoala, about 25 miles to the northwest. Veracruz is an 8-hour drive on coastal Highway 180 from Tampico and about 265 miles east of Mexico City. A fast toll road (150-D) from Mexico City via Puebla leads to the coast.

Villahermosa, on the Gulf Coast highway (180) southeast of Veracruz, sits at the entrance to the land of the Mayas. Many tours to the Yucatan Peninsula begin here. Travelers also come to see the huge Olmec heads in La Venta park, fashioned by a civilization of some 3,000 years ago. The majestic pyramid at Palenque, about 90 miles southeast of town, can be visited on a 1-day tour from Villahermosa. A paved highway also connects Tuxtla Gutierrez with Palenque via Villahermosa.

Getting around the interior

Oaxaca, capital of the state of the same name, makes a good base for visiting the ruins of Monte Alban, Mitla, and other nearby archeological sites. It's also a fine destination in its own right, with well-priced handicrafts from surrounding Indian villages, beautiful buildings, friendly people, good climate, and an unhurried pace.

San Cristobal de las Casas, a smaller city in the Chiapas highlands below the Isthmus of Tehuantepec, is one of Mexico's most charming locations. A colorful Indian market town, it was also a Spanish settlement and capital of the state until 1892. From Oaxaca, it's a drive of about 12 hours; scheduled air service from Mexico City and Oaxaca to nearby Tuxtla Gutierrez (capital of Chiapas) is a better way to get there.

Prepare for the weather

Oaxaca's moderate year-round temperature is due to its 5,000-foot elevation; even when summer days are hot, nights are pleasantly cool. San Cristobal de las Casas, some 2,000 feet higher, can be cold; bring a wrap. Beach towns on the Pacific side are hot in the summer. Late winter and early spring are the best times to visit towns along the Gulf of Mexico. Summer brings rain, high temperatures, and high humidity.

Along the Gulf Coast

From Tampico (see page 113), motorists have a choice of two routes along the Gulf of Mexico—Highway 180 along the coast or a combination of highways 105 and 127 inland through Panuco and Tempoal. The short route is via Highway 180, but you'll have to cross the wide Panuco River on a car ferry, which is big and business-like. The long line-up of cars and trucks waiting their turn to board can be a bit discouraging, and the steady pounding of huge Pemex oil field equipment has ruined the road in places.

The inland route (highways 105 and 127) crosses the bridge over the river at Panuco. This road has been rebuilt as far as Tempoal, and you drive through ranching and sugar-cane country among pleasant, rolling foothills. Beyond Tempoal the road is uneven and hilly. At Alazan Junction the two routes meet and go on into Tuxpan.

South of Tuxpan near Poza Rica the road splits; the right fork is Highway 130, which winds through beautiful mountain country to Pachuca on Highway 85—one route to Mexico City. Take the left fork, Highway 180, to continue down the coast to Veracruz.

Tuxpan. Tuxpan is known as a quiet paradise for tarpon fishermen. Tarpon can be caught from Rio Tuxpan at any time, but June is the peak season. The most important activity of this port town, though, is the shipping of cattle and petroleum. To the east of Tuxpan lies the Gulf of Mexico and a beautiful beach. Delicious tiny shrimp, taken from the nearby lagoon and served with *salsa picante* (hot sauce) are a specialty of local restaurants. An attractive riverside adds to the charm of this tidy port.

Poza Rica. Southwest of Tuxpan is one of Mexico's leading oil towns, Poza Rica, or "Rich Hole." This booming town has one industry—a huge Pemex oil refinery. The city grew rapidly in recent years; most buildings were erected hastily—and look it. Oil is king, and if you happen to forget it for a moment, the penetrating stench of petroleum will soon remind you.

El Tajin. The ruins of El Tajin, a site rivaling any of the other major archeological zones in Mexico, are 10 miles south of Poza Rica on an alternate road into Papantla. The Totonacs settled here around A.D. 800, but the site was inhabited as early as the 5th or 6th century. The buildings were erected over a span of six centuries.

Here, in the steamy coastal foothills, you can understand the effort it took to build the many multifaceted structures. Study the exquisite carved panels on the walls of the south ball court. The seven-story Pyramid of the Niches definitively reigns as the most important building. The structure has a total of 365 niches: 364 in its exterior walls, with the door to the temple on top counting as the final "niche." This number probably represents the days of the solar year.

In front of the pyramid is a tall steel pole around which the *voladores*—the famed Flying Pole Dancers from Papantla—perform on special occasions. Five performers climb to a platform at the top of a 100-foot pole; one remains to play a flute and beat a drum while the other four tie ropes that have been wound around the pole to their ankles, and leap into space, whirling around the pole as they descend to the ground.

Papantla. The Flying Pole Dancers come from this trading and cultural center of the Totonac Indians. Major industries around Papantla and the nearby town of Gutierrez Zamora are the growing of vanilla beans and chili peppers. The voladores usually perform Sunday afternoon and during a week-long fiesta in June, when the whole town celebrates the sale of last year's harvest and prays for rain for this year's crops.

At Gutierrez Zamora a bridge over the placid Tecolutla River replaces a former ferry. The highway proceeds alongside the Gulf for about 20 miles, past sandy dunes and beaches, through Brahma cattle country and magnificent groves of coconut palms. At an old lighthouse junction called El Faro, you have a choice of two routes to Veracruz. Highway 180 continues down the coast; on the other highways you wind inland by way of Teziutlan, Perote, and Jalapa.

Zempoala. The last capital of the Totonacs lies 70 miles south and 2 miles west of Nautla. The ruins—not as impressive as those of El Tajin—have been partially restored and reconstructed; among them are the extensive Temples of the Sun, Moon, and Goddess of Death. Zempoala's cemeteries are worthy of note: tombs are miniature temples about 4 feet high.

Veracruz

If you travel much in Mexico, you're bound to pass through Veracruz, the oldest colonial city on the Gulf of Mexico. Hernan Cortes launched his conquest of the country from here in 1519, the French army landed to install the ill-fated puppet emperor Maximilian in 1864, and twice (in 1847 and 1914) U.S. forces invaded and occupied the city.

Today, the republic's largest port bustles with foreign freighters, Mexico's naval armada, and fishing boats. Spanish forts, trolleys, old churches, and colonial buildings are almost lost among modern structures. Lighthearted Veracruz doesn't look back; it marches, or rather dances (this is the home of *la bamba*), to a different beat.

Palm-thatched huts are never far from palatial townhouses, and everyone from laborer to company president gathers under the arcades around the Plaza de las Armas. Marimba bands wander through the indoor-

DETAILS AT A GLANCE

Southern Mexico

How to get there

Several daily flights from Mexico City and other major Mexican cities reach Oaxaca, Veracruz, Villahermosa, Tuxtla Gutierrez, and other southern cities.

By air. The capital cities of Oaxaca, Tuxtla Gutierrez, Veracruz, and Villahermosa are well-connected with each other as well as to Mexico City by air. Tuxtla Gutierrez offers flights to the ruins at Palenque. Air charter services reach smaller towns and villages.

By car. The best way to tour craft villages around Oaxaca is by rental car. You'll be able to see as much as possible, and visit all the locations you choose. Oaxaca is about an 8-hour drive from Mexico City.

By bus and train. Bus transportation is inexpensive—but you lose flexibility and may pass through the most scenic countryside at night. Deluxe trains connect Mexico City with Veracruz and Oaxaca.

Accommodations

Simplicity is the keynote for most hotels, motels, and campgrounds in southern Mexico. Luxurious hotels are rare and found only in larger cities, but plenty of small, clean accommodations are available throughout the region (see page 157).

Climate & clothes

Oaxaca is a popular destination all year. November to April is the best time to visit; winter may be crisp and early spring smoky due to burning of the fields. Veracruz is on the torrid side most of the year; late February or early March is pleasant.

outdoor cafes playing an assortment of Caribbean, American, and Mexican tunes. After the April rains come, the heat is almost palpable; one encounter with it helps you understand the paradoxical combination of vivacity and indolence you experience in the tropics.

Above all, you'll notice that Veracruz makes no special preparations for tourists such as those found in most Mexican cities: Veracruz is for itself. Though the pre-Lenten Mardi Gras celebration here doesn't rival those of New Orleans and Rio de Janeiro, it is Mexico's most frenetic, with hotels booked months ahead.

Cuisine. Like New Orleans, Veracruz has a Creole cuisine—an amalgam of Spanish and French styles—featuring local foods. Best known is *huachinango a la veracruzana* (baked red snapper topped with a sauce of tomatoes, capers, olives, onion, and mild chiles). For memorable dining, try one of the outdoor cafes around the plaza (Prendes is reliable). For fresh shrimp or oysters, try one of the rustic restaurants at Mandinga or Boca del Rio, south of town.

Veracruzanos take their coffee as seriously as the English take their tea. Near the plaza, at Cafe la Parroquia on Independencia, locals linger over coffee brewed in century-old espresso machines. A newer Cafe la Parroquia is on the malecon.

What to do. Overlooking the harbor, the Castillo de San Juan de Ulua was begun in 1528. The dungeons and walkways of this lichen-covered fortress-prison are open to visitors. Near the zocalo, the church of Santo Cristo del Buen Viaje (Christ of the Safe Voyage) is rumored to be the oldest church on the American continents. At Museo de Arte y Historia Veracruzano (Zaragoza 397), you'll see Totonac, Olmec, and Huastec artifacts.

Along the malecon, you'll find marine curio shops; you can hire a boat for tarpon or deep-sea fishing here or at your hotel. To visit the good beaches on Isla de los Sacrificios, one of three small offshore islands, catch a boat from the front of the Hotel Emporio.

Shopping. Independencia is the main shopping street, but you'll find few regional crafts. One noted exception is the *quechuemetl,* an embroidered capelike garment, which is made in this area. Best buys are liquor and cigars made from tobacco grown in the Valle de San Andreas. Shops close for the traditional afternoon siesta.

Veracruz to Villahermosa

Just south of Veracruz, a side road leads down the coast to Anton Lizardo, a fishing village. Just beyond the turnoff to Anton Lizardo at Paso del Toro Junction, Highway 150 turns inland toward Cordoba, where it cuts across the Continental Divide toward Puebla and Mexico City.

For 96 miles south of Veracruz, Highway 180 provides glimpses of the Gulf—and of shifting sand dunes that sometimes cover parts of the highway. At Alvarado, you cross the wide mouth of the Papaloapan River over a toll bridge. South of Alvarado, the route heads through rich sugar-cane country, then winds along the shore of Lake Catemaco, up into high volcanic hills, and down into the fertile valley of the Hueyapan River.

At the town of Juan Diaz Covarrubias, a sugar refinery, a molasses plant, and an alcohol distillery provide employment for the inhabitants. At Acayucan, Highway 185 branches south across the Isthmus of Tehuantepec to La Ventosa Junction on the Pacific side.

Minatitlan, 13 miles farther along Highway 180, is headquarters for sulfur and oil expeditions into the jungles up the tropical Coatzacoalcos River. Beyond Minatitlan, you drive through about 10 miles of marshy mud flats to the leading town of the area—the oil and sulfur seaport of Coatzacoalcos. The highway by-passes the town and crosses the Coatzacoalcos River on a toll drawbridge that carries both a railroad track and the highway.

The highway winds through oil fields to the Tonala River, crossed by another bridge. Beyond the bridge, a side road to the left leads to the La Venta oil-producing area. In the La Venta swamps archeologists found giant heads and other stone figures sculpted by the Olmecs; these were later removed for exhibition in Villahermosa's Museo La Venta and in Jalapa's Juarez Park.

Villahermosa

An attractive state capital little known by tourists, Villahermosa is worth visiting even if you do not plan to continue into the Yucatan area. For many years the city had no road to the outside world; most transportation of both goods and people was by water, on the Grijalva River. This water culture has not appreciably diminished. Villahermosa still has a beautiful riverfront; an impressive boulevard and flowered plazas border it. You can climb aboard a boat for a cruise up the river.

Pre-Columbian culture. The archeological museum, Museo Regional CICOM (Centro de Investigacion de las Culturas Olmeca y Maya), on the bank of the Grijalva River, has a fine collection of Olmec, Maya, and other pre-Columbian art.

Villahermosa's outdoor archeological museum, Museo La Venta, is worth a visit. Located on the western outskirts of town, this unique tropical park reproduces the original site of La Venta. Tremendous, heavy Olmec stone heads were transported here from the Tabasco–Veracruz border; stone altars and sculpted animals brought from the region also contribute to the setting's realism. You can take a guided tour to La Venta (transportation and admission fee included in the price) or go on your own. Either way, take along insect repellent. A light-and-sound show, in Spanish, is presented nightly.

Around the city. The flower-lined malecon divides the river from the modern hotels and shops of the downtown area. Many good seafood restaurants offer fresh Gulf catches. All-day sightseeing tours leave Villahermosa early in the morning for the 95-mile trip to Palenque, an important Maya center hidden in the Chiapas jungle. Make arrangements for the trip at your hotel; the tour price includes lunch.

Into Indian land. Two important routes originate at Villahermosa. The first, Highway 195, heads inland to Tuxtla Gutierrez in the state of Chiapas. Paved for its entire length, the road has an abundance of curves; allow plenty of time to drive it. Trailers should proceed with extreme caution.

The other route is inland Highway 186, from which a paved side road cuts south to the ruins of Palenque. Beyond the Palenque turnoff, Highway 261 branches off at Francisco Escarcega and heads to Champoton, where it rejoins the coastal route, Highway 180, to Campeche. At Chencoyi, 18 miles east of Campeche, Highway 180 continues north to Merida and Highway 261 branches east 32 miles to Hopelchen, and then north to Merida. This affords motorists a circle route to impressive ruins south of Merida.

Palenque's magnificent ruins

About 70 miles east of Villahermosa via Highway 186, a paved road leads south some 20 miles to the archeological site of Palenque in the Chiapas jungle. Considered by many to be the most beautiful pre-Hispanic site in Mexico, Palenque was a Maya center, inhabited before A.D. 100 and at its height from A.D. 600 to 900.

Most of its buildings are gems of light, airy construction. The Temple of Inscriptions contains an elaborate sarcophagus rivaling those discovered in Egypt. The magnificent burial chamber is reached by a narrow stairway down into the body of the pyramid. Though the priceless collection of jewelry and an elaborate jade death mask are now on display at the Museum of Anthropology in Mexico City, the mummy of Lord Pacal, who died in A.D. 683, still lies in its original resting place.

In April 1982, the eruption of El Chichon, a volcano 75 miles west of Palenque, covered the site with a heavy layer of ash. Traces of the eruption can still be found.

The site is open daily from 7 A.M. to late afternoon, though the museum's hours are much shorter. There are small fees for admission and parking.

Sunlight tints the water around a sailboat anchored in Veracruz harbor.

Mexico City to the Gulf

A fast toll road east from Mexico City (Highway 190-D) takes you to Puebla. To continue to the Gulf of Mexico, pick up Highway 150-D, also a toll route. From Orizaba, this road passes through rich coffee plantations and flower-garlanded resorts en route to the coast.

In the shadow of mighty Orizaba

Beyond the Tehuacan turnoff, Highway 150 climbs to a 7,500-foot summit, offering one of the most spectacular views in Mexico—the Valley of Acultzingo. The gradual descent of 4,000 feet is breathtaking. If you're squeamish about hairpin turns and abrupt drop-offs, though, take the Puebla–Orizaba toll expressway, which misses the Acultzingo descent.

As you approach the city of Orizaba, you'll see magnificent Pico de Orizaba, also called Citlatepetl ("The Star Mountain"). This is Mexico's highest mountain—an 18,701-foot peak with perpetual snows on its volcanic cone. The first town of notable size in this warm, lush valley, Orizaba blends industrial claptrap with colonial ambience: textile mills stand next to long rows of tile-roofed dwellings and shops.

Two breweries, coffee and fruit-packing companies, and cement plants are central to the city's industrial economy. The Municipal Palace, on the plaza northwest of Castillo Park, was purchased by the city from Belgium. (Originally, the building was part of the Belgian Pavilion in a 19th-century Paris Exposition.)

Fortin de las Flores

Less a town than a flower garden, Fortin de las Flores was a Spanish outpost during the colonial period. Today it's a resort area, noted for exceptionally beautiful gardens filled with gardenias, camellias, and orchids. You can visit the plantation that each day supplies a large resort hotel with a truckload of gardenias to be floated on its swimming pool. The best of the area's flowers can be appreciated at the annual flower fair in April.

Snow-shrouded Orizaba, Mexico's highest mountain, peeks out from behind the clouds.

Prickly poppy

Flame vine

Cordoba

Cordoba, a little farther down the highway, is a tropical town dominated by pinks and blues. It's a center for rail shipping of crops you see along the road—coffee growing in the shade, tobacco drying on racks or in smoke barns, and vast emerald sugar-cane fields surrounding sugar mills. Cordoba's tropical personality is emphasized by the presence of peacocks and other vibrantly plumed creatures, and by the numerous groves of sweet, colorful tropical fruits.

Founded by the Spaniards in 1618, Cordoba has a vital heritage. Originally the Totonacs inhabited this area; the Aztecs, led by Moctezuma, conquered them in 1456. The culmination of the War for Independence took place in Cordoba: The last Spanish viceroy, arriving in Veracruz after the war was over, met Iturbide (first ruler of the independent country) in Cordoba in July 1821, and formally acknowledged Mexico's independence.

Down toward the coast are the fields and groves that make eating here a delight. You'll see ragged banana patches, papaya groves, spreading mango trees, trees that bear enormous avocados, and fields of pineapples. Beyond the cultivated areas, agriculture gives way to rank jungle growth; only a thatched hut in a clearing relieves the monotonous greenery.

You reach the coast at Boca del Rio, a ramshackle, tropical-looking village with coconut palms, pink or buff thatched huts, a weedy plaza, and a tiny church. Stop to watch the townspeople fishing from their boats. Nearby coffee plantations are open for touring.

Jalapa

If you want to make a loop trip from Mexico City to the coast and back, you might consider taking Highway 190-D east to Puebla where it intersects Highway 150 and heads on to the Gulf via Cordoba. The return trip to Mexico City along Highway 140, by way of Jalapa, repeats many of the impressions you get on the Cordoba road, but the climb is steadier and you reach pine forests and the plateau sooner. If you're familiar with the history of the Spanish conquest of Mexico, this trip will be much more vivid and absorbing. The road follows the route Cortes took in 1519, after he scuttled his ships at Veracruz and marched on to Moctezuma's capital.

Jalapa is worth more than just a fleeting stop. This quiet state capital has colorful hillside streets and exuberant vegetation; photographers will be able to get delightful close-ups as well as panoramas.

Built on a sloping hillside, Jalapa is known for the variety of tropical fruits and flowers that blossom profusely in its many gardens. The city is home to the University of Veracruz, which has its own symphony, publishing facilities, and museum housing Totonac and Olmec artifacts. Juarez Park, near the massive restored Metropolitan Cathedral, contains colossal Olmec heads and pieces of Aztec and Huastec work.

Clavijero Botanical Gardens, about a mile southwest of the city on the road to Coatepec, contains an arboretum, a palmetum, and research gardens; many cultural events take place here on Sunday during spring and summer. Coatepec is famous for its orchids; one of the large nurseries is on the town's main square.

You'll appreciate the resolute drive of the conquistadors when you cross the 8,000-foot pass beyond the town (near the 14,048-foot peak of the volcano Cofre de Perote) and see the desolate, windswept highland plains.

Near the town of Perote you'll see grim Fort San Carlos, built 200 years ago by the Spaniards to accommodate troops protecting Mexico City–Veracruz stagecoaches from attack by bandits. During World War II, the fort served as a prison for aliens; today it's a rehabilitation center where Mexican inmates produce and sell craft items.

Mitla's intricately carved ruins, dating from A.D. 500, were part of a fabled city of the gods and a pre-Hispanic burial site.

Handmade yarn dolls are sold by Indian women in the small village of Mitla. A pair of girl and boy dolls costs around $15.

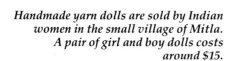

Oaxaca

Oaxaca has given many travelers some of their warmest, richest memories of Mexico. The city lies 340 miles southeast of Mexico City—a day's drive by way of Cuautla (a faster route than through Puebla), about 18 hours by overnight train with Pullman accommodations, 12 hours by first-class bus, or 45 minutes by commercial airliner. This Indian community is worth a stop on any trip continuing south of Mexico City.

An Indian city

This far south of the border, you're less conscious of being a *turista* and are treated more as one of Mexico's own people. Even the climate of Oaxaca is friendly.

Capital of the state of Oaxaca, the city is set in a broad valley at the center of a constellation of Indian villages. Founded as Antequera in 1522 by a group of Spanish soldiers, the city was renamed Oaxaca—a corruption of the Indian word *quauhxyacac* ("place of trees")—in 1529 by Charles V, who granted the valley to Cortes as his private estate.

The city's many colonial buildings are noteworthy for their massiveness and for the lovely pale green color of the local stone used in their construction. Ambling along the wide one-way streets is a pleasure. You'll notice that one street is occupied only by doctors, another by lawyers, and so on. The city is immaculate.

In contrast to Mexico City, Oaxaca's pace is low-key, and its small-town atmosphere is unspoiled. Yet with a population of around 200,000, it's the most important urban center between the capital and the Guatemalan frontier. Descendants of the Zapotec and Mixtec builders of prehistoric Monte Alban (see page 124) comprise two-thirds of the state's population.

Oaxaca is not known for its night life and offers practically none of the tourist amusements available in other parts of Mexico. Instead, its main attractions are the majestic ruins nearby and the market towns of the colorfully garbed Indian people.

Around town. One of the liveliest spots in Oaxaca is the zocalo, heart and soul of the city. On one side stands the cathedral, which boasts a clock donated by a Spanish king; around the plaza, streetside cafes accommodate diners and drinkers. Every evening a band performs in the zocalo, attracting tourists and townspeople alike.

Five blocks north of the zocalo is the imposing, incredibly beautiful Santo Domingo Church; its interior displays the most gorgeous baroque decoration in all of Mexico. The cloistered ex-convent next to it contains the state's Regional Museum, where priceless pre-Hispanic treasures excavated at Monte Alban and Mitla are displayed. A visit is well worth the small admission fee.

The Rufino Tamayo Museum of Pre-Historic Art (Avenida Morelos 503), housed in a lovely colonial villa, contains the personal pre-Hispanic art collection of this world-famous artist. There is a charge for admission.

A massive 16th-century structure on Avenida Independencia is dedicated to the Virgin of Solitude, who is said to have arrived miraculously at the site of the church during construction. The well-dressed, black stone statue is believed to have special healing powers.

The home of Benito Juarez and his former teacher contains period furniture, books, and memorabilia connected with the two men. You pay an admission fee to visit the small house at Garcia Vigil 609.

Markets. The old Benito Juarez Market, 2 blocks southeast of the zocalo, still bustles on Saturday morning. Two blocks south of that site you'll see a crafts market. But the real action takes place at the Saturday Market, south of downtown.

It's a crowded, fascinating place where you can see the Oaxaqueños and learn about their lives. People from surrounding villages come to barter under billowing canvas sun shades. They may bring flowers, rope, or tin-can mousetraps. There may be a woodcarver who has brought his year's work—a few treasured mythical beasts, lovingly painted—or a seamstress from the state's Pacific side, whose traditional blouses are colored with the purple ink of the sea-dwelling *caracol* (snail).

Woven items are still made with a backstrap loom; pottery is coiled without benefit of a wheel. You'll want to bargain. Take along a piece of paper to write down the price you want to pay; show it to the seller and he or she will respond with another figure. You can continue crossing out numbers until you arrive at a mutually satisfactory amount. Not much Spanish is spoken; most of the conversation is carried on in the local Indian dialect.

Crafts. You don't have to attend a market to look for handicrafts—they will come to you. Settle back in the shade of the porticoes facing the zocalo. While you sip a cool drink, vendors parade by with striped serapes, bright rebozos, and lacy golden necklaces. You can bargain right from your table.

It's an easy walk to craft shops in town; you'll find most of them in a small area north and east of the zocalo. Long-time favorites include Yalalag (corner of Alcala and Morelos), Casa Brena (on Piño Suarez), and the government-run Fonart store (Garcia Vigil and M. Bravo). Look for some of Oaxaca's specialities: pottery, gold and silver jewelry, skirts, blouses, men's shirts, rugs, and tablecloths. Oaxaca's knives are famous for their horn grips with handcarved eagles and for their fine steel blades (often etched with a proverb).

Best prices for crafts are in the villages where they are made. Indeed, so many colorful markets take place in surrounding villages, that you could keep busy for a week visiting them all. Tours to many of these villages are available from your hotel.

Monte Alban

The ruins of Monte Alban, on a hilltop 6 miles southwest of Oaxaca, are a monument to the master builders of pre-Hispanic Mexico. For the best sense of the past, visit the brooding ruins early in the morning or at sunset. This is probably the country's most impressive sight. The hill's summit was leveled and reshaped, and artificial esplanades and structures were raised in harmonious groupings over a period of 17 centuries (700 B.C.–A.D. 1000). The earliest buildings are those found in the inner structure of the Temple of the Dancers, and the arrowhead-shaped observatory.

In its glory, Monte Alban covered 25 square miles and had a population of some 50,000. As you see it today, the city is composed of a huge central plaza, limited to the north and south by acropolis-type platforms and enclosed on the east and west by lower buildings. At a lower level behind the northern platform are several tombs open to the public—among them the famous Tomb 7, where archeologists discovered the magnificent jewelry now on display in Oaxaca's Regional Museum.

Originally inhabited by Zapotecs, Monte Alban was taken over by Mixtec invaders around A.D. 1200. The Mixtecs rejuvenated the site and buried their rulers in the former Zapotec temples. Over 150 of the elaborate burial sites have been excavated.

Monte Alban is open daily. You can buy a guidebook to the site at the small shop near the entrance. A museum displays some of the artifacts. Though guides discourage vendors, you may be approached by people offering to sell "artifacts" they have uncovered. Don't be tempted; they're probably fakes. All bona fide discoveries belong to the Mexican government and it's against the law to take them out of the country.

Mitla

You drive through the tidy village of Mitla (about an hour from Oaxaca on a paved road) to visit the remarkable ruins on the outskirts of town. Mitla is another of the Zapotec-Mixtec ceremonial centers, although much smaller than Monte Alban.

Intricately carved stone fretwork characterizes the façades of Mitla's temples; designs are geometric, arranged in repetitive patterns. This was the fabled abode of Mictlantecuhtli, Lord of the Underworld, and a sacred city for the burial of Indian kings. The exhibits in the Frissell Museum of Zapotec Art off the village plaza will help to explain the site.

Mitla ruins are open daily. As with other archeological sites, a small admission fee is charged.

Villages around Oaxaca

You can drive easily to most of the villages near Oaxaca; you can also reach all of them by local bus (station on Trujano, 3 blocks west of the zocalo) or by taxi (be sure to settle the fare before leaving). Some tours to Monte Alban or Mitla include a stop at market towns.

Etla, 12 miles north of Oaxaca, has a Wednesday market. You need not arrive until 11 A.M. or later to see peak activity. The village is noted for its *quesillo,* a cheese boiled into long ribbons and then rolled into a ball. Also look for toys woven from straw.

Santa Maria Atzompa produces pottery—pots with a green glaze and small figures of animals playing musical instruments. English is rarely spoken in the village. The road to the village from Highway 190 is not recommended for the family car.

Culiapan, 7 miles southwest of Oaxaca on the road that passes Monte Alban, contains a Dominican church and one of Mexico's most massive former convents. Begun in 1555, the building was never finished. Zaachila, a few miles past Culiapan, was once a Zapotec center and later a Mixtec community. Its weekly market is on Thursday.

San Bartolo Coyotepec, about 6 miles south of Oaxaca along Highway 175, is easily reached by car. (But take note that there are two "Coyotepecs" along the highway; San Bartolo is the second.) Black, unglazed pottery, made without the help of a wheel, is a trademark of this area.

Santo Tomas Jalisco, beyond Coyotepec, specializes in *fajas* (sashes) woven in the ancient manner, using the backstrap loom—one end tied around a tree and the other to a strap around the waist of the weaver. The villagers also make handsome jackets and shoulder bags.

Ocotlan, 12 miles beyond Coyotepec, has a colorful bustling Friday market; it's unusually clean. Occasionally, an Indian girl brings in a beautifully embroidered and pleated blouse to sell. Tall stacks of baskets in all sizes and shapes are for sale.

Santa Maria del Tule, 4 miles southeast of Oaxaca on Highway 190, is renowned as the home of Mexico's largest tree, a 2,000-year-old cypress growing in front of a colorful little church. A small handicraft market is directly across the street.

Tlacochahuaya, a rural pueblo a short distance farther along the highway to Mitla, is noted for its monastery. Indian artists decorated the interior with colorful traditional paintings. Teotitlan del Valle, beyond Tlacochahuaya about 2 miles, dates back to pre-Hispanic times. Its center is a 17th-century church. Best buys are woolen serapes and rugs.

Tlacolula, beyond Tlacochahuaya and about 1 mile to the right of Highway 190, is the site of a fascinating Sunday market. Bargain for extremely well-made serapes.

South of Oaxaca

Several highways from Oaxaca take travelers deeper into Southern Mexico. Highway 175 leads over to the Pacific coast, joining Highway 200 at Puerto Angel. Highway 190, the Pan American Highway, passes through the state of Chiapas en route to the Guatemalan border.

Coastal Oaxaca

Several years ago adventurous travelers in search of inexpensive accommodations, good fishing and swimming waters, and uncrowded beaches discovered the two coastal villages of Puerto Escondido and Puerto Angel (see page 44). Today the sleepy villages' wide stretches of sand and their unhurried atmosphere continue to attract visitors who demand little more from a vacation than relaxation.

Better accommodations, additional tourist facilities, and an airport have been added. A paved road connects Oaxaca with Puerto Angel; Puerto Escondido lies 50 miles away on paved Highway 200. (The road from Oaxaca to Puerto Escondido is not completely paved.)

But the sleepy coast is waking up. Mexico's newest multimillion dollar resort, Huatulco, is taking shape on the neighboring nine bays (see page 45).

To the border

Highway 190 continues south from Oaxaca to the Isthmus of Tehuantepec, where the Gulf of Mexico and the Pacific Ocean are only 120 miles apart. The highway follows the south side of the isthmus through flat country covered with scrubby, thorny brush, then climbs through a series of thickly forested mountains and broad, soft, uncultivated river valleys to the area's largest cities, Tuxtla Gutierrez and San Cristobal de las Casas.

Oaxaca's Christmas Fiestas

 December's colorful holiday festivities in Oaxaca start about a week before Christmas. Make reservations well in advance if you plan to attend.

Fete for a saint

A three-day fiesta in Oaxaca, beginning December 18, honors the city's patron saint, the Virgin of Solitude. At this time of year her name seems singularly inappropriate for the festivals held in her honor. Carnival-like activities lasting well into the evening center around the Sanctuario de la Soledad, an ornate baroque church a few blocks west of the central zocalo.

As soon as that fiesta is over, the Oaxaqueños begin decorating the town for Christmas. Moss, an essential item for the numerous nativity scenes, is brought from surrounding areas by the Zapotec Indians. Trees and shrubs are adorned with ornaments and gay piñatas, and amusement stands arise overnight around Oaxaca's cathedral at the north side of the zocalo.

Restaurants under arcades around the plaza provide the best seats for watching the gaiety. It won't be long before the serape and rebozo vendors are stopping by your table to show their wares.

Night of the radish

By December 23 you smell the *buñuelos* frying. These light, crispy pancakes, sprinkled with pink sugar and drizzled with syrup, are served from many booths around the plaza. Custom demands that, after eating the buñuelo, you smash the saucer in which it is served.

That same evening, the radish contest is decided. This yearly competition of imaginative designs created entirely from special elongated, twisted radishes displays some unusual creative skills. The designs typically depict religious scenes, but one year's winner was an Apollo spaceship complete with astronauts. After the prizes are awarded, the radish figures are sold.

Christmas Eve parade

The traditional Christmas Eve parade starts around 9 P.M. Many villages throughout the state participate, each contributing a float and band. People marching ahead of the floats carry colored lanterns and ornaments, little boys shoot firecrackers, and all the bands play different tunes—simultaneously! It all ends with a spectacular fireworks display and midnight Mass.

. . . south of Oaxaca

Few settlements can be found along this road. If you're driving the route, it's wise to fill up with gasoline before leaving Juchitan; though there is a station at La Ventosa Junction (where Highway 185 crosses the isthmus from the Gulf of Mexico), it may not have unleaded fuel.

At Tapanatepec, you can take an alternate road (Highway 200) south to the Guatemalan border. This lowland highway is popular; it goes through Arriaga, then on to Tapachula.

Both routes from Tapanatepec are paved all the way to the border, but the coast route avoids the dangerous El Tapan stretch of Highway 190–a winding 23 miles of road through a canyon where landslides and flash floods sometimes create difficulties and delays.

Tehuantepec

If the day is hot and humid when you arrive on this west side of the Isthmus of Tehuantepec, you may wonder why you've ventured this far south into Mexico. The towns and villages seem lackluster. The countryside is tropical, but not as dramatic or luxuriant as in other areas. You'll soon discover that Tehuantepec's main attractions are the tall, graceful Tehuana women and the uncrowded Pacific beaches.

In Tehuantepec the women run the marketplace and the men stay home or in the fields. In fact, in this matriarchal society, women are the community's most active members, even in local governmental affairs.

As to the beaches, you can swim inside the breakwater (surf can be rough) at Salina Cruz, a fast-developing port about 10 miles from Tehuantepec. Swimming and the general atmosphere are even more delightful about 4 miles to the south, at the small fishing village of La Ventosa.

Juchitan

Juchitan is 17 miles east of Tehuantepec in open country. The two towns have been rivals over the years. One manifestation of this rivalry is a tacit competition in dress—residents of the towns strive to outdo each other in the splendor of their traditional costumes. Juchitan is about the same size as Tehuantepec, but more spread out; it has larger squares and the streets are wider and gracefully shaded by trees. The marketplace overflows from a high-ceilinged shed into a series of arches or *portales* on one side of the main square.

Marimba music is favored, and it is here that the *sandunga* is danced. In rhythm a waltz, the obligatory turns display the skirted costume to swirling advantage.

Tuxtla Gutierrez

Five driving hours—160 miles—separate Juchitan from Tuxtla Gutierrez, capital of the state of Chiapas. Tuxtla Gutierrez is a prosperous, modern commercial center that serves the coffee plantations scattered throughout the surrounding hills. The state museum on the east side of town has a collection of colonial and pre-Hispanic artifacts.

San Cristobal de las Casas

San Cristobal de las Casas, clean and quiet, is set 7,000 feet above sea level, in a fertile basin ringed with green mountains. One of these mountains, El Chichon, 50 miles northwest of the town, erupted in 1982, covering the city with a layer of ash.

San Cristobal's charm lies in its setting and its solid colonial architecture, and in the comings and goings of the many Indian groups who live in the region. This is truly a photographer's paradise. A note of caution: Indians may refuse to have their photographs taken, or may expect payment.

Visit the 16th-century cathedral on the plaza; it hides a magnificent interior behind an ordinary façade. The plaza itself is charming, with a lacy ironwork bandstand surrounded by shrubs and brilliant flowering plants. The Church of Santo Domingo, 6 blocks away, is impressive on the inside and has a dazzlingly ornate façade; the adjacent convent houses a museum displaying Indian handicrafts, most of which are for sale. The Na-Bolom archeological and ethnological museum and library (Calle Vicente Guerrero 33) is also worth a visit; admission is charged.

Calle Guadalupe is the street of the shops—not the curio shops of tourist centers but *tiendas* (stores) that sell to the Indians. For several blocks north of the plaza, you look through unmarked doorways at stacks of sombreros, large quantities of leather shoulder bags, and dozens of serapes and rebozos in vivid colors and interesting weaves and designs. The market on the eastern edge of town is of interest because, like all Mexican trading centers, it mirrors the area's economic life.

San Cristobal is the departure point for several exciting trips, especially if you enjoy horseback riding. Pack expeditions, arranged locally, can take you into the tropical highland forests for a look at half-buried Maya sites and a visit to Lacandon Indian villages.

Nearby caves attract speleologists, and the beautiful Montebello Lakes are a day-long excursion away. If you're a hardy soul, take a 2½-hour jeep trip to the Indian town of Tenanapa—where two rivers meet, cascade down in two waterfalls, and then plunge underground. Tenanapa's busy Sunday market is worth a visit, too.

Colorful Indians of Chiapas

Tired from dancing, Chiapas men doze at San Cristobal de las Casas festival

Deep in the jungles of the southern state of Chiapas some of Mexico's most fascinating Indian tribes are found.

Lacandons. The Lacandon Indians, descendants of the Mayas, cling valiantly to their peaceful primitive culture. Though their population has decreased to around 300, many of their old ways of life remain. They still paddle rough-hewn dugout canoes up and down the jungle rivers on their way to Yaxchilan, a difficult-to-reach Maya ruin where they worship the ancient gods believed to inhabit the site.

Some are so completely isolated from modern innovations that they still rely on primitive tools such as wooden knives and bows and arrows. The comfort of a warm blanket is a luxury unknown to many of these people; they sleep in hammocks at night, kept warm by the embers of a fire.

Chamulas. If the Lacandons are the recluses of Chiapas, the Chamulas are the area's most progressive and aggressive Indians. In the mid-19th century, they rose in open warfare against the "white" town of San Cristobal de las Casas. Today their aggressiveness takes the form of hard trading in the marketplace.

Chamula men can be distinguished by their black, or sometimes white, tunics; the colored decoration and woven pattern of the tunic indicate the village from which each man comes. The women wear black *huipiles* (blouses) with red tassels.

Zinacantecos. The Zinacanteco Indians of Chiapas provide local color. Their handwoven straw hats with wide brims are profusely decorated with brightly colored ribbons. The Zinacantecos' basic attire consists of white cotton shirts and trousers, tunics, colorful serapes, and kerchiefs worn around the neck. On their feet are traditional Mexican huaraches, with heelguards reminiscent of ancient Indian footwear.

Beribboned straw hat quickly identifies this Zinacanteco Indian

Stalwart visitors climb the Great Pyramid at Uxmal on the Yucatan Peninsula.

Yucatan Peninsula

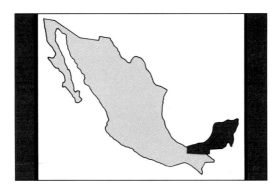

The Yucatan Peninsula—that immense outthrust of land dividing the Gulf of Mexico from the Caribbean—is so uniformly flat that it approaches monotony. But behind its cloak of sameness you'll find a wealth of archeological treasures and some of Mexico's finest resorts. Images that will linger in your mind: the smooth, brown faces of Maya Indians, the charm of the colonial city of Merida, the unexpected beauty of temples rising in the middle of nowhere, and the gemlike brilliance of the Caribbean.

Reasons to visit

The peninsula is shared by the states of Yucatan, Campeche, and Quintana Roo—all of which were once the land of the Maya. For years, the Maya sites of Chichen Itza, Uxmal, Kabah, Tulum, and others less well known to the casual traveler have lured archeologists and adventurers to this remote part of Mexico. The Yucatan would be interesting even without its ruins, but they make the peninsula one of the world's most fascinating tourist areas. As time and restoration funds allow, more ruins are becoming easily accessible to visitors.

Three islands lie close to the mainland just off the northeast tip of the peninsula: Cozumel and Isla Mujeres are accessible by boat and air, and a short causeway reaches Cancun. Many tourists come to the Yucatan just for the sparkling white beaches and the clear aquamarine waters that surround these resort spots, ignoring the region's antiquities.

Whatever your choice, the Yucatan Peninsula has a lot to offer. In addition to temples and beaches, you'll become acquainted with the cuisine, crafts, and lifestyle of today's Maya Indians, a friendly people with sparkling eyes and spontaneous smiles.

Before the resort development, the Yucatan was famous for henequen (sisal) rope and twine. Until the end of World War II, the Yucatan supplied most of the world's high-grade sisal. Since then, synthetic fibers have cut sharply into the market, but you'll still see vast carpets of agave (the plant from which sisal is made) throughout the area.

Getting around

You need a car to thoroughly explore the Yucatan Peninsula. Though it's far easier to fly into Merida or Cancun and rent one, many people drive from Mexico City, some 25 hours away. U.S. motorists who take the highways along the northeast coast enter the land of the Maya at Villahermosa.

With the area's good paved roads and the short driving times between major cities, you can make a loop through the peninsula, visiting archeological sites en route. From Campeche, Merida is about 3 hours away, Cancun is 4 or 5 hours from Merida, and Chetumal is about the same distance from Cancun.

Mountains of Panama-type hats line shelves of small store in Campeche.

The Gulf Side

Driving Highway 180 south from Villahermosa to Campeche involves two ferry crossings and two toll bridges. It's best not to use this route if you're driving a trailer; the undercarriage has a good chance of being severely damaged. Instead, make the trip on inland Highway 186, a longer route that rejoins 180 at Laguna de Terminos.

The first toll ferry along Highway 180 crosses the San Pedro River 15 miles south of the town of Frontera. The ferry runs frequently throughout the day; the trip takes just 10 minutes. The second ferry leaves from Zacatal, just beyond the lighthouse community of Xicalango. It runs to Ciudad del Carmen on the tip of Isla del Carmen, an island separated from the mainland by Laguna de Terminos. This crossing takes about 30 minutes.

Beyond the Ciudad del Carmen, the island stretches for 22 miles to Puerto Real, where a toll bridge connects the island and mainland. From here, you proceed along palm-lined Highway 180 for 65 miles to the seaside ship-building town of Champoton and the junction with Highway 261, an alternate route to Merida.

Highway 186 from Villahermosa, the inland route, is more monotonous—you won't see much tropical vegetation for most of the way—but you won't have to depend on the ferries. At Escarcega, the highway turns east to Chetumal on the Caribbean, traversing the peninsula at its base.

If you want to go on to Campeche, take Highway 261 north from Escarcega to Champoton, where Highways 180 and 261 meet. It's 40 miles from Champoton to Campeche, a leg that alternates between straight stretches along beaches and winding stretches through hills.

Campeche

Campeche, the progressive and increasingly modern capital of the state of Campeche, is one of Mexico's most photogenic spots. It was the first permanent Spanish settlement on the peninsula, founded shortly after the Spanish crown granted the area to Francisco de Montejo in 1526. A fascinating old seaport, Campeche has a wall topped by forts built in the 17th century as protection against pirates. Today, the city's new section rises directly from the beach.

With minimum splash and maximum wing spread, Gulf flamingos take to the sky.

The city is an important shrimp-fishing center. Along the waterfront south of town, you'll see craftsmen building shrimp boats, all the fittings made by hand from local hardwoods. Most of the shrimping activity centers around a pier a little to the south of town; you can wander along it to watch the shrimp being unloaded. North along the waterfront, thatched huts are sprinkled among the palms that grow down to the water's edge. Here, anglers work on their boats or dry and mend nets.

Around town. Some moderately priced hotels and the tourism office are centrally located. The area has some good shopping buys, including finely woven Panama-type (*jipijapa*) hats, hammocks, and wooden items. A state-operated crafts store is located in Fort San Carlos, at the beginning of Calle 8.

You can visit the old wall and ancient forts either on your own or with an English-speaking guide. Two museums are located within the city's fortifications: the Archeology Museum, in Fort San Miguel a couple of miles west of town, contains Maya artifacts; the History Museum, at Fort Soledad in town, has mementos of the area's piratical past. Both museums are open daily, except Monday and Sunday afternoon.

Edzna. About 40 miles west of Campeche lie the ruins of Edzna, best known as the place that the Maya calendar was devised. The most interesting building is a five-story structure resembling a Greek ruin and called the Acropolis.

Merida

The hospitable city of Merida, capital of Yucatan state, makes a good base for exploring the important Maya ruins at Chichen Itza and Uxmal as well as the lesser-known sites of Kabah, Labna, Sayil, Dzibilchaltun, and Izamal. The city lies 20 miles inland from the Gulf of Mexico on the western side of the peninsula. Once, all flights to the Yucatan landed here; with the advent of Cancun, however, this delightful city is too often bypassed.

Two highways reach Merida from Campeche. Highway 180 branches off north from Highway 261 at Chencoyi. This is an interesting route through Maya villages that have changed little over the centuries. At Hecelchakan, there's a museum with artifacts discovered on the island of Jaina—the site of a pre-Hispanic Maya cemetery.

. . . the Gulf side

Highway 261 provides access to the ruins south of Merida. At Muna, Highway 184 takes off southeast to Chetumal, capital of Quintana Roo.

The city. Merida is a charming blend of large, old colonial buildings downtown, modern homes on the outskirts, and thatched Indian huts on the streets in between. The town has a large, open market, well-kept parks and boulevards, good hotels, and excellent restaurants.

Merida was founded in 1542 on the site of the Maya city of T'Ho, but its Spanish heritage is predominant. The Yucatan was long isolated from the rest of Mexico and, for a few years, even politically independent; during its isolation, the area cultivated European markets and manners instead of Mexican ones. Now the largest city on the peninsula and linked by highway, rail, and air to central Mexico, Merida plays a vital role as the processing and distribution center for local products.

The people. Merida's people are friendly and very cordial to foreigners. They consider themselves Yucatecans, distinct and apart from Mexicans. Often you'll see faces that closely resemble those on the stone carvings in Uxmal or Chichen Itza. The dress of many of the women is the *huipil*, a long white overblouse, embroidered at neck and hem; it extends below the knees and may be worn with or without a lacy petticoat.

In other parts of Mexico, homes are closed and surrounded by high walls; but in Merida, doors and windows are open to the street. In the evening, people sit in chairs on their front stoops and chat with passers-by.

Highlights. Many visitors remark on the beauty and tranquility of Merida's zocalo, tree-shaded Plaza de la Independencia, with its topiary and its S-shaped benches. Two buildings that face the plaza are of particular historic interest—the fortresslike cathedral and the Montejo mansion (now a bank), both built in the mid-16th century by the Spanish conqueror and founder of the city, Francisco de Montejo. Notice the statues of armored soldiers standing on the heads of Indians on the mansion's beautifully carved façade. The façade, lighted at night, is truly an impressive sight.

The City Hall, also facing the plaza, dates from the Montejo era; the State House is much newer and noted for the abstract murals over the stairway and for its Hall of History (free admission).

Other notable attractions downtown include the restored Peon Contreras Theater and three of the city's 17th-century arches, built originally as part of a defense system against Maya uprisings. Four blocks southeast of the plaza, a colorful market offers a good selection of authentic crafts.

The restored Palacio Canton on Paseo Montejo, once the impressive home of a prominent Merida family, now houses the Museum of Archeology and History. Admission is charged to view the impressive collection of Maya relics.

The Hermitage of Santa Isabel at Calles 66 and 77 was built in 1748 and soon became known as the Convent of Safe Travel, a place for colonial travelers on their way to the port of Campeche to stop and pray for a safe journey. The restored hermitage is surrounded by a spacious botanical garden, the location of weekend musical performances.

Getting around. It's not difficult to get around Merida on foot, though it is somewhat tricky to drive within the city. As in most older Mexican towns, streets are one-way and very narrow. All streets running north to south are even-numbered; those running east to west are odd-numbered. You can tour all of Merida for a few pesos in a *calesa* (horse-drawn cab). Best place to find one is at Cepeda Park.

On the Paseo Montejo (Merida's equivalent of Mexico City's Paseo de la Reforma), you pass splendid buildings painted in pastel blues, yellows, and pinks—some Victorian or French in style. Many of these large mansions were formerly town houses of henequen barons.

Food. Don't miss savoring the delicious food of the Yucatan; it's a cuisine different from any other in Mexico. *Cochinita pibil* (*pib* means "barbecue pit" in Maya) is pork baked in banana leaves and flavored with *achiote* (red seeds ground into a paste whose flavor combines beautifully with meat and fish). Another specialty is *queso relleno*—an Edam-type cheese hollowed out and stuffed with ground meat, raisins, nuts, and spices.

Shopping. Many shops are found on Calle 57 between Calles 60 and 68. You'll find a variety of henequen items, ranging from bags to mats and hammocks. Straw hats are popular buys, as is inlaid coral jewelry. Stay away from tortoise-shell items; you're not allowed to bring them into the U.S.

Entertainment. The park behind the city hall is often the site of free music and dance performances on Monday evening. Musical events also take place in Santa Ana Park on Wednesday evening, and in Santa Lucia Park on Thursday. *Jarañas* (Yucatecan dances and music) are offered on most Friday evenings at the Hermitage of Santa Isabel. Peon Contreras Theater often showcases concerts and other events.

Dzibilchaltun

North of Merida on the highway to the Gulf, a 6-mile paved turnoff to the right leads to the ruins of Dzibilchaltun, an ancient ceremonial center. One of the largest known Maya sites, it covers almost 20 square miles. For the most part the ruins are unrestored, though a major

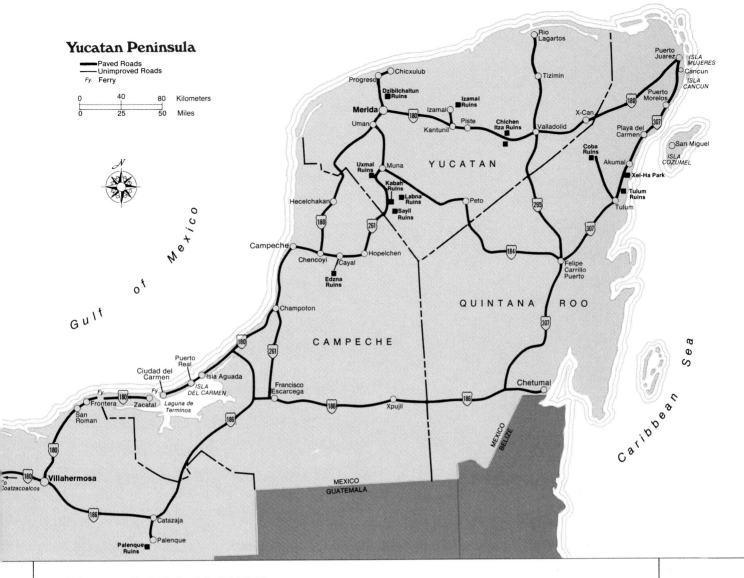

DETAILS AT A GLANCE

Yucatan Peninsula

How to get there

Paved highways to towns and major ruins make this area easily accessible to motorists, but it's a long, dull drive through Yucatan scrub.

By air. Many U.S. travelers jet directly to the Yucatan. From Mexico City it's a 90-minute flight; Cancun takes about 2 hours. Merida and Cancun have jet terminals.

By road. The easiest and most flexible way to tour the Yucatan is to fly into a large city, rent an air-conditioned car, and explore on your own. Regular bus and train service is only for the patient.

Tours

Package tours from Merida and Cancun stop at the major ruins of Chichen Itza, Uxmal, and Tulum, but you won't have much time at each site (see the "Essentials" section on page 158).

Accommodations

Interesting colonial-style hotels (many with pools) make Merida a good base for exploring the Yucatan. Cancun's accommodations range from condominiums and villas to deluxe beachfront hotels. Cozumel offers a variety of resorts, most geared to skin divers. You'll also find simple hotels in other cities and some comfortable accommodations at Uxmal and Chichen Itza (see page 158).

Climate & clothes

Usually humid, Yucatan weather is best from October to March, with clear sunny days and cool evenings. Expect brief tropical downpours in summer. Dress for heat and bring a bathing suit for the beautiful warm water. Wear comfortable clothes and rubber-soled shoes for climbing around ruins.

Chichen Itza's immense ball court, once scene of ancient Maya games, still sports side wall hoop.

. . . the Gulf side

portion of the central area has been cleared. Within this clearing is a *cenote,* a large, deep, natural well, into which offerings (including some human victims) were thrown to the water gods, and from which a great many artifacts have been recovered.

Also in the cleared area is the site's most imposing structure, the Temple of the Seven Dolls, so named because archeologists discovered seven rubber dolls during excavation. At the entrance to the site is a small but well-organized museum that, for orientation's sake, should be the first stop on your tour. The site also has a small crafts center.

The port of Progreso

Progreso, Yucatan's most important seaport for the fishing and henequen industries, is located on the Gulf of Mexico about 22 miles north of Merida. Freighters tie up in the deep water at the end of a mile-long concrete pier. To watch the activity, you can drive out to the end of the pier on a roadway flanked by a railroad track and a pedestrian walkway.

Izamal

Izamal, the ancient holy city of the Maya, lies 45 miles east of Merida. To get there, take the turnoff from Highway 180 en route to Puerto Juarez. The ruins on the outskirts of present-day Izamal are largely overgrown and difficult to see. In the late 1500s, a Franciscan church-monastery was erected over some of the ruined buildings; the huge monastery and the Kinich Kakmo Pyramid (dedicated to the god of the midday sun) are excavated.

Modern Izamal is a charming town; horse-drawn carriages and the tranquil plaza contribute to the restful, unhurried atmosphere. A large religious festival takes place here on October 25, with processions, dances, and musical performances.

Chichen Itza

About 35 miles beyond Izamal (80 miles from Merida) on Highway 180, just past the village of Piste, are the ruins of Chichen Itza—the most visited of all Maya cities unearthed to date in the Yucatan.

The Olmec, Mexico's Mother Culture

Until 40 years ago, considerable mystery surrounded the Olmecs. Today archeologists agree that their civilization had its beginnings around 2000 B.C. and that their homeland was on the Gulf Coast, in the jungles of the present states of Veracruz and Tabasco.

Though their origins and the reasons for their disappearance are still being debated by the experts, it is believed that this ancient race was Mexico's earliest advanced civilization. They are thought to be the initiators of all that became known as "high culture" in the pre-Columbian world of Mexico.

The majority of Olmec artifacts date from around 1100 B.C., the time when most of their religious centers were started along the Gulf of Mexico.

The Olmec civilization

Their name comes from the Indian word *ulli*, or rubber, and means "inhabitants of the country of rubber."

Stone was scarce in the Olmecs' jungle home, and that prevented them from developing a lasting architecture. Structures found at La Venta, San Lorenzo, and Tres Zapotes are earthen—temple bases arranged around plazas, forming ceremonial centers. The stone they were able to bring into the area was used for carving colossal figures, notably the so-called baby-face heads.

Almost everything the Olmecs constructed was on a large scale. The gigantic heads (some with Negroid and others with Oriental features) stand as high as 10 feet and weigh in the neighborhood of 20 tons. A circular pyramid at the La Venta ceremonial center in the jungle rises over 100 feet from a base of over 500 feet in diameter.

Though their architecture wasn't sophisticated, the Olmecs possessed impressive intellectual and artistic skills. They developed a numbering system, hieroglyphic writing, and a prototype for the Maya calendar—the most exact ever devised in the ancient world.

Brooding majesty characterizes stone head in Villahermosa's outdoor museum.

The Olmecs were also masters at carving stone and jade. Particularly notable in their culture was the deification of the jaguar; feline motifs in pottery, figurines, and masks all signal Olmec influence.

As an ethnic entity, the Olmecs had disappeared by the beginning of the Christian era. Groups of them wandered and merged with other peoples, spreading Olmec achievements throughout Mexican territory, into Oaxaca, the central highlands, as far north and west as Colima and Guerrero on the Pacific coast, and even into Guatemala and El Salvador.

Viewing their world

The center at La Venta, close to the mouth of the Tonala River, was one of the few Olmec sites that visitors could reach without too much difficulty. But access is now limited due to oil discoveries in the area.

Though earth mounds and a few stone monuments still remain, most of the sculptures unearthed have been removed for display at the open-air museum in Villahermosa.

Other Olmec heads can be seen at the park in Jalapa in the state of Veracruz. Smaller Olmec relics are also exhibited at Mexico City's National Museum of Anthropology.

La Venta museum. You can view many of the ancient Olmec sculptures at La Venta Park and Museum in Villahermosa. Thirty sculptures have been transported from the archeological zone upriver and placed on exhibit in a lush garden. Included in the displays are three colossal stone heads, a tomb, and seven altars.

Laced with winding paths, the park is a pleasant place to wander at your leisure. Take along mosquito repellent. There is a small admission charge.

Tabasco's Museum of Anthropology. On the left bank of the Rio Grijalva in Villahermosa, the state's museum contains other mementos of the Olmec culture, including maps and photos of the archeological sites. Start your tour on the second floor. You'll pay a small admission fee to view the exhibits.

. . . the Gulf side

According to archeologists' theories, construction began in the city about A.D. 450. It was invaded by the Itza branch of the Mayas early in the 10th century and occupied late in that same century by the Toltecs, who superimposed upon it their architecture and culture.

Toltec ruins. North of the highway is the extensively restored group of structures preferred by sightseers. These buildings reflect the influence of the Toltecs, who occupied the city some time after the close of the Maya Classic period in A.D. 900.

The most imposing building is called El Castillo ("The Castle") on the Great Plaza. It's a pyramid some 75 feet high; each side of its square base is approximately 180 feet long. The pyramid is topped by a temple to Kukulkan, a god (called Quetzalcoatl elsewhere in Mexico) represented by a feathered snake. Inside the temple a remarkable spotted stone jaguar with green eyes may have served as a high priest's throne.

Also on the north side of Chichen Itza are the ruins of a huge ball court and many other buildings; one, the Temple of the Warriors, has an inner structure that may be visited during certain hours. Like the castle's inner temple, this structure was the original temple; the pyramid you see was built over it.

Central and Old Chichen ruins. On the south side of the highway older ruins, less impressive but equally interesting, are spread out over a large area reached by paths cut through the underbrush. El Caracol ("The Snail") is the predominant structure. Cylindrical in shape, it may have served as an observatory.

Visiting the site. Chichen Itza has a modern visitor center (museum, bookstore, restaurant, handicraft market). A sound-and-light show is presented each evening. Several hotels lie nearby (see page 158); make reservations, especially between Christmas and Easter week.

You'll need 2 days—preferably longer—to explore all the ruins in the area thoroughly, but you can take in the most significant structures in a day. Guides and cars may be secured in Merida and Cancun; package tours from these cities are also available.

Cave of Balancanche. The Cave of Balancanche, a labyrinth of passages and chambers 3 miles east of Chichen Itza, contains Maya and Toltec artifacts. A cenote filled with small, blind fish is located at the end of one passageway.

Valladolid

One of Yucatan's larger cities, Valladolid is 25 miles east of Chichen Itza on Highway 180. Near the center of town, an attractive park surrounds a large cenote, once the city's water supply. As you drive into town on the main highway, the cenote is a few blocks to the north. In late January, a festival called *Las Candelarias* features folk dances and colorful parades. If you're continuing on to the coast, it's wise to fill up here with gasoline and buy any necessary supplies.

Uxmal & other Maya ruins

One of the most successful architectural achievements of Maya civilization, the ancient city of Uxmal is noted for the symmetry and proportions of its buildings, constructed in the Puuc style of veneer masonry. Uxmal reached its peak in the last half of the Classic period (A.D. 600–900). From the 10th century on, it was ruled by a family of Mexican origin, and suffered a gradual decline under its foreign conquerors—as did all centers of Maya culture.

A heavy chain stretched along the almost vertical stairway at the oval pyramid of Temple of the Magician aids height-wary visitors in making the trip (120 steps) to the top. To the west, the Quadrangle of the Nuns is a great patio flanked by long rows of chambers; the façades are richly ornamented at roof level. A spectacular light-and-sound show is presented here nightly.

The majestic Palace of the Governor rises beyond the ball court. Its main façade is entirely covered with a frieze composed of thousands of tiny stone pieces fitted together to form serpents, latticework, thrones, huts, and columns. On the same great platform that gives added importance to this palace stands the elegantly simple, and comparatively small, House of the Turtles.

The front of the Great Pyramid, to the southwest, has been reconstructed. (This is a good spot for taking photos of the entire complex.) West of the pyramid lies a quadrangle known as the House of the Pigeons.

Uxmal, 50 miles south of Merida, is easily reached by car or on an organized tour. If you wish to spend some time exploring the ruins, stay in one of several hotels nearby (see page 158).

Kabah. The archeological site of Kabah lies 15 miles to the south. Its outstanding building is the Codz Poop (Rolled Mat), the façades of which are completely covered by masks of the long-nosed rain god, Chac. Many of the upturned noses are missing—taken as souvenirs by thoughtless sightseers. A large corbeled arch at Kabah marks the start of a road that once carried Maya religious processions to Uxmal.

Labna, Xlabpak & Sayil. To visit these lesser-known sites, reserve a car and driver at Kabah. The trip through the towering Yucatecan bush will take a full day. Highlights of the partially restored ruins include Labna's monumental arch, the Temple of Chac in Xlabpak, and the elegant three-story Palace of Sayil.

The Mexican Caribbean

On the Caribbean side of the Yucatan Peninsula the vegetation changes from thick bush to jungle—not dense, humid jungle, but the South Sea Islands variety—with palms fringing gleaming white beaches and turquoise waters. This is the location of Mexico's first planned resort, Cancun, and other popular destinations.

Isla Mujeres

The embarkation points for ferries to Isla Mujeres are just north of Cancun at Puerto Juarez and Punta Sam (a few miles north of town). There's also air service to the small island from Merida and Cozumel, but the boat ride shouldn't be missed. It's a photographic bonanza. The 12-mile round trip can be made in a day if you get to the port early enough; but since the number of hotels on the island is growing, you may want to stay overnight and revel in the tranquility and solitude.

The island is only 7 miles long and less than a mile wide. A popular boating excursion includes a look at the crumbling Maya ruin, a stop for swimming or snorkeling, and a seafood lunch. Sailing, fishing, and water-skiing are other activities available.

Cozumel

Cozumel, an island about 30 miles long and 12 miles wide, has long been attracting visitors: the first Spanish explorers landed in 1518; it was an off-duty recreation area for servicemen during World War II; and snorkelers began arriving after Jacques Cousteau extolled the grandeur of the Palancar Reef off its shores. You reach the island by plane (from Cancun and Merida) or by boat. It's a short ferry ride from Playa del Carmen.

All of the action is centered around the water. Resort hotels line the beaches north and south of the island's one town, which boasts a number of good restaurants and shops. Most visitors scoot around on motorbikes.

Cancun

Just south of Puerto Juarez, a coast-hugging road leads to the posh Mexican resort development called Cancun. Crystal-clear seas and spectacular offshore coral reefs are a few of Cancun's assets. Other attractions include deluxe hotels, a golf course, a marina, fine restaurants, and a variety of shops. Once a village of just 120 inhabitants, Cancun has grown explosively; its population now numbers around 150,000. More than 30 hotels and a variety of condominiums accommodate visitors.

Sports. Cancun's configuration makes it ideal for every type of water sport. Less than a mile wide and 12 miles long, the resort is bounded to the east by the Caribbean, and on the mainland side by Nichupte Lagoon, a body of water that covers 30 square miles. Cancun's southern tip, famous for its beautiful coral outcropping, is popular with scuba divers. The crystalline turquoise water is also ideal for skin diving, snorkeling, swimming, water-skiing, and wind surfing; or you can go sailing, power boating, and fishing. For the more passive, there are picnic cruises to Isla Mujeres, and houseboat tours of the lagoon.

The island's causeway bisects the Pok-ta-Pok Golf Club; the course was designed by Robert Trent Jones. At the club and at island hotels, tennis buffs will find plenty of lighted courts. A 6-mile moped path, bordered by palms and flowering plants, parallels the north beach.

Other activities. Good shopping can be found in major hotels and at El Parian Mall (in the Convention Center) and Villa del Caribe (also called the Mauna Loa Shopping Center). Cancun is a duty-free zone for perfumes, cosmetics, crystal, china, and European designer goods; it's also a good place to buy black coral jewelry.

Sightseeing is big business: half-day city tours, bird-watcher cruises, amphibian-plane tours, and bus trips to such attractions as Tulum, Laguna Balacar, Xel-Ha, Akumal, Chichen Itza, and other sites. It's only a 20-minute flight from Cancun to the island of Cozumel.

South of Cancun. Gorgeous stretches of beach perfect for snorkeling, deep-sea fishing, or just plain relaxing lie to the south. Akumal, once a Maya center, is now a resort; Xel-Ha Lagoon, to the south, is a national park for divers and snorkelers. For a small fee you can rent a mask, snorkel, and fins, and plunge into another world.

A trip to Tulum, 17 miles south of Akumal, is rewarding. Tulum's dominant structure, El Castillo, perches atop a 40-foot cliff above the Caribbean. A different type of Maya ruin, Tulum was a fortress city and one of the last bulwarks of the Maya culture. It was inhabited from the 11th century until just before the Spanish Conquest. Long stretches of the wall that once enclosed the city are still standing.

From the village of Tulum, a paved road heads north 25 miles to the ruins of Coba, an immense site with towering pyramids. Founded about A.D. 600, Coba was apparently a very important Maya center; it's at the hub of a network of sacbes—wide Maya thoroughfares that led traders and pilgrims from town to town.

South of Tulum, the scenery along Highway 307 takes on a new look as the road passes through hardwood jungle en route to Chetumal, capital of Quintana Roo. North of the city, pretty Balancar Lagoon stretches along the highway for 50 miles. Chetumal has a large, busy harbor. The town is a free port, so all imports are inexpensive. Accommodations and good restaurants are available.

Akumal resort overlooks a palm-fringed Caribbean beach popular with swimmers, snorkelers, and anglers.

The Yucatan's Green Gold

Part of the Yucatan's wealth is stored in its green gold—henequen. All over the peninsula, for as far as the eye can see, vast expanses of the henequen-producing agave plant form a gray-green, prickly carpet. Razor-sharp, swordlike leaves similar to those of the yucca grow from the plant's core.

The climate of the Yucatan provides ideal conditions for henequen cultivation: adequate rainfall and porous limestone soil.

Henequen is also known as sisal. The name "sisal" comes from a town near Merida that was once the peninsula's leading port—shipping henequen to all parts of the world. The henequen fibers are made into twine, rope, hammocks, table mats, sandals, and a variety of other woven products.

Visitors view Hacienda Yaxcopoil, 200-year-old henequen farm

Baler collects henequen

Rise and fall of an industry. The henequen industry got its greatest economic boost in the early 1900s, when the invention of the self-binding harvester created a need for twine and rope to tie bales of cotton, wheat, and other harvested crops on farms.

Synthetic substitutes were discovered and manufactured by the mid-1900s, damaging the Yucatan's importance as the world's foremost fiber producer. Despite competition and the industry's gradual decline, henequen is still important to area economy.

Henequen harvest. Henequen harvesting and processing is simple but laborious. The plants grow for six or seven years before being harvested for their fiber.

The old, outer leaves are cut off with machetes and taken to the defibering plant. The cut plants continue to produce spiky leaves that are harvested annually for another 10 to 15 years.

At the defibering plant the leaves are crushed and the fiber extracted. The henequen is then dried and baled for shipment.

Know Before You Go

Planning a trip is not only part of the fun—it's essential for a smooth stay. Fortunately, going to Mexico, North America's nearest "foreign" country, is extremely easy. Because of its proximity, transportation is frequent and convenient—and you don't need a visa.

What you will need to get and have handy at all times is a tourist card. If you're planning to take a car, trailer, camper, boat, or any other vehicle into Mexico, you'll have to arrange the necessary permits, licenses, and insurance ahead of time.

Tourist cards

All U.S. citizens visiting the Mexican interior must have tourist cards. In Baja California, tourist cards are required when traveling beyond Maneadero (a few miles south of Ensenada), south of Mexicali on Highway 5, or in the border area if your stay exceeds 72 hours. On the mainland, tourist cards are required when traveling beyond the border towns for a stay of more than 72 hours.

These free cards are available at Mexican consulates, Mexican government tourist offices, and border crossing stations. You can also get cards from auto clubs, Mexican insurance agencies, travel agents, tour operators, and offices of airlines, cruise ships, and bus companies serving Mexico.

When you apply for your tourist card you will need to show your proof of citizenship: a valid passport or certified birth certificate. A driver's license is *not* proof of citizenship. Naturalized citizens must carry an original naturalization certificate, citizenship certificate, or valid U.S. passport.

Single-entry tourist cards are valid for 90 days; multiple-entry permits enable you to enter Mexico anytime within a 180-day period. To obtain a multiple-entry card, you'll need two passport-type photographs.

A minor (under age 18) traveling alone or accompanied by someone other than a parent, must present a notarized letter of consent in duplicate signed by both parents or guardians and authenticated at a Mexican consulate. Even if one parent goes along, a minor must submit a notarized and authenticated letter from the absent parent.

Aliens residing in the United States are subject to special requirements. They should contact their nearest Mexican consulate well in advance of departure date.

Carry your tourist card and proof of citizenship with you at all times in Mexico. At the time of your return, the tourist card will be surrendered to Mexican authorities.

Vaccinations

A smallpox vaccination certificate is not necessary when you're entering Mexico from the U.S.—or when you're reentering the U.S. from Mexico, as long as you've traveled only within Mexico. If you're entering Mexico from Central or South America, you must have evidence of a smallpox vaccination given within the last three years.

Though not required by either Mexican or U.S. health authorities, tetanus and typhoid shots may be a wise precaution, particularly if you plan to spend much time in tropical areas or remote sections of the country. Consult your physician for other immunizations.

Entering Mexico

Special restrictions apply on what you may bring into Mexico, including personal belongings, automobiles or recreational vehicles, and pets. U.S. automobile insurance is not valid in Mexico, so you'll need to arrange for coverage with a reliable Mexican insurance carrier.

Baggage is examined by Mexican customs officers at the border. You can save time by carefully observing Mexican laws and regulations.

Automobile paperwork

Automobile permits, required for every entry into Mexico, are valid for 90 days; extensions of 90 days can be obtained from Mexican customs offices. The free auto permits, available at the border, are issued to the principal driver. Permits are not required for visits to Mexican border towns for periods of less than 72 hours. In Baja California only, you may use your vehicle for the length of time that your tourist card is valid without an automobile permit. You must, however, obtain a permit if you plan to transport the car by ferry to the mainland.

To obtain an automobile permit, you'll need proof of ownership: a current license registration or a notarized bill of sale. Although not recognized as proof of ownership, a copy of the vehicle ownership certificate (legal title or "pink slip") should be carried at all times. If you don't own the car, you'll need a notarized statement from the legal owner giving you authority to drive the car into Mexico. If the vehicle is rented or leased, you'll be asked to produce the notarized statement from the owner or a copy of the formal rental or lease agreement.

Your car must return with you; it cannot be sold in Mexico. If it's impossible to return your car to the U.S. before the permit expires, a bond must be posted with the Mexican customs department to cover duties.

Your valid U.S. driver's license is also valid in Mexico, but your U.S. automobile insurance is not. Mexican insurance company agents on both sides of the border issue short-term policies at reasonable daily rates. Some automobile clubs also issue insurance for a trip into Mexico.

Automobile accidents in Mexico are handled from a criminal rather than a civil standpoint. This means that drivers are liable to jail sentences in cases where fatal injury results, and even in minor accidents drivers may be held pending proof of innocence. Because of this arrangement, it's very important that you take out Mexican insurance.

Signs for good driving

DESVIACION	CURVA PELIGROSA	VADO	DESPACIO	CONTINUA		
DETOUR	DANGEROUS CURVE	DIP OR FORD	SLOW	RIGHT TURN AT ALL TIMES	HILL	NARROW BRIDGE

CONSERVE SU DERECHA — KEEP RIGHT
2.50 m ANCHO LIMITE — MAXIMUM HORIZONTAL CLEARANCE
NO — DO NOT ENTER
100 MAXIMA — SPEED LIMIT IN KILOMETERS
PARADA — BUS STOP
ADUANA — INSPECTION
8 a 21 H DIAS HABILES — NO PARKING 8 A.M. TO 9 P.M. WEEKDAYS

TRANSITO — ONE WAY
TRANSITO — TWO WAY
CIRCULACION — ONE WAY, YIELD RIGHT OF WAY
PREFERENCIA — ONE WAY, RIGHT OF WAY
CEDA EL PASO — YIELD RIGHT OF WAY
ALTO — STOP

Displayed above (from left) are festival masks from the state of Michoacan, pineapple-shaped water coolers from Guerrero and Michoacan, trees of life from the state of Mexico, and storage vessels from Oaxaca

A shopper's paradise, Mexico offers a wide array of tempting merchandise in all parts of the country. Best buys are the beautiful handcrafted items that represent Mexican folk art at its best. For the U.S. shopper, accustomed to a machine-made world, part of folk art's appeal lies in its handmade quality. It represents a way of life that has changed little over the years.

Many of these objects could not emerge from our secular modern culture—for example, Tarascan altar offerings of bundles of wheat, Huichol ceremonial animals in yarn, or Metepec visions of paradise in ceramic. Nor are we accustomed to everyday bowls, baskets, or birdcages designed individually and made by hand.

The Mexican techniques vary from primitive pottery making to refined lacquerwork, from weaving of rough-textured fabrics to intricate embroidery. Designs are nearly always geometric, often with a childlike simplicity that is anything but naive. And they are frequently traditional, using age-old motifs.

Whole villages in Mexico do one kind of work. But from village to village and from region to region, you'll find astonishing diversity; the country's mountains have provided the long isolation that is a prime ingredient in the development of distinctive local cultures.

Government-sponsored craft stores. All major cities, and even smaller towns, have shops sponsored by the country or the state where you can see the best of the handicrafts produced in that area.

These serve as both folk-art museums and stores, providing a good introduction to regional crafts. Prices are set; no bargaining is accepted. While the prices will probably be a bit higher than you may find elsewhere, you can be assured that you are getting top-of-the-line goods.

Where can I bargain? Bargaining is expected at native markets, shopping stalls, and when dealing with streetside and beachside vendors. Though shops have fixed prices, you can always ask for a discount, especially if you are paying in U.S. dollars. As a general rule, the larger the order, the lower the price per item.

In the Indian country of southern Mexico, the prices are so low that it's often embarrassing to bargain. In the resort areas, on the other hand, merchandise is often overpriced, and bargaining is the only way to get the price down to a reasonable figure.

How do you do it? Start the bargaining game by asking if this is the lowest figure they will accept, then offer about half of the asking price. When bargaining ensues, increase your offer slowly and only in small increments. Don't ever show too much interest; slowly walking away is a final ploy if the price remains too high.

Best buys in Baja California: Some leather goods and basketry, rare black-coral jewelry, well-made silver jewelry at lower prices than on the mainland (always look for the hallmark of sterling silver—a spread eagle), onyx, shells (spiny murex and other unusual varieties), and beach attire. Baja is a duty-free area for perfumes, cosmetics, and other imported luxuries; the tax is only 6 percent rather than the 15 percent charged elsewhere in Mexico.

Best buys on the west coast: Resort wear, sun tan creams, leather goods in Mazatlan and Puerto Vallarta, papier-mâchè, some jewelry.

Colorfully dyed fiber creates vividly chromatic chair seats

Best buys in and around Mexico City: Almost anything—paintings, unusual jewelry, papier-mâchè, silver, tinware, pottery, tiles, furniture, leather, glass, vanilla, and fashionable clothing, to name only a few items. Taxco is noted for its fine silver (you may pay more here than in Mexico City, but the array is astonishing). Cuernavaca has the Emaus store, with fine silver and wood creations; the city also has a good selection of leather goods. Go to Puebla for Talavera tiles and ceramics, and to Toluca for heavy woven jackets, shawls, and rugs, as well as reed furniture.

Best buys in and around Guadalajara: Yarn paintings, woven goods, pottery, wood carvings, serapes, lacquerware from Uruapan, ceramics, handblown glass, copperware from Santa Clara del Cobre, blouses and embroideries from Morelia and Patzcuaro, handwoven textiles, guitars from Paracho, silk rebozos, white serapes from Jocotepec, and semiprecious stones from Queretaro. At Tequila, you can buy spirits from the source.

Best buys in Northern Mexico: Saddles, woolen serapes, rugs, beer. Lead glass and crystal are good finds in Monterrey. Embroidered and handpainted items can be found in the Huasteca region along the Gulf of Mexico.

Best buys in Southern Mexico: Oaxacan knives and black pottery, handwoven serapes and rugs from surrounding Indian villages, yarn dolls in Mitla, gold filigree jewelry modeled after Monte Alban treasures, wood carvings, replicas of pre-Columbian art, and native dress. The state of Chiapas produces sturdy embroidery.

Best buys in the Yucatan: Panama-type hats, *guayabera* shirts, basketware, mats, and hammocks.

Ornate ceramic bird is a traditional handicraft

. . . entering Mexico

Basic baggage

Clothing and other personal items within reason may be taken into Mexico duty free. Each adult tourist may take into Mexico 3 liters of wine or other alcoholic beverage and two cartons of cigarettes (or one box of cigars or 250 grams of loose tobacco). Up to 500 grams of unopened perfume may also be taken into the country. Be sure all medications are properly identified and carry only the quantity you'll need during the trip.

Pets

It's advisable to leave pets at home because of special inspections, health certificates, and possible hotel policies against animals. (Rodent poison is often placed on the floors in seaport rooms; check carefully before you let your pet roam.) If you must take your pet to Mexico, you will need both an International Health Certificate from a U.S. veterinarian and a rabies inoculation permit valid within the past six months. The pet health certificate cannot be issued more than 72 hours before the animal enters Mexico.

If your pet is out of the U.S. for more than 30 days, you'll need inoculation certificates to reenter the country. Dogs can be left at kennels on the border in Texas, California, and Arizona while their owners travel in Mexico.

Hunting & fishing gear

Very strict regulations govern the temporary importation of firearms into Mexico for hunting. Check with your nearest Mexican consulate or tourist office regarding gun permits and regulations. All hunters need a current Mexican hunting license; the consulate can provide assistance with details.

Any reasonable amount of fishing tackle may be brought into Mexico duty free. You may pick up fishing licenses at the border or from local fish and game wardens. A fishing license is good in any state in Mexico.

All private boats entering Mexican waters must obtain certification and a boat permit from a Mexican consulate or customs broker. Naval authorities must be informed of each new port of destination before arrival. Permits are issued for six months and can be extended for another six months. For detailed information, check with your automobile club or the closest Mexican consulate or tourist office.

Photographic equipment

Each tourist is permitted one still camera and one 8-mm or 16-mm movie camera with up to 12 rolls of unused film for each as well as one video camera and 12 blank cassettes per person. Don't forget to register foreign-made cameras at your point of departure so that you can prove your camera wasn't purchased in Mexico.

Film is available in most cities. Photographic supply stores in larger Mexican cities can process film; it's best, though, to get your film developed in the U.S. All film should be hand-carried and hand-inspected at airline boarding points to prevent possible damage from baggage inspection equipment.

When photographing throughout Mexico, remember that you're a guest. Respect the Mexicans' privacy. Professional photographers will need special permits to shoot with tripods and flash equipment in archeological sites, museums, and colonial monuments.

Tips on Visiting Ruins

 The Mexican government's National Institute of Anthropology and History (INAH) charges a modest admission to visit its archeological zones.

Sites are open daily, usually from 9 A.M. to 5 P.M. or sunset. If you can, visit early in the morning or in the late afternoon.

Wear comfortable shoes and a hat, and carry water (bring a canteen). A few of the largest sites have restaurants; at others you may want to take along a picnic lunch.

At major sites you can hire a licensed, English-speaking guide for a small fee. Stay on main trails, and watch where you step and sit. Do not leave any valuables unattended.

For a more enriching trip, be prepared with good guidebooks.

Real aficionados may want to join a guided group tour led by experts in Mexican archeology or anthropology. Operators with scheduled trips include the American Museum of Natural History (New York), National History Museum of Los Angeles County (Los Angeles), Nature Expeditions International (Eugene, OR), and Smithsonian Institution (Washington, DC).

Returning from Mexico

When you leave the country, immigration officials will stamp and retain your tourist permit. If you're flying home from an international airport, save enough money to pay the departure tax (about $10). You can pay in either dollars or pesos, but your change will be in Mexican currency. Motorists surrender their tourist permits at the U.S. border. En route you will be stopped at Mexican agricultural inspection stations along the highways (see the "restricted items" listed below).

When you return to the U.S., you must present proof of citizenship; if you have a passport, the procedure is very rapid. After you pass through immigration, your baggage is inspected. To expedite the process, keep sales slips handy and have all your purchases in one bag.

What you may bring back

U.S. residents returning from Mexico are permitted to bring back up to $400 worth of articles duty free within any 30-day period. Each member of a family, regardless of age, gets the same exemption and these exemptions may be pooled. Though there is no time restriction for tourists returning through Arizona, California, New Mexico, and Texas ports of entry, at least a 48-hour stay in Mexico is required at all other ports to obtain the exemption.

If you are over the age of 21, your allowance may include one liter of alcohol, 100 non-Cuban cigars, and 200 cigarettes. Some perfumes are limited to one bottle; some are prohibited all together. Be sure to inquire before you buy.

For detailed information on what can be brought into the country, pick up a copy of *Know Before You Go* from your local customs office, or write to U.S. Customs, P.O. Box 7407, Washington, D.C. 20044, to get this helpful booklet.

Restricted items

The list of items you cannot bring back to the U.S. from Mexico includes most fruits and vegetables, plants, livestock, poultry, meats, uncured hides, and imports originating in Cuba, North Korea, Vietnam, Cambodia, Libya, and Nicaragua. Lottery tickets and endangered wildlife species (or products made from any part of such species) are also prohibited. Some products protected by U.S. trademark are restricted.

Valuable archeological and religious relics are the property of the Mexican government and may not be taken out of the country.

Duty-free imports

In addition to the duty-free items mentioned above, Mexico is included among the many nations whose economies are improved by exports. Most Mexican handicrafts can be brought back duty-free and need not be included in the $400 exemption. There is also no duty on art or on antiques over 100 years of age, but you may need an export certificate.

Gifts

Any gifts you bring back across the border are considered to be for personal use and are included in the $400 exemption. You may send gifts valued at less than $50 to people in the U.S. without including them on your customs declaration, provided the addressee does not receive more than one such package in a single day. Perfumes valued at more than $5 retail, tobacco products, and alcoholic beverages may not be included in gift packages.

If you intend to have purchases sent home for you, choose well-established shops that enjoy a good reputation. Factories and stores that sell frequently to tourists are usually very experienced at arranging for merchandise shipment and will handle all details for you.

The words "Unsolicited Gift," the name of the donor, and the retail value of the contents must be written clearly on the outside of the package. Merchandise shipped to your home address cannot be included as part of the $400 exemption. Any article that you ship to yourself will be taxed on its appraised value at the applicable rate of duty.

For assistance—in the U.S. or Mexico

Detailed information on Mexico is available at the following Mexican Government Tourism Offices in the U.S.: 10100 Santa Monica Blvd., Suite 224, Los Angeles, CA 90067; 2707 North Loop W., Suite 450, Houston, TX 77008; 233 N. Michigan Ave., Suite 1413, Chicago, IL 60601; and 405 Park Ave., Suite 1002, New York, NY 10022.

If you have questions or require help while you are in Mexico, the phone number of the U.S. Embassy in Mexico City is (5) 2-11-00-42. Their office has compiled a brochure on *Tips for Travelers to Mexico*. To get a copy before you go, write to the Department of State, Public Affairs, Bureau of Consular Affairs CA/PA, 2201 C St. N.W., Washington, D.C. 20520.

A 24-hour hotline for tourist information and assistance is provided by the Mexican Government Tourist Secretariat in Mexico City; call 2-50-01-23.

How to Get There— & Back

Whether you enjoy, flying, driving, cruising, or riding the rails, choosing a means of transportation for your trip to Mexico can be the most crucial decision in planning your trip. When you're deciding, keep in mind the length of your stay, distance to be covered, budget allowance for transportation, number of people in your party, and the areas you wish to visit. More and more visitors to Mexico opt for the ease of leaving their own cars at home, flying to Mexico, and then renting a car or joining an organized tour to see the countryside.

A "Details at a glance" feature accompanies the regional maps for each area of the country and offers some suggestions for reaching that specific area—by car, plane, or other means of transportation.

Driving in Mexico

In general, the main highways in Mexico are good and well marked. (All distances and speed limits are shown in kilometers; to convert to approximate mileage, multiply by 0.6.)

Precautions. Highways are often unfenced, and animals are apt to wander onto the road. For this reason alone, driving at night is not recommended. As one Mexico guidebook mentions: "Burros don't wear taillights."

Motorists may encounter roadblocks set up by the Mexican government to control the transportation of such ilicit items as drugs and guns. If you are stopped by soldiers for a car search, patience and polite cooperation will usually get you on your way quickly.

Occasionally reports are heard of unauthorized roadblocks operated by those trying to collect illegal tolls. The American Automobile Association offers the following suggestions to minimize this type of encounter: travel only during the day; never travel alone; stay on the main roads; and be especially careful on Highways 15 and 1 in the state of Sinaloa, Highway 2 near Caborca, Highway 40 from Durango to the west coast, Highway 57 between Matehuala and San Luis Potosi, and Highway 147 between Palomares and Tuxtepec in the state of Oaxaca.

If you encounter an unofficial roadblock, remain calm, patient, and polite. It's never wise to exhibit large amounts of cash; keep small amounts handy for tips, which can often free you from unnecessary hassles.

Gasoline. Only one brand of gasoline is sold in Mexico—Pemex, which gets its name from the words, "Petroleos Mexicanas," the government-owned oil company. There are two grades of this gasoline: Pemex Extra (unleaded fuel similar to regular unleaded in the U.S.) and Pemex Nova (leaded fuel below the ratings of leaded U.S. gas). Pemex Extra is found in silver pumps; Pemex Nova in blue pumps. The red pumps contain diesel fuel. U.S. brands of oil are sometimes obtainable in independent repair shops and stores.

Gasoline is sold in *litros* (liters). One liter equals about one quart. Consequently, if you order *diez*, you will get about 10 quarts instead of the 10 gallons you would get in the U.S. Your U.S. oil company credit card will not be good in Mexico; be prepared to pay in pesos as traveler's checks may not be accepted.

Though the supply of unleaded gasoline has been increased to meet tourist demands, it's regularly available only in major cities. Because the continued use of leaded gasoline will damage catalytic converters, vehicles with this equipment are best used only near border cities where no refueling is anticipated.

Camping & trailering

Attitudes about camping in Mexico are sharply divided. Some travelers recommend it as the only way to get away from the tourist crowds, to mingle with the people of Mexico, and to explore some out-of-the-way places. Others, though experienced campers north of the border, wouldn't attempt to camp in Mexico.

Members of the first group of tourists—avid campers—are usually adaptable souls willing to adjust their normal camping routines to meet the special safety and health precautions in Mexico. The second group—the doubters and disclaimers—are simply people who decide that camping loses its appeal when they must cope with the health problems of food and water and campground improvisations necessary in Mexico.

Beaches can serve as primitive campsites if you can find a suitable access road; all beaches in Mexico are public. Camping or RV facilities are extremely primitive at most lakes, but you can use them for overnight campsites. When trailering, go with a caravan; it's not wise for a single car or camper to park overnight along highways or to stop at length in a lonely spot.

AAA lists recommended trailer parks in its accommodations guide to Mexico (available free to members). Another excellent source of information on Mexican highways, accommodations, and trailer parks is the series of bulletins and road logs published by Sanborn's Mexican Insurance Service, McAllen, TX 78501.

If you're pulling a trailer, check with your insurance broker to find out just how well your policy protects your trailer while in Mexico. Stay on the main highways with a trailer; unusually high centers, sharp curves, and narrow bridges are sometimes encountered on secondary roads. If you plan to make a side trip to a small village, check first to find out if the road is suitable for travel with a trailer and if you can pull one into the town.

Bus touring

If you're young and/or hardy, traveling throughout Mexico by bus can be a great way to see the Mexican countryside and offbeat villages, as well as the big population centers and favorite tourist destinations.

Mexico City can be reached inexpensively and not too uncomfortably by bus from border cities such as Tijuana, Nogales, El Paso, Eagle Pass, Laredo, and Brownsville.

Take only first-class or deluxe buses. Reserved seats (standard or first-class buses) are of the reclining type and usually well upholstered. Several companies (such as Tres Estrellas de Oro, Transportes del Norte, and Omnibus de Mexico) feature stewardesses, background music, and restrooms on some runs.

Package tours, which include all arrangements, are offered by Greyhound and Continental Trailways, Gray Lines (in Baja California), as well as by some smaller operators. Tours will take you anywhere from the dry deserts of Chihuahua (where you can visit Pancho Villa's home) to the high mountains in the interior to the colorful resorts down the west coast. Most tours return via the west coast—inland through Sonora to the border.

Drawbacks to bus travel in Mexico are too infrequent rest stops and the inadequate restroom facilities and lunch counters at many of the smaller stops. One must be prepared to travel four (and sometimes more) hours without a stop on some routes. The bus traveler will always do well to follow a common Mexican practice and take along a box lunch. Or break up your trip with overnight reservations in towns along the route.

To get there fast, fly

Travel by air is the fastest and easiest way to reach your destination in Mexico. Airlines fly into Mexico from all parts of the world. Even if you're going to some out-of-the-way spot, you can usually fly to an airport not too far from it and take local transportation from there, saving yourself tedious and sometimes rugged driving.

Airlines offering service to Mexico from points within the U.S. include Alaska (Baja), American, Continental, Delta, Mexicana, Northwest, Pan American, Resorts (Baja), United, and Wardair (Baja). These airlines serve principal cities along the tourist routes. Other, smaller Mexican carriers reach spots off the tourist track. A travel agent can help you work out the air routing that is best for you.

If you enter Mexico by private plane you will, like any other traveler, need a tourist card and you'll be required to pass through customs and immigration inspection at the airport of entry. Bring along your proof of ownership and airplane registration papers. Your first landing in Mexico must be at a Mexican port of entry.

Gasoline at airports costs slightly less than it does in the U.S. You may not always be able to get the kind of oil you want, so take along enough for your stay.

One important caution: Remember that all of central Mexico, including Mexico City, is at a high altitude; you must have a plane that will perform adequately at altitudes from 7,000 to 13,000 feet. Another caution: Runways are sometimes unpaved.

When you return home, you must land at a U.S. port of entry for customs and immigration inspection. Notify the field in advance of your expected time of arrival. You can do this by telephoning the field from the Mexican side of the border or by calling a U.S. CAA communications station by radio.

Railroading in Mexico

Mexican rail companies connect with U.S. lines at El Paso and Laredo, Texas; Nogales, Arizona; and Mexicali and Tijuana, Baja California. Direct service to Mexico City passes through the following major cities: Nuevo Laredo to Mexico City by way of Monterrey, Saltillo, and San Luis Potosi; Ciudad Juarez to Mexico City via Chihuahua, Torreon, Zacatecas, Aguascalientes, and Queretaro; and from Nogales to Mexico City through Hermosillo, Guaymas, Mazatlan, Tepic, Guadalajara, and Irapuato. From Mexico City other lines serve southern and eastern Mexico.

Mexico's National Railways continue to upgrade their passenger service. Among the newest trains are the *Constitucionalista* (between Mexico City and San Miguel de Allende), *Expreso del Mar* (connects Nogales with Guaymas), *Purepecha* (sleeping car service between Mexico City, Morelia, Patzcuaro, and Uruapan), *El Regiomontano* (with sleeping cars between Nuevo Laredo and Mexico City), *El Tapatio* (sleeping car service between Mexico City and Guadalajara, and *Jarocho* (between Mexico City and Veracruz).

These trains feature new or refurbished cars, Pullmans with compartments and bedrooms, diners, and club cars. For information on the new trains contact a U.S. travel agent or Wagons-Lits Mexicana in Mexico.

Rail tours are offered by a number of U.S. operators. Several use private Pullman cars to ensure good accommodations and food. Many tours include the Copper Canyon (see page 112).

Private yachts & public liners

Some people prefer to sail their own craft down to Mexico. To get up-to-date information on practicalities and problems, get in touch with people who have already done it, or contact your nearest Mexican government tourist office or Mexican consulate. Several cruise lines offer schedules to Mexico (see page 39).

Travel Essentials

On the following pages we list some of the first-class and deluxe hotels and campgrounds in each region in Mexico, provide an overview of how to get around particular cities and areas, and list some of the tours you can take to get more from your trip.

Hotel listings may also be obtained from AAA, insurance companies serving Mexico, and Mexican tourist offices. Travel agents are often your best source for trip planning and hotel reservations; make sure you always receive confirmation for any hotel you have booked.

Language

Though a knowledge of Spanish isn't essential, it does make a visit more enjoyable to know a few phrases. You'll naturally learn a great deal more about the country if you are able to converse with its people. You can get along surprisingly well with an improvised sign language, though, and it's almost always possible to find someone who speaks a little English. Most personnel involved in serving tourists speak good English.

Time zones

Mexico is divided into three time zones: Pacific Standard in Baja California Norte (Daylight Saving from April through October); Mountain Standard in Baja California Sur and the west coast of the mainland south to, but not including, Puerto Vallarta; and Central Standard in the rest of the country.

Pesos, centavos & dollars

U.S. traveler's checks and currency in any denomination may be taken into Mexico. Traveler's checks can be cashed in most cities, and it's advisable to carry the bulk of your money this way. Purchase most of your traveler's checks in small denominations ($20 and $50); Mexican establishments may not be able to cash checks for larger amounts. Personal checks drawn on U.S. banks are virtually impossible to cash, but major credit cards are accepted almost everywhere.

Dollars and traveler's checks may be exchanged for pesos at banks, exchange houses (casas de cambio), or at most hotels. Banks offer the best rates of exchange, hotels the worst. Exchange desks at airports are convenient and usually offer good rates of exchange.

The Mexican peso is currently fluctuating; for latest official rates, check with local banks, money exchange firms, or Mexican tourism offices and consulates.

Dining

Mexico's best restaurants rank among the finest in the world, and the service is equally impeccable. Unless you choose to dine alone, it's wise to note the customs of the country: breakfast service starts about the same time as in the U.S.; lunch, often the day's main meal, is taken around 2 P.M.; in the evening in large cities, it's not fashionable to dine until 9 or 10 P.M. The ever-popular discos start around 11 P.M. or later and often perform until 3 A.M. or later.

As a rule, dining well is less expensive in Mexico than it is in the U.S. However, in the capital and in some of the major resort areas, you can easily spend as much for dinner as you do at home. A 15 percent sales tax is added to restaurant, bar, and nightclub checks.

Tipping

In hotels, restaurants, and bars, tip the same percentage as you would at home. Normally, service charges are not included in bills. Tipping elsewhere depends on service. You should plan to tip maids, porters, bellhops, doormen, gas station attendants, and the person who watches your parked car. Taxi drivers do not expect a tip unless they provide extra service. Tour guides should receive about 20 percent of the tour price.

Staying healthy

Regardless of the stories you've heard, there are no serious health hazards involved in traveling in Mexico if you take certain precautions.

Most hotels throughout Mexico provide bottles of purified water in the rooms or have installed their own purification systems. If you're ever in doubt about the water, ask for agua mineral or agua purificada. Unless the water is purified, do not use tap water for drinking or brushing teeth. Remember also to avoid ice cubes in drinks unless you know they're purified. One tip—take along a tray of plastic ice cubes that you can freeze in the refrigerator of your room.

Stick to well-recommended restaurants; don't buy from vendors along the street. Don't eat uncooked fruit or vegetables unless you can peel them, and avoid anything that can turn bad from improper refrigeration.

If you do run into the "turista" problem, be prepared. At the first symptoms of stomach upset, take drugs prescribed in advance by your personal physician. If medical attention is necessary, competent physicians and surgeons can be found in all large towns in Mexico. The U.S. Embassy in Mexico City and the U.S. consulate in Guadalajara have lists of approved physicians. Your hotel will also be able to recommend a doctor.

ESSENTIALS

Baja California

Accommodations

Baja accommodations run the gamut from modest roadside inns to deluxe seaside resorts. Only in large cities or south along the tip of Baja, at Los Cabos, will travelers find much choice. Along Highway 1 the chain of moderately priced La Pinta hotels is your best bet for an overnight stay in San Quintin, Cataviña, Guerrero Negro, and San Ignacio. These hotels are also among your choices in Ensenada and Loreto.

Most hotels have U.S. reservation offices; check with a travel agent for additional information on location, rates, and types of rooms.

Camping facilities range from primitive sites with no amenities to fully developed RV parks in popular resort areas. Self-contained campers can park along beaches marked *playas publicas* (public beaches) for a few dollars a night. AAA members can get a free listing of all campgrounds and trailer parks.

Bahia de los Angeles. Casa Diaz (on beach), Villa Veta (trailer park adjoins), Guillermo's Trailer Park.

Cabo San Lucas. Deluxe resorts include Cabo Baja (4 miles east), Finisterra, Hacienda, Hotel Cabo San Lucas (10 miles east), Solmar, and Twin Dolphin (7 miles east). Mar de Cortez is a modest motor inn. El Faro Viejo and San Vicente trailer parks have spaces for tents and hookups for RVs.

Ensenada. Most hotels are motels; El Cid, Estero Beach (south of the city), San Nicolas, and TraveLodge are among the best.

La Paz. First-class hotels around town: El Presidente, La Posada, Los Arcos (colonial-style charm), Palmira (on road to Pichilingue ferry terminal), Perla, and Ramada Gran Baja (largest). Trailer parks with hookups: Oasis Los Aripez (9½ miles north), Gran Baja (share hotel facilities), El Cardon, and La Paz.

Fishing resorts south of La Paz: Las Arenas, Punta Pescadero, Palmas de Cortez, Playa Hermosa, Buena Vista, and Punta Colorado. Most resorts have airstrips.

Loreto. Most deluxe rooms are at El Presidente at Nopolo Bay (8½ miles south); in town, try La Pinta, Mision, or Oasis.

Mexicali. First-class hotels: Holiday Inn, Lucerna (nice grounds), Calafia, and La Siesta.

Mulege. First-class hotels: Punta Chivato (resort north on the Sea of Cortez), Serenidad (ranch-style hotel along the river 2½ miles south, trailer park) and Vista Hermosa (formerly Hotel Mulege, air conditioning). RV parks: Jorge's del Rio, Huerta Saucedo, Villa Maria Isabel, Posada Concepcion, plus several public beaches.

San Felipe. First-class hotels: Castel San Felipe (tennis) and Fiesta; both have pools, restaurants, and bars.

San Jose del Cabo. To the original El Presidente (pool, tennis courts, restaurant) in this small town, have been added Aquamarina, Cabo Castel, Aston Cabo Regis (new condo suites), and the area's first golf course. Deluxe Palmilla resort lies 5 miles west of town on a beautiful bay.

Tecate. Full-line spa: Rancho La Puerta.

Tijuana. First-class hotels: El Conquistador, Fiesta Americana, Lucerna, and Paraiso-Radisson.

Getting around

Distances are great between cities. If you don't drive to Baja, your activities may be limited to one destination unless you choose to use air taxi, rental car (available in larger towns), or cab. Boat rentals are the best way to explore the Sea of Cortez.

Border towns. Taxis are plentiful in Ensenada, Mexicali, and Tijuana. You can charter boats for sport fishing at Ensenada and San Felipe.

Los Cabos resorts. Resorts arrange for guest transportation from the airport and between hotels. Boats can be rented through your hotel or at the Cabo San Lucas marina.

La Paz. Taxis are easy to find in town. From the ferry terminals, you can cross the Sea of Cortez to mainland Mexico. Small planes offer service to Loreto, Mulege, Los Cabos resorts, and Guaymas; car rentals and bus transportation are available to the tip of the peninsula. Fishing boats can be chartered.

Tours

Baja California cities offer little in the way of area sightseeing; fishing is the primary reason for Baja's popularity south of the border cities. Ensenada tours visit the wine country and Punta Banda. Cabo San Lucas boat trips go out to the photogenic offshore rocks. From Loreto you can get a car and guide for a full-day trip to San Javier, or take a boat trip out to Isla Carmen. Whale-watching tours are the major attraction of Scammon's Lagoon at Guerrero Negro.

Entertainment

Sophisticated entertainment is available only along the border; you'll find night clubs in Tijuana, Ensenada, Mexicali, La Paz, and the Los Cabos area.

West Coast

Accommodations

Accommodations along the Pacific coast are usually more expensive than in the interior of Mexico. Listed below are hotels that fall into the deluxe and first-class categories. Air conditioning, restaurants, tennis, golf, and swimming are just a few of the facilities you'll discover. Rates tend to drop between May and October (off season).

Most hotel chains have reservation offices in the U.S.; check with your travel agent for additional information on location, prices, and types of rooms.

Acapulco. Acapulco's hotels get bigger, better, and more flamboyant each year. One of the most deluxe resort hotels is the Acapulco Plaza near the Acapulco Center. This huge complex has over 500 suites and a variety of restaurants and lounges, but it's not on the beach. The tower of the stunning Acapulco Princess adds more pools and restaurants to their attractive complex. Also polished to perfection are Las Brisas (pink casitas and jeeps and a dramatic beach club), the two Hyatt facilities (Hyatt Continental and Hyatt Regency), and hideaway Villa Vera. Other first-class to deluxe hotels: Acapulco Malibu, Acapulco Sheraton Playa Secreto, Calinda, Condesa del Mar, El Presidente, Maralisa, Pierre Marques, and Ritz (newly remodeled). Creative Leisure offers deluxe private villas.

Bahias de Huatulco. First-class hotels: Binniguenda, Club Med, Sheraton Tongolunda, and Veramar.

Guaymas. First-class to deluxe hotels: Nuevo Posada de San Carlos and Playas de Cortes; Club Med's facilities are at Playa los Algodones in San Carlos.

Ixtapa. First-class to deluxe hotels: Aquamarina, Camino Real (top of the line), Dorado Pacifico, El Presidente, Holiday Inn, Krystal Ixtapa, Riviera del Sol, and Sheraton Ixtapa. Club Med's operation and an inexpensive trailer park, Playa Linda, are at Playa Quieta north of town.

Manzanillo. Deluxe hotel: Las Hadas. First-class hotels: Club Maeva (north of town), Club Santiago, Roca del Mar, and Villas del Palmas.

Mazatlan. First-class to deluxe hotels: Balboa Club, Camino Real, El Cid, Hacienda, Holiday Inn, Los Sabalos, Oceano Palace, and Playa Mazatlan.

Playa Blanca. Club Med facilities include a variety of sports and other activities.

Playa Careyes. Plaza Careyes is a first-class hotel in this somewhat remote spot.

Puerto Angel. Angel del Mar hotel sets on a hill atop the bay.

Puerto Escondido. Hotels include Castel Puerto Escondido, Paraiso Escondido, and Hotel Santa Fe.

Puerto Vallarta. First-class to deluxe hotels: Buganvilias Sheraton, Camino Real, Fiesta Americana, Fiesta Los Tules, Garza Blanca, Holiday Inn, Las Palmas, and Posada Vallarta. Puerto Vallarta Villa Rentals has condos.

Zihuatanejo. First-class to deluxe hotels: Fiesta Americana, Sotavento, Villa del Sol, and Villas Miramar.

Getting around

Rental car companies have offices throughout the west coast, at airports, in towns, and at assorted hotels.

If you're hiring a car or taxi, agree on the price beforehand. Public transportation is worth investigating—it can be an efficient and inexpensive way to travel.

Acapulco. Yachts are popular for cruising Acapulco Bay; several are available daily, each with a different tour. Some hotels include a car or jeep with the room, inexpensive buses run along the waterfront, and horse-drawn carriages will carry you back in time.

Guaymas. Ferry service departs for Santa Rosalia in Baja three times weekly; check schedules upon arrival. Boats, ranging from small craft to large cruisers, can be rented by the hour or day. A train and buses are available for travel to nearby San Carlos.

Ixtapa/Zihuatanejo. Boats are available at the pier; shop around for the best price. Water taxis provide transportation from pier to beaches around Zihuatanejo's waterfront. Cycling is popular.

Mazatlan. To get around the beaches, you can hire a *pulmonia* (an open-air three-passenger taxi). Ferry service departs for La Paz several times weekly; check schedules upon arrival. Limousines, cabs, and buses transport visitors from the airport to town; public buses offer service to beach hotels from other parts of town.

Fishing boats can be chartered; be sure to shop around for the best price.

Puerto Vallarta. Boats are a popular means of transportation around the beautiful bay. Ferry service connects Puerto Vallarta with Cabo San Lucas in Baja; check schedules upon arrival. Taxis are easy to find; agree on a price before the ride.

Tours

Larger resort areas offer an assortment of guided tours worth investigating. Smaller areas are best seen on your own—by rental car or on foot. You can hire guides for explorations into the surrounding countryside. Some travelers combine a trip to the west coast with a 1-day (or longer) visit to another area. From Puerto Vallerta, for example, Guadalajara is less than an hour by air.

Acapulco. The city tour picks you up at your hotel and covers the major attractions around town (including La Quebrada) in just over 3 hours; a full-day tour explores the area around the city. For an introduction to Acapulco's famous night life, consider the night tour; it departs from major hotels at 9 P.M. and takes in Acapulco's hot night spots.

Glass-bottom boats tour La Roqueta Island, Acapulco Bay, and the underwater Shrine of Our Lady of Guadalupe. Cocktail and dinner cruises are a good way to get a look at the entire bay.

Guaymas. No organized tours are offered of the city, but you can take a harbor cruise. Check with your hotel for details. Fishing boats can be hired at the dock.

Ixtapa/Zihuatanejo. Boat tours include trips to Isla Ixtapa (where *Robinson Crusoe* was filmed) and uninhabited Isla Grande—a tropical island abounding with bird life and lush greenery. Daily excursions head out to Playa Las Gatos for swimming, snorkeling, and diving.

A Sunday tour of Agua de Correa Market gives you a look at local crafts; tours of Cabritero anthropological ruins and the ruins at Cocolmeca provide an introduction to Mexico's past.

Manzanillo. Both land and sea tours cover the town of Manzanillo and take you past the exclusive resort of Las Hadas.

Mazatlan. Take a city tour, or see the town on your own. A full-day tour takes you to San Blas, a remote seaside town, or to the old mining town of Copola. Boat tours explore the island-dotted bay.

Puerto Vallarta. A city tour takes about 3 hours. You can also visit Mismaloya beach, site of the original set of *Night of the Iguana.* During the winter months, spend a day sunning and swimming at one of several streamside restaurants and resorts in the jungle canyons about 10 miles south of town.

Day-long boat tours take visitors to the secluded village of Yelapa. Sunset boat tours are a good way to view lovely Banderas Bay.

Entertainment

Mexico's west coast offers some of the most varied entertainment in all of Mexico. The resorts know what you come to the west coast for, and are geared to keeping you happy and busy. So take advantage of it, and experience all the activities for which you have time and energy.

Acapulco. Described by many as Mexico's "playground," Acapulco can keep you entertained 24 hours a day. La Quebrada divers perform several times a day. Bullfights take place every Sunday during the winter months.

Parasailing is popular; tennis, and swimming facilities can be found at most hotels. Golfers find several 18-hole courses. Acapulco offers a choice of lively discos and night clubs (many in hotels).

Guaymas. The International Deep-Sea Fishing Rodeo is every July; the Fiesta de la Pesca is in May. If you don't like to fish, you can go riding, snorkeling, or water-skiing.

Beautiful stretches of beach beckon the visitor; the water is ideal for swimming, the sand perfect for relaxing or playing. Golf and tennis can be arranged through your hotel; fees are reasonable.

Ixtapa/Zihuatanejo. Parasailing, snorkeling, and scuba diving are only a few of the choices. Golfers will enjoy the Palma Real golf course (designed by Robert Trent Jones). Ixtapa has several lighted tennis courts for the aficionado. Sailboats and water-ski boats can be rented, usually in front of the larger hotels. Charter a fishing boat in either Ixtapa or Zihuatanejo. Shell collecting is also a productive pastime.

Discos and occasional live entertainment are evening diversions.

Manzanillo. Water sports are excellent. There's good deep-sea fishing from October through June, and Manzanillo hosts an annual fishing tournament in mid-January.

If tennis is your game, you'll find courts at all the large hotels. Good golf courses are located at Las Hadas and Club Santiago resorts.

Mazatlan. Fishing—especially for sailfish and marlin—is good all year. Skin diving, water-skiing, and hunting are excellent. Spectator sports such as baseball and bullfights occur in the winter months. Concerts take place regularly in the main plaza; night clubs and discos can be found throughout town.

Horseback riding along the beaches is inexpensive; take some binoculars for bird watching, a popular sport. Shell collecting is quite rewarding.

Puerto Vallarta. Parasailing, golf, and tennis are favorite pastimes. The Annual Deep-Sea Fishing Tournament takes place in the first week of November. During the season, "polo burro" is played on the beach and at the Camino Real. Night clubs and discos are plentiful in Puerto Vallarta.

Skin-diving equipment is available for rent; lessons are also provided. Snorkeling equipment can be rented either in town or at the beaches, and speedboats can be rented for water-skiing. There's horseback riding—or muleback, whichever you prefer—along the beaches or in the hills.

Mexico City

Accommodations

Hotel accommodations in the capital range from good to great. You'll also find a few motor inns off Paseo de la Reforma, conveniently located for most sightseeing. As in most large cities, trailer parks are located in the suburbs.

Most of the hotels center around four areas: Zocalo, Paseo de la Reforma, Chapultepec Park, and Zona Rosa. Each of the areas has advantages. The listing below covers major first-class and deluxe hotels in these areas. See your travel agent for reservations and for additional information on price, exact location, and type of room.

Zocalo. Moderate to first-class hotels: De Cortes (18th century, lovely garden), Majestic (dining on the roof), Metropol, and Ritz.

Paseo de la Reforma. First-class to deluxe hotels: Crowne Plaza Holiday Inn (rooftop supper club), Maria Isabel Sheraton (deluxe, completely refurbished), and Reforma (moderate).

Chapultepec Park. Deluxe hotels: Camino Real (one of the world's best hotels), El Presidente Chapultepec (walk to the park), and Nikko (new).

Zona Rosa. First-class to deluxe hotels: Aristos, Century, Galeria Plaza (same owners as Camino Real), Geneve (great ambience), Krystal, and Plaza Florencia.

Getting around

Fixed-price minibuses transport passengers from the airport to most downtown hotels. Taxis are inexpensive alternatives. Don't take the Metro from the airport; no luggage is allowed on the trains. Driving in Mexico City is nerve-frazzling. Use local transportation.

Around town, you have a choice of first-class buses, taxis, and cars or limousines with drivers and/or guides. Along the Reforma, you can catch buses or *peseros* (jitneys that travel main city streets). English-speaking guides with private cars cluster around major hotels. Check at the hotel desk for recommendations, and be sure that your guide has a license from the government.

Whenever you engage a driver-operated vehicle, settle the one-way or round-trip fare before entering. If you plan to spend a few hours at a location outside the downtown area, be sure you can get transportation back to your hotel before letting your vehicle leave.

Riding the Metro, the city's subway, is an inexpensive experience. Clean, quiet, attractively decorated marble stations (many with archeological treasures) may change your image of underground transportation. Don't attempt the trip during rush hours.

Tours

You'll have a wide choice of tour operators offering a variety of city excursions covering major points of interest in the capital city and surrounding countryside. Book them through your hotel.

Local tours last from half a day to all day, depending upon the attractions and events included. Prices for full-day tours usually include lunch. Even if you've been to Mexico City before, a half-day orientation will refresh your memory on location and keep you up to date with changes in the capital.

City tours. A full-day city tour normally covers such destinations as the Zocalo, Reforma attractions, Chapultepec Park (Castle and Anthropology Museum), markets, University City, Pedregal residences, San Angel, and Xochimilco. Saturday tours also include the Bazaar Sabado; Sunday ventures might add the Ballet Folklorico (see below) and the bullfights.

Area tours. The most popular excursion goes to the pyramids of Teotihuacan, the Guadalupe Shrine, the Plaza of Three Cultures, and an Indian market.

Day-long tours also will take you to Cuernavaca and Taxco, Puebla and Cholula, and to Toluca for Friday market. (Overnight stays can usually be arranged on these longer excursions.)

Entertainment

Mexico City is a lively town; you can find something to do until early in the morning.

Nighttime activity isn't limited to restaurants, hotel lounges, night clubs, and discos, though you'll find plenty of these. Don't sally forth for cocktail hour until at least 7 P.M. or you'll be all alone. Dinner begins around 9 or later, and evening entertainment goes on until the wee hours of the morning.

A 5-hour night club tour (by private car or bus) includes dinner and several stops for mariachi music and flamenco dancing. You can also take an evening excursion to Teotihuacan for the light-and-sound spectacle or visit Garibaldi Plaza to hear the mariachis compete.

The highlight of any trip to Mexico, though, is a visit to the Ballet Folklorico. Nightly presentations (Wednesday and Sunday) are an experience in dance, music, and costuming. (Ballet Folklorico also performs on Sunday mornings.) Get tickets in advance; excursions include reserved seats and transportation to and from your hotel.

Around Mexico City

Accommodations

The area around Mexico City contains accommodations in a variety found nowhere else in the country. Centuries-old haciendas offer rooms in the countryside around the capital. Lush gardens and high walls hide gemlike inns in the hills. Quaint colonial hotels offer a touch of the past. Resort spas add landscaped grounds and beauty regimens. All hotels have restaurants and many other amenities.

For more information on some of the colonial haciendas, turn to the special feature on pages 80–81.

Some travelers prefer to pick one site as a base for sheer relaxation; others sample different area's offerings. A few choices are listed below. For details on these hotels (and for other suggestions), check with your travel agent.

Cholula. First-class hotel: Villa Arqueologica.

Cuernavaca. First-class to deluxe hotels: Cuernavaca Racquet Club (open to the public), Hacienda de Cortes, Hosteria Las Quintas, Las Mañanitas (Mexico's top restaurant is located here). First-class hotels: Posada Jacarandas, Posada San Angelo.

Trailer parks: KOA (pool, tennis courts), San Pablo (en route to Cuautla, pool).

Around Cuernavaca. First-class hotels: Hacienda Vista Hermosa (between Cuernavaca and Taxco), Hacienda Cocoyoc (pools, tennis courts, riding, restaurants, nightclubs).

Ixtapan de la Sal. Resort: Hotel Ixtapan (full facilities, train). First-class hotel: Bungalows Lolita (dining room).

Puebla. First-class hotels: Aristos, El Meson del Angel (balconies or terraces, pools), and Mision. Moderate hotels: Del Portal, Lastra (grand volcano views from roof garden), and Royalty.

Taxco. First-class to deluxe hotels: De la Borda, Hacienda del Solar, Los Arcos, Montetaxco, Posada de la Mision, and Rancho Taxco Victoria.

Tehuacan. First-class hotels: Mexico, Spa Peñafiel (northwest of town, tennis court, nine-hole golf course).

Toluca. First-class hotels: Castel Plaza las Fuentes, Del Rey Inn (steam baths, sauna).

Valle de Bravo. First-class hotel: Golf Hotel Avandaro (resort motor inn).

Zitacuaro (San Jose Purua). First-class hotel: Spa San Jose Purua (resort motor inn on canyon brink).

Getting around

This area is best traveled by car; half the delight of visiting the region is the fun of exploring. Rental cars are available in larger towns such as Cuernavaca, Taxco, Puebla, and Toluca. Some areas can be reached by bus from Mexico City; bus transportation to small towns is unreliable, though, and should be avoided by tourists.

Some of the regions are so small they can easily be explored on foot. Guides with cars are available in Cuernavaca and Puebla.

For 2- or 3-day trips, you may prefer to take advantage of guided tours, using Mexico City as a base. Though driving in the capital is not for the timid, touring outside the city is remarkably easy. You can rent a car near the edge of the city.

Tours

Not many organized tours are available. From Mexico City, tour organizations offer excursions to principal attractions in Cuernavaca, Taxco, Toluca, Puebla, Cholula, and surrounding villages. Good information on Cuernavaca attractions is available through most Mexico City hotels.

Setting up your own tour from Mexico City through the countryside is relatively easy. Local travel agencies can assist you in hiring a car and driver or guide. They can also arrange advance accommodations for popular spots.

If possible, plan your countryside exploring during the week, when accommodations are easier to locate and traffic is considerably lighter. On weekends, families in the capital leave town for vacations, inundating small resorts. Also avoid popular holiday periods.

Entertainment

Long days in the sun exploring caves or visiting Indian sites; swimming, golf, and tennis; shopping; gazing at waterfalls, lakes, and volcanoes—these are the major attractions around Mexico City. At night, you can dine well at one of the region's excellent restaurants; then enjoy mariachi music or go dancing at a disco.

Your choice of destination determines your activity. Don't expect much in the way of gala entertainment in quiet haciendas or small spas. Best bets for late-night activity might be Cuernavaca, Puebla, or Taxco.

Guadalajara

Accommodations

Accommodations in Guadalajara range from inexpensive to deluxe; first-class and deluxe hotels are listed below. It's wise to make reservations in advance; check with your travel agent for additional information on location, prices, and type of room.

There are four trailer parks in the Guadalajara area—either within the city or just outside of it.

Guadalajara. Deluxe hotels: Azteca (new), Camino Real (nightclub), El Tapatio (golf, tennis, horses), Fiesta Americana (three restaurants), Guadalajara Sheraton, Holiday Inn (remodeled), Hyatt (within a mini-city), Lafayette (in heart of Pink Zone), and Quinta Real. First-class hotels: Aranzazu (downtown), Best Western Fenix (Mexican decor), Hotel de Mendoza (downtown), Quinta Real (new), Qunita Quetzalcoatl (Lake Chapala inn), and Plaza del Sol (bar and disco).

Getting around

Guadalajara's streets are clearly laid out; you won't have to worry about getting lost. Many downtown streets are pedestrian malls, perfect for strolling and browsing. Take advantage of them and explore the city on foot. Metered cabs are available around town; make sure the flag has been lowered once you've entered, or agree on the fare before-

hand. If you want to drive yourself, you can rent a car—offices are located throughout Guadalajara (many at the major hotels). Bus service is efficient and inexpensive.

Clopping along the streets in a horse-drawn *calandria* (carriage) is a good way to relax and view the downtown attractions. Look for them in front of the market, museum, and San Francisco Park.

Tours

A 4-hour city tour of Guadalajara's highlights includes the village of Tlaquepaque. Bus tours leave from San Francisco Park or Los Arcos; check schedules upon arrival. Hotel desks will have all the necessary tour information.

To Tlaquepaque and Tonala. Some tours include visits to these attractive handicraft centers, but it's often best to plan your own itinerary. Check with your hotel for a car and driver, and plan to spend the day. Tlaquepaque contains more than 200 shops, restaurants, and other attractions. Nearby Tonala, an important pottery center, offers colorful markets and fine studios and shops.

A tequila tour. Tours are available from Guadalajara to several tequila distilleries. Here you'll see the complete process of making Mexico's national drink, from harvesting the maguey heart through bottling the liquid (see page 96). The Sauza family estate, across from their distillery, is also open to visitors.

To Lake Chapala. A 6-hour tour from your hotel to Lake Chapala also includes lunch. You'll get a look at the charming residential communities of Ajijic and Jocotepec, and have time for shopping. Handloomed fabrics are good buys.

Other tours. Do-it-yourself tours to Barranca de Oblatos (Monks' Canyon) about 5 miles east of the city give you a good look at a 2,000-feet-

deep scenic gorge, a good place for a picnic.

Interested in opals? Drive out to Magdalena, about an hour northwest of Guadalajara on Highway 15. The San Simon opal mine is still operating. Your best bet for genuine gems is to buy from one of the city stores.

Entertainment

Activity in Guadalajara doesn't end when the sun goes down; there's plenty of night life. Hotel bars have the most action; entertainment ranges from mariachi bands to discos. Many restaurants have musical entertainment (in addition to great food).

Guadalajara is the center for mariachi music; expect to hear the sound everywhere. Plaza de los Mariachis is where the groups congregate. You can hire them for a song—or for an evening.

For a cultural experience. The Degollado Theater schedules opera, symphony, and ballet performances; check schedules upon arrival or with a travel agent before you begin your trip. Folkloric productions—traditional music, dancing, and theater—are performed by the University of Guadalajara troup at the theater on Sunday morning.

Strolling through stores. Shopping is a major form of entertainment in Guadalajara, and every visitor should take advantage of it. Visit the markets, as well as the shopping areas on the west side and in the Pink Zone. You'll find excellent buys in Mexican handicrafts in the villages of Tonala and Tlaquepaque and in communities along the shore of nearby Lake Chapala.

Sports for all. Hotels have the usual recreational facilities; you can enjoy tennis, golf, and swimming. Bullfights, baseball, polo, and *futbol* are available for those who prefer spectator sports.

Colonial Circle

Accommodations

Accommodations in the towns within the Colonial Circle are generally first-class, clean, and simple; in many cases, hotels are built in charming colonial style. If you're traveling by car, plan to reach your destination by nightfall. Depending on the time of year, it's wise to make advance reservations; check with your travel agent for additional information on location, prices, and types of rooms.

Campers will find trailer parks outside of Patzcuaro and San Miguel de Allende. A trailer park adjoins the Azteca Hotel in Queretaro.

Guanajuato. First-class hotels: Castillo de Santa Cecilia, Real de Minas, and San Gabriel Barrera (a converted hacienda).

Morelia. First-class hotels: Posada de la Soledad (originally a colonial monastery), Villa Montaña (cliffside), and Virrey de Mendoza (originally a colonial residence).

Patzcuaro. First-class hotels: Posada de Don Vasco (hacienda-style), and Meson del Cortijo (converted hacienda).

Queretaro. Deluxe: La Mansion Galindo (16th-century elegance with 20th-century comfort, tennis, golf). First-class hotels: Holiday Inn, Jurica (golf, riding), Meson de Santa Rosa, and Real de Minas.

San Miguel de Allende. First-class hotels: Casa de Sierra Nevada (bedrooms with fireplaces), Hacienda de las Flores, Hacienda Taboada (resort with mineral spas), Rancho Hotel El Atascadero (fireplaces and bungalows) and Villa de Club (Club Med new on the scene).

Uruapan. First-class hotels: Mansion del Cupatitzio (next to national park), Motel Pie de la Sierra (terraces and fireplaces).

Getting around

If you really want to capture the flavor of the Colonial Circle, travel by rental car. Rental offices are located in Guadalajara (many in the major hotels). The roadways in the area are well laid out, but roads in the towns themselves can be confusing, so tour on foot here. Stroll the village streets and browse in the shops; this way, you won't miss a thing. In Guanajuato, you can either walk (arm yourself with a good map) or hire a car and driver. Taxis serve San Miguel de Allende.

To visit archeological sites around Patzcuaro, it's best to hire a car and driver. One is on the lake's east shore; the others lie off roads leading into town.

Tours

You'll find few formal sightseeing tours in the Colonial Circle; these towns were meant for exploring on your own—be sure to wear comfortable shoes.

Guanajuato offers a city tour twice daily; another way to see the town is to hire a car and driver. In Patzcuaro, you'll find information on reliable city guides at the Posada de Don Vasco. San Miguel de Allende often has house and garden tours.

Highlights of some of the towns in the Colonial Circle include:

Guanajuato. See the central plaza, Jardin de la Union, Teatro Juarez, Church of San Diego, Plaza de la Paz, Basilica of Our Lady of Guanajuato, Mercado Hildago, the museum of Alhondiga de Granaditas, (Spanish fort), and Diego Rivera's house museum.

Morelia. See the Plaza de los Martires, the cathedral, the churches of San Agustin and Santa Rosa, and the Sanctuary of Our Lady of Guadalupe. Browse through Museo de Arte Colonial, and Casa de las Artesanias.

Patzcuaro. Visit the Plaza Principal (surrounded by Spanish buildings), the Basilica de Nuestra Vergine de la Salud, and Casa Gigante—once the home of the Count of Menozal. Shop at the Plaza Grande market; stop in at the Museo de Arte Popular (lovely Tarascan artifacts).

San Miguel de Allende. Visit the Plaza Insurgentes Allende, the church of La Salud, the lovely chapel of San Miguel Viejo, and the church and convent of San Francisco.

Uruapan. On Sundays, the band still plays on the Plaza Principal; facing it is an excellent museum.

Entertainment

Travelers will find surprisingly good restaurants in the Colonial Circle, especially in San Miguel de Allende. (Case de Sierra Nevada and Hacienda de las Flores are two good choices here.)

Shopping is another form of entertainment here, and this is one of the best shopping areas in Mexico; Morelia and Patzcuaro are noted for handicrafts.

You'll also find many facilities for tennis, golf, and horseback riding throughout much of the area. Night life is limited; there are no discos or night clubs. The towns and the people living there are the best entertainment.

Northern Mexico

Accommodations

Scattered across central and eastern Mexico are clean, simple, moderately priced hotels. You'll also find some deluxe facilities here and there, usually in the larger cities. If you're traveling by car, plan your trip to reach a town (the larger the better) by nightfall, to ensure a wider choice of accommodations. Hotel amenities usually include a restaurant.

Check with your travel agent for additional information on location, prices, and types of rooms. Trailer hookups can be found in most large cities.

Aguascalientes. First-class hotels: Francia, Las Trojes, and Medrano (free airport transportation).

Chihuahua. Deluxe accommodations: Castel Sicomoro, El Presidente (great view), and Hyatt Chihuahua. First-class hotels: Posada Tierra Blanca (in older section).

Durango. First-class hotels: Campo Mexico Courts (adjoining trailer park), El Presidente.

Monterrey. First-class hotels: Gran Hotel Ancira, Monterrey Plaza, Holiday Inn, Monterrey (night club), Rio, and Westin Ambassador (colonial rooms with balconies).

San Luis Potosi. First-class hotels/motels: Cactus Motel (trailer park), Hostal de Quixote (best), Hotel Panorama (rooftop restaurant).

Tampico. First-class hotels: Camino Real (rooms, bungalows set in tropical gardens), Inglaterra (rooftop night club), Posada de Tampico (putting green, tennis courts).

Zacatecas. First-class hotels: Aristos (view of the city), and Best Western Gallery.

Getting around

The best way to see the area is to rent a car in one of the large cities and tour the surrounding towns and villages on your own. You can take buses to larger cities, but you'll miss trips to the out-of-the-way places that make this area so special.

Car rentals are available in most large cities. One caution: plan your stops carefully; there's often a shortage of good accommodations in smaller towns.

Tours

You'll find half- and full-day city tours offered in the larger cities, along with organized excursions to some of the surrounding areas. To visit attractions at a leisurely pace, arm yourself with a good map and do some exploring on your own.

Aguascalientes. Tour the wine-growing areas and the farms where fighting bulls are bred; your hotel will make arrangements. Highlights of the city are the churches.

Chihuahua. Local travel agents offer city tours. Highlights are the baroque cathedral, the Palacio Federal, Quinta Luz (Pancho Villa's former home, now a museum), the Palacio Gobierno (where Father Miguel Hidalgo was executed) and, to the north, the spectacular views from Cumbres de Majalca.

Durango. See the colonial homes (the best is that of Count Kuchil), the Ichnographic Gallery of Bishops, and the cathedral.

Monterrey. Highlights are the 3-hour city tour, Carta Blanca brewery tour (free beer included), a shoppers' tour to Saltillo, an hour burro ride to Horsetail Falls, and a 4- to 5-hour excursion to the spectacular Garcia Caves.

San Luis Potosi. Take a self-guided tour; include the cathedral, the colonial-era Convent of San Francisco, the Governor's Palace, the Plaza de Armas, Our Lady of Carmen Church, the Potosi Regional Museum, the Loreto Chapel, and the Guadalupe Shrine.

Tampico. A half-day city tour includes a boat ride on the Tamesi River. See the Plaza de Armas, the cathedral, and the Palacio Municipal.

Zacatecas. Visit the lovely baroque cathedral, the Church of San Francisco, Santo Domingo Church, and the Museum of Huichol Art; for something different, tour a silver mine or take a cable car ride over town. About 30 miles to the southwest are the restored ruins of Chicomoztoc.

Entertainment

For the most part, you won't find much night life in northern Mexico. A few night clubs and discos may be found in the larger cities, usually in the bigger hotels. The attractions of this area are the people—their traditions, their towns, and their lives. You'll also discover a curiously refreshing lack of tourist-oriented facilities in the countryside.

Sporting activities are big throughout the region—fishing, hunting, golf, and tennis. Monterrey hosts major baseball games, soccer matches, bullfights, and charreadas.

Southern Mexico

Accommodations

You can be assured of clean, simple, and moderately priced accommodations in the interior of southern Mexico. Most visitors to this area are interested in ancient ruins and Mexico's Indian heritage, so the hotels won't be deluxe. Along the coast, top accommodations are located at the new resort of Bahias de Huatulco.

If you're touring the area by car, plan to reach your destination by nightfall (your choice of accommodations will be greater in large towns). Check with your travel agent for additional information on location, prices, and rooms.

You'll find trailer parks in Oaxaca, Palenque, and Veracruz.

Bahias de Huatulco. First-class to deluxe hotels: see page 150.

Oaxaca. First-class hotels: El Presidente (originally 16th century Convento de Santa Catalina), Mision de Los Angeles, (newest), San Felipe Mision, Victoria (overlooks city), and Villa Antequera.

Palenque. First-class hotels: Chan Kah Cabañas (overlook the river), Mision Palenque, (pool and golf course), Villa Arqueologica.

Puerto Escondido. First-class hotels: Villa Sol and others on page 150.

San Cristobal de las Casas. First-class hotels: Bonampak, Molino de la Alboriada (dude ranch), and Posada Diego de Mazariegos (rooms with fireplace).

Veracruz. First-class hotels: Colonial (on the plaza), Hostal de Cortes (across from the beach), Emporio (overlooks harbor), Puerto Bello (pool and entertainment), and Torremar (newest).

Villahermosa. First-class hotels: Cencali (entertainment), Holiday Inn, Hyatt, Maya Tabasco (modern), and Villahermosa Viva (pool and tennis courts).

Getting around

Southern Mexico is best seen on your own in a rental car—you'll avoid set schedules, and be able to spend more time in the areas that interest you most. Rental cars are available in Oaxaca and other large cities.

Buses serve Oaxaca and offer transportation to and from Monte Alban and Mitla. Cabs are reasonably priced. They'll stop off at such Indian villages as Tule and Tlacolula; agree on the fare before entering the cab. Major hotels in the city have minibuses that serve the airport.

Buses commute between San Cristobal de las Casas and Tuxtla Gutierrez several times daily; the fare is reasonable. Air transport is a popular form of transportation from San Cristobal de las Casas to the surrounding ruins and small villages.

From Mexico City, a fast train deposits you in Veracruz, site of a lively pre-Lenten Mardi Gras.

Buses serve Palenque from Villahermosa; check schedules upon arrival. Small (three-passenger) planes fly into Palenque's airport from Tuxtla Gutierrez; four passengers can charter a flight to Palenque that includes stops at Bonampak and Lacanja. The plane will wait for up to 3 hours while you tour the ruins. Taxis carry passengers to and from the airport.

Tours

Half and full-day tours cover main attractions in most major cities. If you choose to tour on your own, arm yourself with a good map and comfortable shoes. Take advantage of group tours to the ruins; English-speaking guides are usually quite knowledgeable.

Oaxaca. Travel agents in the area offer half-day tours of the city, as well as tours to Mitla, Tule, Tlacolula, Ocotlan, Coyotepec, Monte Alban, and other areas. If your time in Oaxaca is short, hire a car and driver at your hotel for a quick condensed tour. Be sure your driver speaks English; agree on the price in advance.

San Cristobal de las Casas. The city tour lasts 4 hours. Air tours are available to the unrestored ruins of Bonampak and Yaxchilan.

Veracruz. You can take a half-day city tour or see the city on your own.

Villahermosa. Full-day guided bus tours to Palenque depart from your hotel. If you prefer to determine your own schedule, hire a car and driver.

Entertainment

Until Bahias de Huatulco is firmly established, Oaxaca offers the most sophisticated entertainment in the central and western reaches. Regional dances often take place on the plaza. There are mariachi concerts almost every night; the plaza is the scene for Saturday night concerts. The Victoria Hotel boasts a disco. In Veracruz, the major form of entertainment is people-watching and relaxing around the plaza. There's a disco in town, and a band concert takes place a couple of times a week. For the most part, though, travelers visit southern Mexico to view the ruins and experience a virtually untouched landscape.

Yucatan

Accommodations

Travelers will find the greatest range of accommodations in the resort areas of Cancun and Cozumel and in the city of Merida. The archeological sites of Chichen Itza, Coba, and Uxmal have Villas Arqueologicas, inns managed by Club Med and geared to explorers. You'll find simple and comfortable accommodations scattered throughout the Yucatan. Check with your travel agent for additional information on location, prices, and types of rooms.

Campers will find sites outside Campeche, Merida, and Chichen Itza.

Campeche. First-class hotels: Baluartes (open-air dining), El Presidente.

Cancun. Deluxe hotels: Casa Maya, Club Lagoon, Club Med, Crowne Plaza (late 1988), Fiesta Americana, Hyatt Caribe, Hyatt Regency, Krystal, Sheraton, and Westin Camino Real. First-class hotels: Aristos (refurbished), El Presidente (renovated), Mision Miramar, Villas Plaza Cancun, and Viva.

Within driving distance of Cancun. First-class hotels: Balam-ha (45 minutes from Cancun), Blue Parrot Inn (small inn on beach at Playa del Carmen), Club Akumal, and La Ceiba Beach Hotel (cottages).

Chetumal. Continental (near the market) and El Presidente (entertainment).

Chichen Itza. Deluxe hotel: Mayaland (5-minute walk to ruins). First-class hotels: Mision (1½ miles from ruins), and Villa Arqueologica (tennis courts, library, 5 minutes from archeological zone).

Cozumel. First class to deluxe hotels: Cabañas del Caribe, El Cozumeleño (marble baths), El Presidente (good bay swimming), La Ceiba Beach Hotel (beachfront), Mayan Plaza (good scuba diving), and Sol Caribe-Cozumel (across from Paraiso beach).

Merida. Deluxe hotel: Holiday Inn. First-class hotels: Casa del Balam (colonial style), Mision Merida (refurbished), Montejo Palace (night club), and Panamericana (nightly entertainment).

Pez Maya Resort. A deluxe fishing camp complete in itself; accessible from Cozumel or Cancun. All-inclusive packages (prices include accommodations and plane fare) are available from Cozumel.

Uxmal. Deluxe hotels: Hacienda Uxmal (luxurious), Mision (1 mile from ruins), Posada Uxmal (same grounds as the Hacienda, but smaller rooms), Villa Arqueologica (near ruins).

Getting around

If you plan to explore the ruins, it's a good idea to rent a car (rentals at Merida or Cancun airports). Taxis can be found in Merida; buses at Cancun will take you to any part of the island for a low fare. A ferry serves Cozumel from Playa del Carmen on the mainland; hydrofoils connect Cancun and Cozumel.

Tours

In the larger cities, half- and full-day city tours are offered. Excursions to the ruins are a must if you're in the vicinity—you can take a tour starting from your base city or hire a guide at the entrance to the archeological ruins.

Campeche. The whole city is worth exploring; be sure to visit the Archeological Museum (Maya artifacts).

Cancun. Full-day trips are offered to Chichen Itza, Uxmal, and Merida; half-day trips are available to Tulum. Go snorkeling or diving at Xel-Ha or charter a boat to snorkel off Isla Mujeres or visit a nearby national park and bird sanctuary. Water-ski on the lagoon.

Cozumel. Cruise to one of the beaches (San Francisco or Passion Island) on the Robinson Crusoe tour, take a day trip to Tulum, or go on a glass-bottom boat ride.

Merida. A 2-hour city tour covers the city; there's often a 3-hour home and garden tour that takes in four elegant homes. Or take a day trip to Chichen Itza or Uxmal (some tours visit Kabah). You can also make arrangements to visit Yucalpeten, a new resort area on the Gulf (windsurfing, sailing, water-skiing) with two hotels, Sian Ka'an and Fiesta Inn.

A 1½-hour carriage ride takes you from the main plaza past the grand mansions on Montejo Boulevard and back. Prices are surprisingly low.

Entertainment

You'll find evening entertainment in the form of discos in Cancun. The Ballet Folklorico performs at the Convention Center nightly except Sunday. Merida's nightly gala evening at the Panamericana Hotel features Yucatecan folk dancing; other regional dances and concerts are held in the Peon Contreras Theater, Santa Ana and Santiago parks, and the gardens behind the Municipal Palace.

The rest of the area offers little organized entertainment, but you'll find music in most hotels.

Index